Global and Local Polemics of Development

VOLUME– I

Disquieting Divides: Politics of the Self and the Other

By the same Author

— Development Ethics

About the Editor

Dr. Prasenjit Maiti (1971-) is presently an Assistant Professor at the Public Systems Management and Human Resource Management Departments of the Indian Institute of Social Welfare and Business Management, Kolkata. He has written three books and several papers on the problems of governance and development. He was invited to the University of Southern Denmark as a Guest Professor in 2007. Dr. Maiti has also worked as a Consultant on different projects funded by the World Bank, Asian Development Bank and the Department for International Development, United Kingdom.

Global and Local Polemics of Development

VOLUME–I

Disquieting Divides: Politics of the Self and the Other

Edited by

DR. PRASENJIT MAITI

CONCEPT PUBLISHING COMPANY, PVT. LTD.
NEW DELHI-110059

ISBN-13: 978-81-8069-661-9 (set)
ISBN-13: 978-81-8069-662-6 (Vol. I)
ISBN-13: 978-81-8069-663-3 (Vol. II)

First Published 2010

Published and Printed by:

Concept
Since 1974

Concept Publishing Company Pvt. Ltd.
Regd. Office:
A/15-16, Commercial Block. Mohan Garden
New Delhi-110059 (India)
Phones : 25351460, 25351794, *Fax* : 091-11-25357109
Email : publishing@conceptpub.com,
Website: www.conceptpub.com

Editorial Office:
H-13, Bali Nagar, New Delhi-110 015, India.

Cataloging in Publication Data--*Courtesy*: D.K. Agencies (P) Ltd. <docinfo@dkagencies.com>

Global and local polemics of development / edited by Prasenjit Maiti.
2 v. cm.
Contributed articles.
Includes bibliographical references and index.
Contents: v. 1. Disquieting divides : politics of the self and the other -- v. 2. Sustainable development and inclusive growth : histories, institutions, ideologies and praxes.
ISBN 13: 9788180696619 (set)
ISBN 13: 9788180696626 (v. 1)
ISBN 13: 9788180696633 (v. 2)

1. Globalization--Economic aspects--India. 2. Globalization--Economic aspects-- Developing countries. 3. India.--Economic policy. 4. Developing countries-- Economic policy. 5. Sustainable development--India. 6. Sustainable development--Developing countries. 7. Rural development--India. 8. Rural development-- Developing countries. I. Maiti, Prasenjit, 1971-

DDC 338.954 22

Preface

I am honoured to introduce the present Volume to academics worldwide. The central problem of this edited anthology is structured around the debates of poverty, human rights, local problems and global resolutions among other fascinating negotiations between the dynamics that have provoked the ideology of Globalization and even Globalization. This edited Volume is expected to contribute new knowledge and facilitate innovative research to better understand the interactions and interplay between the local and the global.

The politics of Globalization and local identities are generally underpinned by the interplay between issue-driven conflicts and strategic reconciliations. Such problems of multicultural specifics and puzzling reflexes can often incite unmanageable crises both at the levels of the State and the Civil Society. The Market happens to be the predominant actor so far as the praxes of Globalization are concerned along with the agora of Politics where choices are exercised as tactics and tools of critical polemics. So we are more concerned nowadays in our post-postmodern world with structures that fall apart, ideologies that are dead and realities have become like readably texts with more than one possible interpretation.

We more often than not hear that Globalization is both an opportunity and a threat. It has its strengths and weaknesses that have to be interrogated against the established parameters of our own cultural root paradigms. But what is our own and who constitutes the other in a localized world? Meanings change, attributes undergo metamorphosis while attitudes and beliefs are no more our own, as they are now subverted by disquietingly new texts of power. Do borders actually disappear and discriminations get reduced in a globalized scenario? It is convenient to deny the benefits of Globalization but it is rather more difficult to understand why the forces of this phenomenon have resulted in an uncomfortable mode of production.

The new debates on human rights world-wide centre around the multiple politics of empowerment and identities. Civil liberties and human rights constitute the critical polemic that happens to inform current Globalization debates. We have proposed to read the current rhetoric of human rights in this Volume in the context of tension and reconciliations between the State, Civil Society and Market.

The dynamics of neo-institutionalism and neo-liberalism also impinge upon the metaphors of Empowerment, Gender and Inclusive Growth in an era when on the one hand barriers are collapsing only to create new obstacles to the emancipation of the Self. The Orientalism discourse is also especially relevant in this connection, as the polyphony of new discourses often engage in serious tussles with emergent signifiers and signifieds.

So new identities and new meanings have evolved to facilitate better understanding of this project of human rights in our global era when we have engaged with the Millennium Development Goals as an imperative of human development and well-being. But it also remains a fact that neo-imperialism in its dynamic *avatar* of Coca-Colonization and war against terror has instigated fresh debates that lead to fundamental doubts about the Politics of Self.

Can we determine the sovereignty of our Body, let alone the sovereignty of our political systems? Can we in fact synergize and strategize new ways of thinking about politics, society and our culture root paradigms? These are disturbing questions that impact upon the basis of the new human rights projects that have attracted critical gazes world-wide.

Are we still within the panoptican discourse of discipline and punish that the state had once assumed to streamline its own grand narratives of power and hegemony? Or are we ready to interrogate new debates on the small narratives of the microphysics of knowledge and the archaeology of an arrangement we often tend to confuse with the prevalent notions of Legitimacy and Democracy?

These are rather problematic inquiries with no readymade answers to be made available in pocketbook philosophies. The Contributors to this Volume have painstakingly tried to arrive at their own answers by deploying their own methodological tools and paradigms of knowledge learnt in their individual as well as collective contexts of deschooled pedagogics.

I had various occasions in the past to study poverty in both the rural and urban sectors while working on urban development and rural livelihood projects. It had repeatedly come to my notice in this connection that poverty is more often than not caused by inadequacies of access and capabilities and entitlements on the part of individuals or groups *vis-à-vis* the limited basket of civil societal and market resources.

Such an understanding of poverty is not new or unique. But I also had the opportunity during my academic-turned-practitioner career to analyze the causes and effects of poverty from the angle of human development. What had generally struck me during my interfaces with poverty at the empirical and theoretical levels is the fact that poverty is also an attitude as well as an ethos that are antipodally posited to our common understanding of the phenomenon of well-being.

Predatory market forces often cause incidence of poverty while lack of access to information can also lead to widespread famines, as established by academics worldwide. So the next question that arises is whether the available political systems can actually determine the structure of poverty and dictate the courses of redress of such uneven socio-economic impacts so far as vulnerable groups are concerned?

Food security, gender issues, child labour and other important concerns happen to underpin the discourses of poverty that are to be analyzed more on a comparative basis rather than by adopting a standalone approach. The cultural and psychological aspects of poverty have to be also interrogated in a holistic manner by utilizing the insights obtained from prevalent social, political and economic realities.

So poverty is now the domain of study for social scientists in general rather than economists in particular. Why do government-sponsored poverty alleviation programmes fail? Why do hunger deaths occur? Why cannot the beneficiaries be assured of livelihood and income generation programmes during the course of implementation of projects that adversely impact upon their Common Property Resources, land and structures?

The issue of poverty is also related to the larger concern of social development. So poverty cannot simply be understood as a localized phenomenon but has to be studied as a construct of multiple realities, especially when hunger asks uncomfortable questions.

The *problematique* of this book project is also structured around the polemic of civil societal institutions (networks and embeddedness) and democratic governance (inclusive growth and participatory development) among other critical areas of social scientific research. This edited anthology would contribute new knowledge and facilitate innovative research to better understand the interactions and interplay between actors and their institutions.

The politics of everyday life and human development are generally informed by the dynamics of choice and the strategies of cooperation. This tension can be somewhat resolved by adopting the social capital approach, as inclusive growth can more often than not be ensured by empowered choices and delegated actions.

The above contention is supported by the World Bank's perception of social capital. The Bank tends to apply the lessons learnt from various projects funded under its auspices in the light of community fabric, collective trust and networks of cooperation sustained by the ethos of multi-stakeholder dialogues.

This highlights the importance of social capital in all our grand as well as small narratives today in a world where economic signifiers and their signified meanings are more or less in a state of constant flux provoked by the marketplace of politics and the social as well as cultural rhetoric of globalization.

The Bank has also championed the Think Globally Act Locally slogan while the Millennium Development Goals themselves are a construct of social capital that require meaningful negotiations with the perceptions of disengaged civil societies and panoptic state systems.

The Contributors to this Volume have generally made serious attempts to answer such disturbing questions while located within the context of the much-celebrated pedagogics of the oppressed discourse. I thank them for their insights and empathy with the core problem areas of this multi-volume book project. Their sincere and painstaking efforts would be duly recognized if they receive critical acclaim from their readers.

The Contributors have made indepth analyses in their Chapters to scientifically analyze the problems and questions described above and investigate multiple options that may suggest compatibilities between States, Civil Societies, Markets and Politics in a world of dwindling borders and enhanced inequalities. They would be adequately rewarded for their academic efforts if this Volume can provoke new theoretical and empirical research projects on Globalization, human rights and poverty.

The Contributors have also made attempts to best reflect the tensions described above and explore optimum resolutions that may lead to best fits or at least working relationships between individuals and their organized interactions called institutions. They would be amply rewarded if this book project can lead to exciting research in relatively new areas such as social capital theory.

I thank all of them for their brilliant efforts to bring out this Volume that looks both anew and askance to the ongoing human rights debates in the post-Cold War and post-9/11 world when established notions have been subverted by a new politics and fresh strategies of engaging the Self with the Collective. Their efforts would be rewarded if this Volume receives critical academic appreciation on a global basis.

I also avail of this opportunity to thank all the Contributors who have worked tirelessly to make this book project successful. I would always remember the wonderful friendships cultivated and the important scholarly lessons learnt while engaged in this academic exercise. I have enriched myself both in personal and professional terms while dealing with subjects such as trust, ethics and cooperation.

I also wish to thank the Publisher whose editorial staff have worked with commitment to make this book project successful. I would fondly cherish the professional relationships developed and the academic insights derived while working on this Volume. I sincerely hope that this anthology would lead to a renewed interest in the ongoing global versus local debates among researchers and practitioners world-wide.

Salt Lake City
Kolkata (India)

Prasenjit Maiti

Contents

Contributors

Dr. Prasenjit Maiti (1971-) <pmaiti@vsnl.com> is presently an Assistant Professor at the Public Systems Management and Human Resource Management Departments of the Indian Institute of Social Welfare and Business Management, the country's first Business School established in 1953 at Kolkata. He is a political sociologist and has written three books and several papers both in India and abroad on the problems of governance and development. He was invited to the University of Southern Denmark as a Guest Professor in 2007 while he was earlier a Doctoral Research Fellow at the University of Fribourg, Switzerland in 1999. Dr Maiti also worked as a Consultant on different projects funded by the World Bank, Asian Development Bank and the Department for International Development, United Kingdom.

Somesh K. Mathur, PhD (JNU) <skmathur@iitk.ac.in> has nearly eleven years of teaching and research experience at the Department of Economics, Jamia Millia Islamia (Central University), Delhi. While teaching at the Jamia he completed his M. Phil and PhD degrees in economics from the Centre for International Trade and Development, JNU. He joined as Fellow (Associate Professor) at RIS in April 2006 on deputation from the Department of Economics, JMI for two years. At present he has joined on permanent basis IIT Kanpur as Assistant Professor of Economics in the H &SS department of the IIT Kanpur. His area of interest lies in efficiency and productivity analysis, new trade and growth theories, convergence issues, TRIPS and other WTO issues. He has participated in various national and international conferences and has published in referred national and international journals. Dr. Mathur has taught papers like Pure Theory of International Trade, Quantitative Methods (eleven years), Econometrics, International Finance and Banking, Micro-economics and Corporate Finance to the post-graduate students of the University. He has also taught national income accounting, mathematical methods of economics, micro-economics and Indian economy at the graduate level. Dr Mathur has been awarded his PhD in Economics in December 2005 from SIS JNU and has completed his term as a research fellow at RIS (www.ris.org.in). He also works in the WTO areas like TRIPS and Dispute Settlement Process. In addition he is interested in growth and convergence and time series econometrics. He has authored 4 books (including two e-books) on Global Economic Trends and South Asia Economic Growth and Convergence in Selected South Asian and East Asian Economies: A Data Envelopment Analysis , an e-book on Perspective of Economic Growth in Selected South Asian and East Asian Countries (www.ideaindia.com). He has published his fourth book (e-book) on IT Success Model of India.

Raghwendra Pratap Singh<rpsingh@mail.jnu.ac.in> is the Chairperson of the Centre for Philosophy at the School of Social Sciences, Jawaharlal Nehru University, India. He has authored 12 books and over 90 articles. He has also delivered lectures at the University of Massachusetts, Cambridge and Harvard University. His main areas of interest are Epistemology, Ethics, Social and Political Philosophy.

Deane Neubauer <deanen@hawaii.edu> is Professor Emeritus in the Department of Political Science at the University of Hawaii, Manoa, Senior Research Fellow Globalization Research Center (UHM) and Senior Advisor to the Education 2020 Programme of the East West Center. Educated at the University of California, Riverside and Yale University, he has taught additionally at the University of California (Berkeley and Irvine), Waikato University (NZ) and the University of Sydney. His research interests lie in health policy, political economy and globalization. His work explores globalization phenomena as a major vector of social change throughout the world. He served as the founding dean of the

College of Social Sciences at the University of Hawaii, Manoa (1980-88). In 1999 he founded the Globalization Research Center at the University of Hawaii, Manoa and subsequently the Globalization Research Network, a collaboration of four US Universities. He served as Interim Chancellor of the University of Hawaii, Manoa from 2001-2002 and as Interim Vice-President for Academic Affairs for the University of Hawaii System from 2001-2004.

Lynn Anne Mulrooney <lynn.mulrooney@sympatico.ca> is Senior Policy Analyst for the Registered Nurses' Association of Ontario. Her perspective has been informed by her work as a community health nurse in rural Ethiopia and as a relief worker in Somalia. She is affiliate faculty with the Globalization Research Center at the University of Hawaii at Manoa.

Raghu Bir Bista <rbbista@wlink.com.np> is an Economist. He is an Assistant Professor and teaches at the Post-graduate programme at the Department of Economics, Patan Multiple Campus of Tribhuvan University, Nepal. He is an editor of Economic Journal of Development Issues published by Department of Economics. He was associate editor of Nepal Year Book for five editions. His first book publication was on Foreign Direct Investment in Nepal. His present research interests are macro-economics, international economics, environment economics, policy economics, FDI and poverty.

P.R. Bose (1952-) <prbose@yahoo.com> is a Senior Scientist in the National Institute of Science, Technology and Development Studies, New Delhi, a Laboratory of CSIR. Basically, he is economist and did MS degree in S&T from BITS Pilani. He is working in the research area of Science, Technology and Society (STS). He has wide experience in Research of about 30 years. He has written two books and several research papers in the area of rural development, technology innovation and technology transfer. He has brought out a book and papers on different aspects on Aluminium Industry. Presently, he is a participant for Supra Institutional Project at the institute "Indian S&T – manpower mapping and comparative capacity".

Shiben Krishen Raina MA(Hindi & English), PhD; Professor/ Writer; born on April 22,1942 Srinagar (J&K); Edu J&K, Rajasthan and Kurukshetra University; Head Hindi Dept.Govt Post-graduate College, Alwar; Sought voluntary retirement from

Principalship and joined Indian Institute of Advanced Study, Rashtrapati Nivas, Shimla as Fellow to work on Problems of Translation (1999-2001). published—14 books including *Kashmiri Bhasha Aur Sahitya* (1972), *Kashmiri Sahitya Ki Naveentam Pravrittiyan*, (1973), *Kashmiri Ramayan: Ramavtarcharit* (1975 translated from Kashmiri into Hindi), Lal Ded/Habbakhatoon-monographs translated from English (1980), *Shair-e-Kashmir Mehjoor* (translated 1989); *Ek Daur* (Novel translated 1980) *Kashmiri Kavyitriyan Aur Unka Rachna Sansar* (1996 crit); *Maun Sambashan* (Short stories 1999); Awards: Bihar Rajya Bhasha Vibagh, Patna 1983; Central Hindi Directorate 1972, Sauhard Samman 1990; Rajasthan Sahitya Academy Translation Award (1998) Bhartiya Anuvad Parishad Award(1999); Titles conferred: Sahityashri, Sahitya Vageesh, Alwar Gaurav, Anuvadshri etc.Address: 2/537(HIG) Aravali Vihar, Alwar 301001, India. Email: skraina@hotmail.com/skraina123@rediffmail.com/ sk.raina@gmail.comMob.9414216124

Dr Sudha Mohan <sudhamohan1@gmail.com> is Reader/ Associate Professor in the Department of Civics and Politics, University of Mumbai. She has published in the areas of Urban Governance, Civil Society, Decentralisation and Citizen Participation, Globalisation, among others, besides publishing a book entitled Urban Development and New Localism. Dr. Mohan was the recipient of the Sr. Fulbright fellowship (2004-05) to pursue post doctoral research at State University of New York, Pittsburgh and Columbia University, NYC. Her current research projects include Issues in Urban Governance in Developing Countries, Global – Local Interface, and Substantial Democracy and Sustainable Development.

Tapomoy Deb <tdeb1969@rediffmail.com> holds M.Phil (Management), MBA (HRM), MSW (PM&IR), PGDHRD, DLL and B.Sc (Hons) Physics. He is currently working as Dy. General Manager–HR in Spentex Industries Ltd., New Delhi (largest spinning company in India), and has wide corporate experience in HR. He is member of several professional bodies and has published numerous articles (more than 30) on HR Management in leading professional HR journals such as HRD Newsletter, NHRD Journal, HRM Review (ICFAI University), Atlantic Journal of Development Studies, Business Manager, Textile Review, Human Potential, etc. He has authored several text books on Human Resource Management, Human Resource Development, Strategic Talent Management and Training & Development for MBA students. He is recipient of several medals and prizes in his academic career. Currently he is a Research Scholar (HRM) in Jamia Millia Islamia (A Central University), Mohammed Ali Jauhar Marg, Jamia Nagar, New Delhi pursuing his Ph.D. A merit rank holder and a prolific writer.

Louise Warwick-Booth (b. 1976) <l.warwick booth@ leedsmet.ac.uk> is a lecturer in health policy at Leeds Metropolitan University, UK. She was previously a graduate tutor in sociology, social policy and criminology at the University of Sheffield, where she completed her PhD in community based research and evaluation within social regeneration. Her current research interests include community development, community research and social inclusion.

Sam Wong <s.wong@leeds.ac.uk> is a Lecturer in the School of Earth and Environment at the University of Leeds. His research lies in environmental governance, community participation and politics of gender and identity. He has published a book, entitled 'Exploring Unseen Social Capital in Community Participation' (Amsterdam University Press, 2007). His important pre-reviewed journal papers include Urban Change (Vol. 45), Environmental Politics (forthcoming) and Gender and Development (forthcoming). He has obtained research grants totalling £160K and worked in India, Bangladesh, Ghana and China.

Shankar Chatterjee <shankar_nird@yahoo.com> has been working as Senior Assistant Professor in National Institute of Rural Development (NIRD), Hyderabad. Before joining NIRD he worked as Assistant Professor in degree colleges in Assam and Tripura. Dr. Chatterjee served in Eritrea (NE Africa) as Associate Professor for 2 years. He also visited Iran at the invitation of Government of Iran as Resource Person. He has already published 5 books on rural development (Three individually and two as co-author). He has published more than 120 articles in National and international journals.

Tapomoy Deb <tdeb 1969 @rediffmail.com> is a management teacher. He holds M. Phil. (Management), MBA (HR), MSW (PM&IR), PGDHRD, DLL & B.Sc. (Hons) Physics. He is

Guest Faculty to a number of reputed management institutes in Delhi such as Rukmini Devi Institute of Advanced Studies, Skyline Business School, Jamia Millia Islamia, etc. He has authored four MBA textbooks on Human Resource Management, Human Resource Development, Training & Development and Strategic Talent Management besides four derivative books. His latest book is on Performance Management (forthcoming, 2008, with Oxford University Press).

Mohammad Taghi Sheykhi <mtshykhi@yahoo.com> is currently teaching different courses of demography and sociology at Al-Zahra University in Teheran. He has published widely in demography and sociology in the past 15 years. His publications include: Sociology of Population, Principles of Demography, Applied and Analytical Demography, Economic and Social Demography, Principles and Concepts of Demography, Population and Family Planning, Sociology of the Third World, Industrial Sociology, Urban Sociology, Sociology of Women and the Family, Sociology of Development, Sociology of Social Problems and Social Work etc. Dr. Sheykhi has also published more than 35 articles, most of them published/reflected in reputed international journals.

Sasikumar, V.K. is a Research Scholar in Centre for Social Systems in Jawaharlal Nehru University. He had completed his M.A. in Anthropology with distinction. He is now working on Economic Anthropology and this paper is based on his M.A. thesis.

Ali Musa Abakar Eissa alimabakar@yahoo.com> is an Agricultural economist. He joined to the Department of Agricultural Economics and Rural Development at University of Kordofan, Sudan since 1997 to date. He studied his Ph.D. in University of Khartoum. He attended many international, regional and national workshops and presented some papers. Mr. Eissa has published paper on economic egg plant. He is the second author of the research entitled: "Poverty among Social Groups, Effects on Farming Systems and Resources Allocation: The Case Study of Rural Sudan." Supported by the ERF, Egypt (June 2007). He is the second leader of the ongoing project "Livelihood Risk Determinants facing Female Headed Households and Role of the Livestock in Poverty Eradication in Western Sudan."

Introduction

I am honoured to introduce these Volumes to academics worldwide. The central problem of this edited anthology is structured around the debates of poverty, human rights, local problems and global resolutions of development among other fascinating negotiations between the dynamics that have provoked the ideology of Globalization and even Glocalization. These edited Volumes are expected to contribute new knowledge and facilitate innovative research to better understand the interactions and interplay between the local and the global.

The politics of Globalization and local identities are generally underpinned by the interplay between issue-driven conflicts and strategic reconciliations. Such problems of multicultural specifics and puzzling reflexes can often incite unmanageable crises both at the levels of the State and the Civil Society. The Market happens to be the predominant actor so far as the praxes of Globalization are concerned along with the agora of Politics where choices are exercised as tactics and tools of critical polemics. So we are more concerned nowadays in our post-postmodern world with structures that fall apart, ideologies that are dead and realities have become like readerly texts with more than one possible interpretation.

We more often than not hear that Globalization is both an opportunity and a threat. It has its strengths and weaknesses that have to be interrogated against the established parameters of our own cultural root paradigms. But what is our own and who constitutes the other in a glocalized world? Meanings change, attributes undergo metamorphosis while attitudes and beliefs are no more our own, as they are now subverted by disquietingly new texts of power. Do borders actually disappear and discriminations get reduced in a globalized scenario? It is convenient to deny the benefits of Globalization but it is rather more difficult to understand why the forces of this phenomenon have resulted in an uncomfortable mode of production.

The new debates on human rights world-wide centre around the multiple politics of empowerment and identities. Civil liberties and human rights constitute the critical polemic that happens to inform current globalization debates. We have proposed to read the current rhetoric of human rights in these Volumes in the context of tension and reconciliations between the State, Civil Society and Market.

The dynamics of neo-institutionalism and neo-liberalism also impinge upon the metaphors of Empowerment, Gender and Inclusive Growth in an era when on the one hand barriers are collapsing only to create new obstacles to the emancipation of the Self. The Orientalism discourse is also especially relevant in this connection, as the polyphony of new discourses often engage in serious tussles with emergent signifiers and signifieds.

So new identities and new meanings have evolved to facilitate better understanding of this project of human rights in our glocal era when we have engaged with the Millennium Development Goals as an imperative of human development and well-being. But it also remains a fact that neo-imperialism in its dynamic *avatar* of Coca-Colonization and war against terror has instigated fresh debates that lead to fundamental doubts about the Politics of Self.

Can we determine the sovereignty of our Body, let alone the sovereignty of our political systems? Can we in fact synergize and strategize new ways of thinking about politics, society and our culture root paradigms? These are disturbing questions that impact upon the basis of the new human rights projects that have attracted critical gazes worldwide.

Are we still within the panoptican discourse of discipline and punish that the State had once assumed to streamline its own grand narratives of power and hegemony? Or are we ready to interrogate new debates on the small narratives of the microphysics of knowledge and the archaeology of an arrangement we often tend to confuse with the prevalent notions of Legitimacy and Democracy?

These are rather problematic inquiries with no readymade answers to be made available in pocketbook philosophies. The Contributors to these Volumes have painstakingly tried to arrive at their own answers by deploying their own methodological tools and paradigms of knowledge learnt in their individual as well as collective contexts of deschooled pedagogics.

I had various occasions in the past to study poverty in both the rural and urban sectors while working on urban development and rural livelihood projects. It had repeatedly come to my notice in this connection that poverty is more often than not caused by inadequacies of access and capabilities and entitlements on the part of individuals or groups *vis-à-vis* the limited basket of civil societal and market resources.

Such an understanding of poverty is not new or unique. But I also had the opportunity during my academic-turned-practitioner career to analyze the causes and effects of poverty from the angle of human development. What had generally struck me during my interfaces with poverty at the empirical and theoretical levels is the fact that poverty is also an attitude as well as an ethos that are antipodally posited to our common understanding of the phenomenon of well-being.

Predatory market forces often cause incidence of poverty while lack of access to information can also lead to widespread famines, as established by academics worldwide. So the next question that arises is whether the available political systems can actually determine the structure of poverty and dictate the courses of redress of such uneven socio-economic impacts so far as vulnerable groups are concerned?

Food security, gender issues, child labour and other important concerns happen to underpin the discourses of poverty that are to be analyzed more on a comparative basis rather than by adopting a standalone approach. The cultural and psychological aspects of poverty have to be also interrogated in a holistic manner by utilizing the insights obtained from prevalent social, political and economic realities.

So poverty is now the domain of study for social scientists in general rather than economists in particular. Why do government-sponsored poverty alleviation programmes fail? Why do hunger deaths occur? Why cannot the beneficiaries be assured of livelihood and income generation programmes during the course of implementation of projects that adversely impact upon their Common Property Resources, land and structures?

The issue of poverty is also related to the larger concern of social development. So poverty cannot simply be understood as a localized phenomenon but has to be studied as a construct of multiple realities, especially when hunger asks uncomfortable questions.

The *problematique* of this book project is also structured around the polemic of civil societal institutions (networks and embeddedness) and democratic governance (inclusive growth and participatory development) among other critical areas of social scientific research. This edited anthology would contribute new knowledge and facilitate innovative research to better understand the interactions and interplay between actors and their institutions.

The politics of everyday life and human development are generally informed by the dynamics of choice and the strategies of cooperation. This tension can be somewhat resolved by adopting the social capital approach, as inclusive growth can more often than not be ensured by empowered choices and delegated actions.

The above contention is supported by the World Bank's perception of social capital. The Bank tends to apply the lessons learnt from various projects funded under its auspices in the light of community fabric, collective trust and networks of cooperation sustained by the ethos of multi-stakeholder dialogues.

This highlights the importance of social capital in all our grand as well as small narratives today in a world where economic signifiers and their signified meanings are more or less in a state of constant flux provoked by the marketplace of politics and the social as well as cultural rhetoric of globalization.

The Bank has also championed the Think Globally Act Locally slogan while the Millennium Development Goals themselves are a construct of social capital that require meaningful negotiations with the perceptions of disengaged civil societies and panoptic state systems.

The contributors to these Volumes have generally made serious attempts to answer such disturbing questions while located within the context of the much celebrated pedagogics of the oppressed discourse. I thank them for their insights and empathy with the core problem areas of this multi-volumes book project. Their sincere and painstaking efforts would be duly recognized if they receive critical acclaim from their readers.

The contributors have made indepth analysis in their chapters to scientifically analyze the problems and questions described above and investigate multiple options that may suggest compatibilities between States, Civil Societies, Markets and Politics in a world of dwindling borders and enhanced inequalities. They would be adequately rewarded for their academic efforts if these Volumes can provoke new theoretical and empirical research projects on globalization, human rights and poverty.

The contributors have also made attempts to best reflect the tensions described above and explore optimum resolutions that may lead to best fits or at least working relationships between individuals and their organized interactions called institutions. They would be amply rewarded if this book project of ours can lead to exciting research in relatively new areas such as social capital theory.

I thank all of them for their brilliant efforts to bring out these Volumes that looks both anew and askance to the ongoing human rights debates in the post-Cold War and post-9/11 world when established notions have been subverted by a new politics and fresh strategies of engaging the Self with the Collective. Their efforts would be rewarded if these Volumes receive critical academic appreciation on a global basis.

I also avail of this opportunity to thank all the contributors who have worked tirelessly to make this book project successful. I would always remember the wonderful friendships cultivated and the important scholarly lessons learnt while engaged in this academic exercise. I have enriched myself both in personal and professional terms while dealing with subjects such as trust, ethics and cooperation.

I also wish to thank the Publisher whose editorial staff members have worked with commitment to make this book project successful. I would fondly cherish the professional relationships developed and the academic insights derived while working on these Volumes. I sincerely hope that this anthology would lead to a renewed interest in the ongoing global versus local debates among researchers and practitioners worldwide.

These Volumes on sustainable development and inclusive growth is an exciting anthology where contributors from diverse backgrounds and professional disciplines have united in order to share their multicultural experiences and research insights to add both academic value and practitioner worldviews to the ongoing debates on the best practices of sustainable development strategies worldwide.

This multi-Volume book series is a global project that seeks to make available a common platform to academics, researchers, practitioners and activists alike so that they may in turn document their pluralist voices and specific choices of sustainable development interventions and initiatives based on their own local endeavours underpinned by global compulsions.

As the Editor of this book project I must admit that my initial motivation to plan and execute such an academic exercise was catalyzed during my visit to the Danish Institute of Rural Research and Development (IFUL) under the University of Southern Denmark in Esbjerg as a Guest Professor in 2007. I am grateful to Professor Flemming Just of IFUL and his colleagues who had inspired me considerably to edit these Volumes.

It was at IFUL that I first hit upon the idea of designing a book series that would suitably try to incorporate lessons learnt and research methodologies of sustainable development projects (among other related issues and concerns such as the history, institutional arrangements, case studies, land reforms, decentralized governance, community mobilization, gender empowerment, indigenous technologies, multi-stakeholder dialogues and success stories) both from the North and South.

Sustainable development is an important concern at the policy and praxes levels,: as this issue leads to related concerns like political decentralization, good environmental governance, human ecology, legal reforms, institutional rethinking, fiscal readjustments, eminent domain and the overall ethics of development. Sustainable development strategies and practices have recently emerged in the context of the Millennium Development Goals as a *problematique* of Neo-Liberal and Neo-Institutional Globalization that may be ideally negotiated in terms of locally workable strategies.

Participatory development strategies can be supported by an entire array of methodological tools like Focus Group Discussions, Gender Interviews, Community Meetings, Logical Framework Analysis and Risks Assessment. Resource Mapping, for instance, is an imperative requirement for Sustainable Development Projects. Micro-planning at the grassroots must inform the aims and aspirations of the concerned stakeholders. Management of sustainable development is nearly always intrinsic to local level realities. So it is critical to be attuned to the local insights for sustainable development projects to emerge as exemplars at the global level. This leads to our glocal approach as a combination of the global and the local.

Sustainable development and management indicators can be both quantitative and qualitative in nature in order to provide primary inputs to monitor different projects, evaluate progress of project implementation and guide the stakeholders to sustain the benefits of these projects. Such indicators may also evaluate the impacts of these projects on the quality of life of the stakeholders before and after implementation, and also examine the increased level of community participation and awareness-generation *vis-à-vis* project interventions.

Sustainable development plans must also strategize and implement both qualitative and quantitative methods in order to examine the ground realities and design physical interventions for different identified projects. Such interventions should generally be participatory and qualitatively differ from the conventional top-down approaches that involve measurement of project performance against pre-set indicators by using standardized procedures and tools.

Participatory development may be defined as an interactive process during the passage of which the concerned stakeholders gain access to effective decision-making either directly or *via* institutionalized dynamics. This helps to identify the needs and perceptions of the primary stakeholders, sustains project benefits even after withdrawal of the implementing agencies, monitors physical progress, streamlines civil societal institutional arrangements and develops a sense of ownership among community members *vis-à-vis* their collective assets.

Problems of sustainable development and inclusive growth may be identified by deploying participatory processes. The problems identified should be converted into need-based statements. This exercise requires prioritization of development projects. The achievements of sustainable development projects usually depend on how project beneficiaries react to the resources created, managed and/or sustained by the project initiatives.

Management of inclusive growth is generally an arrangement of value-specific interventions where progress indicates contrasting worldviews, where new actors help evolve different modes of production and where dynamic stakeholder interfaces result in participatory mechanisms. Sustainable development so tends to emerge as an ongoing process that tries to resolve (with uneven success) the tension of priorities between the Centre and periphery.

I am grateful to the Publisher who has steadfastly supported my idea of editing this book project. Special thanks are due to Dr. Gunnar Lind Haase Svendsen of IFUL with whom I share common research interests and inclinations in the social sciences. I am also much beholden to the Contributors to these Volumes who kindly responded to my Call for Papers in a prompt manner. I am certain that their valuable papers would duly receive scholarly attention and academic recognition world-wide.

September 2008 **Prasenjit Maiti**
Salt Lake City
Kolkata (India)

1

Globalization Process and South Asia: Opportunities, Challenges and Strategies for Global Governance[1]

SOMESH K. MATHUR

Globalization has been defined as the process by which markets and production in different countries are becoming increasingly interdependent due to dynamics of trade in goods and service and the flows of capital and technology. The growing interdependence is revealed not only by the rising ratio of trade to output, but also by increased foreign investment, international joint ventures, inter-firm agreements, reduced trade barriers, emergence of a relatively open international trading system and liberal trading policy climate created by the various multilateral trading rounds and unilateral and regional liberalization efforts. Information and communication revolution in the 1990s is a major contributor towards rising world trade to output ratio. Rising ratio of world trade to world output can be viewed as an indicator of globalization.

The much more pertinent question is to discuss the opportunities and the constraints imposed by globalization on the ability to undertake autonomous national development and articulate ways and means to manage the tensions and problems of globalization and to seize the opportunities of globalization.

Globalization Process: Historical Background

The last decades of the nineteenth century (from 1870's) to the early twentieth century (up to 1914) was a period of rapid growth of the global economy based on expansion of international trade and free capital mobility under the gold standard. This regime came to an end with the disarray brought about by World War I, which in turn was followed by the big inflations and macroeconomic turbulence of the 1920s in several major European economies and thereafter, by the Great Depression of the 1930s. These events, in turn, radically reshaped prevailing ideas on how to stabilize global and national economies and the role of international trade and capital movements as engines of growth and prosperity. Global capitalism was seen as inherently unstable system; prone both to periods of volatility and inflation, as in the 1920s, or to recessionary trends without self correcting mechanisms that assure full employment, as it was patently demonstrated in the 1930s.

A new set of global institutions emerged in the mid 1940s, known as the Bretton Woods Institutions. The International Monetary Fund was given the mandate of assuring a normal payments under a system of fixed exchange rates, and providing external financing to countries running balance of payments deficits. The role of the World Bank was to provide long term financing reconstruction and development.

A period of considerable stability, rapid growth and prosperity lasted from the late 1940s to the early 1970s; this period, called the 'golden age of capitalism', was based on a (globally and nationally) regulated market economy. This regulated market economy could be defined by a myriad of global institutions in charge of providing stability and development assistance, complemented by national institutions such as the 'welfare state', in industrial countries and a 'developmentalist state', in developing countries, oriented to assure social protection and shared growth. The state also was to implement counter-cyclical macroeconomic policies oriented towards maintaining full employment. The 'golden age of capitalism' ran out of steam in the industrial economies with the two oil price shocks and the ensuing stagflation during the 1970s. Developing countries, in turn, borrowed heavily in the 1970s and 1980s, a process that led to debt crisis of the 1980s and early 1990s. The 1990s and the millennium year have also experienced financial instability in some of the developing economies: macroeconomic disequilibrium due to high fiscal deficits in Latin American countries (Brazil, Argentina, Ecuador), the East Asian banking and currency crisis in 1997, The Mexican Peso crisis in 1994, the EMU crisis in 1992, The Russian crisis of 1998 and by 1999, newly elected President Fernando de la

Rúa of Argentina faced a country where unemployment had risen to a critical point, and the undesirable effects of the fixed exchange rate were showing forcefully resulting in GDP dropping by 4 per cent and the country entering a recession phase (which was to last three years, ending in a collapse), among others.

Financial instabilities can be caused by instabilities in institutions and instabilities in markets. Institutional instability exists when 'failure of one or a few institutions (due to inability to meet their contractual obligations) spreads and causes more widespread economic damage while market instability, on the other hand, is defined 'in terms of the wider impact that volatility in asset prices and capital flows (short-term) can have on the economy' (Crockett, 1997). These apart, another potential source of instability, which has gained prominence in recent times, has been instability associated with disruptions to market infrastructure. Instability in market infrastructure is caused by inefficient working of the payment and settlement systems, inadequate development of prudential regulation, lack of corporate governance and non-workable legal and judicial system. Corporate governance in its wide connotation covers a variety of aspects, such as protection of shareholders rights, enhancing shareholders value, broad issues including its composition and rôle, disclosure requirements, integrity of accounting practices and internal control systems (Reddy, 1999). Another source of banking and currency crises is the asymmetric information existing in capital markets leading to adverse actions by debtors and creditors.

Globalization, boosted by the adoption of market oriented economic policies and high degree of capital mobility in both currency and bond markets, short-term credit and other financial instruments in developing countries and transition economies, is being accompanied by substantial financial volatility characterized by currency and banking crisis of high frequency and intensity, affecting large developing and transition economies. Interestingly, the global economy of the late twentieth century resembles, in several respects, the pre-1914 liberal economic order in the sense of more open regime for international trade, foreign investment, migration and capital movements even by the late twentieth century standards (O'Rourke and Williamsom, 1999). War brought all this to an end and despite the efforts of politicians and organizations such as League of Nations, the interwar period was to see further retreats into protectionism, the erection of barriers to immigration, the final breakdown of gold standard, and a wave of international defaults.

To a large extent, post -1945 integration can be seen as an attempt to recoup the losses of the interwar period (O'Rourke, 2001). There are some differences, however, between pre-1914 and late twentieth century globalization. First, the degree of capital mobility is of unprecedence in nature. In the nineteenth century also one saw a large amount of capital mobility, international factor mobility was much more symmetric, labour being an internationally mobile then as capital. The nineteenth century saw not merely the European migrations to USA, Australia, New Zealand. It saw a large migrations from India and China too. Those days one did not even need a passport to go from one country to another. Secondly, in early twentieth century globalization there was not global financial institutions aimed at stabilizing the world economy, financial development, setting global rules for international trade in goods and services (the WTO), and provide a political and diplomatic forum to settle disputes and address a host of other global issues (e.g., nuclear proliferation, climatic changes, poverty, etc.) such as United Nations. Thirdly, compared with the end of the nineteenth century when international trade was concentrated in generic products (one country sold, say, wheat and bought textiles), today a country quite often imports as well as exports the same product, whether it is cars or computer parts. We call this intra-industry trade. The implication this has is that it makes the traded commodity much more substitutable and, therefore, the competition is much more intense today.

Despite all the talk of globalization, it is overstated sometimes today. Citizens of most countries, even today, like the US and even in India, invest overwhelming proportions of savings within their own country. Most countries have an overwhelmingly large non-trade sector. In the international markets even in tradable goods, price arbitrage and convergence takes place very slowly. In financial markets, even with all the integration in most advanced economies, real interest rates are not equal among them.

However, today, shrinking space, shrinking time and disappearing borders are linking people's lives more intensely, more immediately than ever before. That is, people everywhere are becoming connected—affected by events in far corners of the world. Here, we have new markets (Foreign Exchange and Capital

Markets linked globally, operating 24 hours a day, with dealings at a distance in real time); new tools (Internet Links, Cellular Phones, Media Networks); and new actors (the World Trade Organization with authority over national governments, the multi-national corporations with more economic power than many states, the global networks of non-governmental organizations and other groups that transcend national boundaries); and new rules (multilateral agreements on trade, services and intellectual property, backed by strong enforcement mechanisms and more binding for national governments, reducing the scope for national policy). The challenge of globalization in the new century is not to stop the expansion of global markets but to find the rules and institutions for stronger governance—local, national, regional and global—to preserve the advantages of global markets and competitions; and also to provide enough space for human, community and environmental resources to ensure that globalization works for people (UNDP, 1999).

In this sense, globalization is shaping a new era of interaction among nations, economies and people. It is increasing the contacts between people across national boundaries—in economy, in technology, in culture and in governance. But it is also fragmenting production processes, labour markets, political entities and societies. So, while globalization has positive, innovative, dynamic aspects—it also has negative, disruptive, marginalizing aspects. Today's interactions between nations and people are deeper than ever as shown by global trends and links. During this global integration are policy shifts to promote economic efficiency through the liberalization and deregulation of national markets and the retreat of the state from many economic activities, including the restructuring of the welfare state. Driving integration even faster are the recent innovations in information and communications technology. But global integration is still very partial since the flow of labour is restricted, with borders closed to the unskilled. However, the world today has more opportunities for people than hundred years ago. Child death rates have fallen by half and a child born today can expect to live a decade longer than a child born then. In developing countries, the combined primary and secondary enrolment ratio has more than doubled—and the proportion of children in primary school has risen and form less than half to more than three-quarters. Also, adult literacy rates have risen and more states are now independent with more than seventy per cent of the world's people living under fairly pluralist democratic regimes. But these trends make great unevenness in the advances and in the new setbacks.

Despite the tremendous progress in the twentieth century, the world today faces huge backlogs of deprivation and inequality that leave huge disparities within countries and regions. Global governance, therefore, is the framework of rules, institutions and practices that set limits on the behaviour of individuals, organizations and companies; and hence the inter-governmental policy-making in today's global economy is in the hands of the major industrial powers and international institutions they control (The World Bank, International Monetary Fund, and the Bank for International Settlements). Their rule-making may create a secure environment for open markets, but there are no countervailing rules to protect human rights and promote human development. More so, *ad hoc* and self-selected policy groups have emerged in the past decade to make *de facto* global economic policy, outside the United Nations or any other format system with democratic processes and participation. Some of these groupings includes G-7, G-22, G-15, and G-10. All these groups play a key part in international economic policy-making, yet only the G-22 has any consultation with developing countries, and then only with a select few. And yet, one big development in opening opportunities for people to participate in global governance has been the growing strength and influence of NGOs. They have been effective advocates for human development, maintaining pressure on national governments, international agencies and corporations to live up to commitments. A theme that deserves further attention is the need to strike a proper balance between global, regional and national institutions responses to challenges posed by globalization.

Tensions and Dilemmas of Globalization

As of today global events like possibility of interest hike in major developed economies and volatilities in stocks, property and commodity markets tend to have major impact on growth rates across the regions including the South Asian Economies.

One tension of globalization is associated with the fact that in a more interdependent and interlinked world economy any adverse global or regional shock, for example the Asian and Russian crisis of 1997-98, is rapidly propagated to the other economies including a limited impact on India through changes in the value of exchange rate[2]. The propagation (contagion) mechanism at work can be a decline in the import volume and/or changes in the real price of commodities (oil, copper, timber, rubber, etc). Economies that depends heavily on a few commodities as their main source of export earnings and fiscal revenues can be hit hard by these shocks. This has been the case of Mexico, Indonesia, Ecuador, Venezuela, and Russia with the drop in oil prices, and Chile with the decline in copper prices, to give some examples. Another transmission mechanism is asset markets. Highly integrated markets tend to transmit global, regional or local shocks much more rapidly than in past decades when financial markets were less integrated. Portfolio shifts affect exchange rates, interest rates and economic activity. As the volumes of financial intermediation and currency transactions are enormous now-a-days, shocks can greatly be amplified in more or less synchronized fashion with destabilizing effects on many economies. This source of financial volatility was largely absent in the world's of the 1950s, 1960s and early 1970s when multilateral lending and aid dominated global capital movements although financial crises is a phenomena prevalent throughout the twentieth century. There is ample empirical evidence showing that uncertainty and volatility penalize capital formation (and productivity growth) with adverse effects on economic growth. Thus instability and volatility can be ultimately viewed as a tax on growth and prosperity. In many instances, this instability originates from abroad. However, the quality of the domestic policy response in the face of adverse external shocks matter. These are policies which create sound macro economic (low fiscal deficit with expenditure management) and good micro-economic environment (Prudent supervision and regulations alongwith curb on speculative behaviour) to deal with the instabilities and shocks originating from outside. The problem of moral hazard (Tendency to take risk actions by debtors when the creditors cannot supervise the actions of debtors) and adverse selection (the problem of choosing the right borrowers) is prevalent in capital markets due to asymmetric information between debtors and creditors. Countries need judicious mix of regulations and supervision on assessing the movements of capital and more debtor creditor meet to deal with the above mentioned twin problem of moral hazard and adverse selection. The nature and timing of the domestic policy response can often soften the impact of these shocks.

Another tension of globalization lies in social effects. As globalization is often associated with increased instability of output and employment, this affects, among other things, job security. As labour income is the main source of earnings for the majority of population under capitalism, job insecurity is socially disruptive and brings tension to the fabric of society. In addition, flexibility in labour markets required to compete, successfully, in international markets, tends to erode long-term work and personal relationship between firms and employees, workers and managers that traditionally give a sense of security to people.

Another open discussion is whether foreign trade and globalization narrows or widen income disparities. Large part of the opposition to globalization relates to the damage caused to jobs, wages and incomes of poor people by the dislocation and competition of international trade and foreign investment and the weakening of the ability of the state to compensate for this damage and in general to alleviate poverty (Bardhan, 2006). Traditional trade theory suggesting factor price equalization across countries seem of little relevance in a world of large per-capita income differentials (*e.g.* between South Asian economies and between South Asian and the OECD); moreover, convergence in income levels is, at least, very weak across regions and nations.

In addition, globalization gives a premium to people with sophisticated skills, high levels of education, and entrepreneurial traits. These are people better equipped to survive and succeed in the more competitive world brought about by globalization. The mirror image of this is that unskilled labour, uneducated workers and marginalized population are likely to benefit less in a more competitive world economy. Thus income and wealth inequality can be amplified, underscoring the need for public policy to correct these inegalitarian trends.

Another critique of globalization is that it tends to transmit the cultural patterns of large countries to the rest of the world through imitation of consumption patterns, global mass media and other means of influence. This trend would, eventually, lead to homogenization of values, thereby reducing cultural diversity and national identities.

The Opportunities of Globalization: A Closer Examination

The economic order of the late twentieth century offers many opportunities to developing countries and other actors in the global economy. The drastic reductions in barriers to international trade have opened the door for export led growth. In fact, for small and medium sized economies with limited internal markets, the possibilities for rapid economic growth lie, to a large extent, in production oriented towards international markets. The historical experiences of the last three decades show that countries that have managed to grow at very rapid growth rates, say 7 per cent, 8 per cent or more per year, have all relied on strong export growth, with exports expanding at faster rate than GDP. This has been the case of East Asia since the 1960s (upto their current crisis of 1997), China, since the mid-1970s, Chile since the mid-1980s and others. Sachs and Warner (1995) find that an economy open to trade during the period 1965-90 grew 1.97 percentage points faster per year compared with an economy that was completely closed throughout the period. Even Prime Minister Manmohan Singh's PhD thesis submitted at Cambridge in the 1960s propagated that the country needs to export to earn the foreign exchange for importing the basic requirements of the country at the right time.

Globalization creates, through export-led expansion, the potential of rapid overall output growth, increasing national wealth and contributing to improve living standards in developing countries. However, Rodriguez and Rodrik (1999) have reviewed recent empirical studies that strongly supported the consensus on the virtues of openness. On theoretical grounds, they claim that freer trade raises income once and for all but cannot raise its growth rate in a sustained fashion. Srinivasan and Bhagwati (1999) contest the arguments put forward by the study. They, however, agree that models can be built which show that free trade will reduce current income and even growth compared to autarky if market failures are present. Bhagwati (1958) showed that growth under free trade may even lower welfare. This can happen if distortions are present. Therefore, in the presence of distortions the link between trade openness and growth breaks down and policies may need to be designed that reduce trade distortions. They also contest the Rodriguez-Rodrik critique of the recent findings supporting growth-enhancing aspects of trade openness. It may be pointed out that different growth models (like endogenous growth models) may predict outcomes that show that trade openness may sustain growth rates permanently.

Another benefit of globalization is the access to a wide variety of consumption goods, new technologies and knowledge. Globalization allows the access to ideas and international best practices in different fields and realms: This can be a new product design, a new investment project, a new production technology, a new managerial practice. It can be a certain set of institutions that has proved successful in other places, and, eventually, model of society. Of course the mere acquisitions or imitation of foreign products, technologies or foreign social models to local conditions with all their specificities and idiosyncratic features is not a guarantee of success. It is a just potential benefit (or cost if use in misleading fashion) deriving from broadening the set of choices open to the participants of the global economy. For example, very careful recent work now shows that in developing countries, even when sometimes the countries gain from ideas and goods brought in by multinational company, there is very little spillover of benefits to domestic firms other than the joint ventures in the same industry, contrary to what was thought before (Harrison and Hanson, 1999). Spreading of benefits is necessary so that the economy does not become an enclave economy. It may call for policies designed to invite foreign investment in all sectors. Also, subsidies on the capital flows from abroad may not essentially bring benefits for all and the governments need to rethink the case for such subsidies.

Sometimes what is brought in as new technology is not really new technology, only new brand names. This is particularly true in the case of pharmaceuticals. The pharmaceutical sector is highly research intensive industry, highly protected by patents. Quite often, a patent is taken out for a new drug, but it is not actually not a new drug, but a recombination of the ingredients of the old drug. The companies take out a patent so that it stops competition and they can charge exorbitant prices. The patent issue is discussed under the TRIPS agreement of the WTO. In the context of the TRIPS agreement competition policy coupled with compulsory licensing offers one avenue for mitigating some of the most egregious effects of TRIPS agreement (Mathur, 2001). However, it is important to add that every 73 TRIPS articles relating to different aspects of the intellectual property rights have different impact on the development of the country and one needs to take an objective stand while article 39.3 of TRIPS talks of unfair commercial use but not of data exclusivity, Article 8 talks of technological transfers with balanced growth and equity, TRIPS incorporates the importance of governments in committing to Public Health concerns of the citizens (dealing with Malaria, Tuberculosis, AIDS, Cancer and possibly in future drugs pertaining to the developing countries like dengue and chickengunia, among others) through the Doha Development Agenda of the World Trade Organization, the same TRIPS agreement is silent about benefit sharing, declaration of the "source" of genetic resources and traditional knowledge and prior informed consent). TRIPS allows considerable flexibility in how countries may design their patent systems. Developing countries may stand to lose due to providing extensive patent protection as a means of encouraging research because it may have affect on prices especially of medicines[3]. Therefore, developing countries like India should aim for strict standards of patentability to avoid granting patents that may have limited value in relation to their health objectives. Such systems should aim to promote competition, and provide safeguards in the event of abuses of the patent system. The issue of technology transfer is possibly one of the most important area of interest to developing countries. It was precisely because of this concern that many developing countries were originally opposed to a GATT-driven accord on intellectual property rights. With the growing technological gap between the developed and developing countries, the developing countries like India should increasingly call for creation of mechanisms that promote technology transfer and dissemination. This may be possible if the Article 27 of the TRIPS agreement on patentable subject is extended to protect all types of technologies. Also, Article 7 of the TRIPS Agreement on technology transfers with balanced growth and equity for producers and users should be strengthened and used more often along with the other inbuilt flexibilities in TRIPS like parallel imports, compulsory licenses and Bolar provisions to tackle the egregious impact of TRIPS on the citizens of the country. The threat at this juncture however is coming in the form of "The TRIPS plus" provision inbuilt in many of the bilateral and WIPO agreements and our own patent laws which have gone beyond providing minimum protection (Mathur, 2007).

There is very little support in mainstream international trade theory for charging exorbitant prices for patented drugs in developing countries (Helpman, 1993). The rich countries always tells us that patents and high prices are necessary for foreign invention. One reason this is not relevant is that for many of these products the major market is in rich countries, and whether developing countries protect with the same degree of zeal or not is going to matter very much ultimately for the origin of the innovations. Secondly, there are, many cases where the main demand for the drugs is potentially in the poor countries (as in the case of drugs against tropical diseases like malaria). But even in such cases there is no denying the fact that the monopoly pricing through patents is often socially inefficient. There are now very interesting suggestions by many economists for an intermediate solution to the problem which keeps the private incentives for innovation alive, and yet society pitches in for hard pressed consumers. The idea of international cooperation on malaria vaccine research is very interesting example in which the drug multinationals, the World Health Organization (WHO) and the local governments are now getting together. The latter will contribute towards guaranteeing the market for the drug multinationals if they come up with a suitable product.

Providing education is a necessary condition to take advantage of globalization. The impact of globalization on growth depends on people's ability to absorb and use the information and technology made available to them through trade and investment. However, it will be not only the quantity but also the quality of education which will matter in preparing citizens to better absorb knowledge in the information age. Improvement in quality should be complementary to the expansion of education. If the poor can only go to lower quality schools with fewer opportunities of getting jobs in the future, the incentives for parents to send their children to schools would be lower. When coverage is not universal in low income countries, a win-win strategy is to focus on policy interventions that can raise demand for both the quantity and quality of education services. For example, policies designed to reduce child labour and keep children in schools, such as lunch programmes, cash stipends for schooling can go very well with those for improving quality of schooling as teacher training. A World Bank study on the interaction between education and openness suggests that increase in education and openness might have interacted to produce especially strong returns to investment and that openness facilitates the importation of knowledge-enhancing capital, promotes learning by doing and provides higher payoffs to education. Also, crucial for economic development is a more equitable distribution of quality education across population groups through capacity-building and improvements in infrastructure in schools and colleges and training of teachers by the government.

In the present international set up the process of globalization is making many companies from India global. We have found a new trend when companies from many developing countries especially from India and involved in steel and pharmaceutical business, among others, acquiring firms of higher value abroad. Kumar (2006) finds that Indian enterprises draw their ownership advantages from their accumulated production experience, cost effectiveness of their production processes and other adaptations to imported technologies made with their technological support, and sometimes with their ability to differentiate product. Policy liberalization in India since 1990s turns out to have pushed Indian enterprises abroad.

Conclusion

Globalization implies greater economic integration with the world economy in trade, investment, flow of information, knowledge, technology, financial flows, travel, greater mobility of labour, etc. Today globalization is not an option but an indisputable fact of life. Indian policy-makers needs to take an objective stand to weigh benefits and costs associated with the globalization process and prepare itself to deal with the globalization process through upgrading of skills of their citizens through access and affordability of quality education and public health, improving infrastructure including information networks through ICT technologies, and creating conditions and regulations to support the under-privileged where all have an equal opportunity for upward mobility. Many investments in public health and education have long-term benefits and policies have to be designed looking into the long-term future of the country least it wants to have a change of profile and demography and casualization of jobs in years to come. The Globalization Process re-enforces the need to articulate and achieve national development goals.

The social cost of development through globalization can become onerous for developing countries including India. Integrated management of macroeconomic and social policies is not always easy in situations of continuous change and fluctuations. Indeed national action is essential to capture global opportunities in trade, capital flow and migration and to protect people against the uncertainties and vulnerabilities of globalization. Individual actions require themselves to have multiple identities to better deal with the egregious impact of the globalization process rather than veil the mask of single identities like being a Hindu, Muslim, Christian among other religious identities and then face the upcoming challenges. But the success of national action hinges on how effectively countries can negotiate at the global level. Thus reinventing global governance is not an option but an imperative for the twenty-first century. Global Competition and market efficiency are the big objectives of current efforts to restructure global economic governance. The latter need to incorporate human development priorities for people in all parts of the world (for poverty reduction, equity, sustainability and human development). Here, the institutions of global governance have leaned hard on national governments to adopt their preferred systems of social protection—marginal for the International Monetary Fund, social safety nets for the World Bank and a broader and more pragmatic range of social policy options and mechanisms for other United Nations agencies. But a broader, more coherent set of international principles is required—as some governments are beginning to recognize. Such agreements, carefully defined can raise living standards and protect the environment, without setting back employment or discouraging foreign investment. Collective regional action can ensure that the decisions are based on the needs of people in the countries concerned. In other words, with the new challenges of globalization, and the need to ensure stronger action on old problems and new, the time has to come to rethink the global architecture. Some of the key element of the proposed international architecture are a stronger and more coherent UN System, with greater commitment from all countries; a global central bank; a world investment trust with redistributive functions and transfer mechanism; a world environment agency; a revised world trade organization; a more inclusive Bank for International Settlement, an international criminal court and a broader United Nations. Thus, just as countries need central banks, so the world needs a central bank in the twenty-first century. The recent establishment of the European Central Bank demonstrates the perceived need among some of the richest industrial countries. A World Central Bank would, therefore, help stabilize global economic activity by performing several vital functions: acting as lender of resort; regulating financial institutions and flows; calming financial markets when they become jittery or disorderly; and creating and regulating new international liquidity. Enlarging the mandate of the IMF would be one approach while another would be to establish a world financial authority. Keynes' original proposal was that the global monetary authority should have access to resources equivalent to 50 per cent of world imports. The US counter-proposal was for 15 per cent. Several mechanisms are available to expand the global financial resources, including a renewed issue of special drawing rights and agreements with the main central banks to permit enlarged swap arrangements. Quick access to funding may be as important as the size of the resources available and procedures to achieve this need to be explored such as advance agreement on provisional lines of credit. In addition, there is an urgent need for new mechanisms to generate additional flows of resources to poor developing countries as well as new funding for global public goods. Indeed, relative to today's global economy and the global challenge of sustainability, present structures and levels of global supports are minuscule. Needed is a world environment agency, possibly developed from UNEP, with much larger resources and broader functions. These include to oversee the global environment presenting reports and posing issues for review and policy-making; to broker deals and to serve as a clearing bank. One important focus of that agency would be to encourage the removal of perverse subsidies and shift the resources released to direct support of environmental protection and other measures (including employment creation) for its cleaning house functions, the agency would oversee trade in permits for green house gas emissions, along the lines explored in the clean development mechanism proposed in the climate conferences. Emission rights could be borrowed or lent, but not sold and thus keeping the market competitive and avoiding any risk that developing countries might lose long-term control over their rights. Also, the clearing house would be a new mechanism for mobilizing additional financial resources for developing countries, especially the poorest. Finally, the world is rushing headlong into greater integration that is driven mostly by economic forces and guided mostly by a philosophy of market profitability and economic efficiency. People in all parts of the world need to join in the debate and to make clear their interests and concerns. The process of reinventing global governance must be broader and human development can provide framework for this exploration. These new and stronger international institutions of global governance can be global public goods. At the national level, public goods have been recognized as vital when the market is neither the incentive nor the mechanism to meet a public need. With growing globalization, international public goods are now needed for similar reasons. This new perspective is much more than a change of terminology. To recognize the need for global goods is to accept the importance of actions of global governance beyond the capacity of individual countries to provide, to establish a rationale for new forms of financial support that countries need to ensure but to recognize also that without special efforts such support may not be forthcoming. These issues become matters for political advocacy and education on globalization in which all countries have a role and a stake.

But the greatest challenges may lie in (1) the systemic weakness entailed in huge and still-growing global finance imbalances and rising public debt in high income countries. The current account deficit of the United States surpassed $ 800 billion, matched by increased surpluses elsewhere, particularly in Europe, East Asia and oil exporting countries. In several parts of the world, growing savings surpluses appear to be essentially caused by stagnating or reduced investment rates. This could cause long term interest rates to rise much faster than expected, and dampen growth prospects. How can these be corrected without a world-wide recession? The solution has to build on higher domestic demand in Europe and Japan, but a coordinated international macroeconomic approach that includes the major developed and developing countries; (2) The world economy though has been expanding strongly but unemployment remains a problem in many countries. Globally, almost half the unemployed people are young (aged 15-24), although they make up only 25 per cent of the working-age population; (3) A multilateral round which can negotiate reduction in agricultural subsidies provided by the developed nations and opens up markets for products originating in the Developing Nations. Also, the debates on TRIPS were part of broader issues of the role of technology in development and could not be addressed in narrower legalistic terms pertaining to enforcement. However, in case of India the open definition of the new chemical entities that the TRIPS agreement uses has opened a Pandora Box and there is possibility that it may affect affordability and accessibility of medicines in future; and (4) The ongoing challenge of poverty—

> *South Asia faces an enormous challenge. Home to 1.4 billion people, the region accounts for about half of the world's poor with five hundred million people living on less than $1 a day. Beyond income poverty, human deprivation remains deep. South Asia has the world's highest illiteracy rate at 44 per cent and accounts for one-third of all maternal deaths in the world.*

Although the Asian region has been growing faster economically than most parts of the world for two decades or more, the eradication of poverty remains a challenge.

In tackling the problem of poverty it is important to remember that rapid economic growth along with poverty reduction directed programmes and land reforms remains the surest route for reducing both income poverty and non-income poverty. Rapid economic growth provides opportunities for employment in both the formal and informal sectors of an economy and it generates resources for the public sector. In this manner, issues of non-income poverty, such as insufficient or poor-quality public goods, that is, education, health, transport and housing, can be meaningfully addressed. However, rapid growth alone may not be enough. It appears that in countries where poverty is widespread, jobs and income growth alone will not have a positive impact on non-income poverty. In such cases, the governments concerned need to intervene to make the growth process more equitable by expanding the provision of, and access to public goods, particularly for and by the poor. Inequitable growth is an important issue in many smaller economies, including LDCs. The world decided in the year 2000 to launch a concerted attack on poverty and the problems of illiteracy, hunger, and discrimination against women, unsafe drinking water and a degraded environment. Meeting at the United Nations at the dawn of the new Millennium, leaders from virtually all countries agreed to a set of eight ambitious Goals. Developing countries, the most highly victimized by poverty, have been taking the lead in this campaign, especially regarding the first seven Goals concerning direct improvements in human well-being. The eighth Goal includes steps that developed countries need to take in support of the campaigns of developing countries to win the first round in the fight to ultimately eradicate poverty. Most of the targets set for progress on the Millennium Development Goals are benchmarked for the period 1990 to 2015—promising clear and measurable

The Chart 1.1 shows progress upto September 2005, drawing on the latest information from all countries of the world and from the UN family of operational agencies. The Chart 1.1 depicts that Southern Asia and Sub-Saharan African countries have moderate success in achieving the MDGs and the process and planning needs to be done judiciously and adequately on attaining parity with the goals. In 1990, China and India each had about 470 million living under the $1 a day poverty line, with 230 million in Sub-Saharan Africa. By 2015, there could be under 12 million poors in China, around 205 million in India, but over 330 million in Sub-Saharan Africa[4]. Sustaining growth rates with more equitable distribution of benefits through unilateral, multilateral and regional liberalization efforts remains the best instruments of achieving the MDGs for the South Asian countries. Apart from this, technology gap between developed and developing nations hinders achievement of the MDGs[5].

Most developing countries are unlikely to narrow the technology gap without making Science and Technology top priorities in their development agenda. The process of technology creation, diffusion and use is not automatic. It requires carefully designed strategies and policies. Local adaptation, effective use and improvement upon existing technologies require more than technology transfer. It requires building a solid scientific base, domestic capacity-building and raising human capital. Raising human capital and skills through education and training is essential to building domestic capabilities. Special attention should be paid to young students, especially women, to enter the fields of science and technology. Efforts should also be made to reverse the impact of brain drain. Upgrading both physical and services infrastructure are important strategies for domestic capacity-building. Also, this calls for new analytical and evaluation tools to help decision-makers make infrastructure choices that deliver vital services. These services include energy, transportation and water, which facilitate growth and achieve the

Chart 1.1: Millennium Development Goals: 2005 Progress

Goals and Targets	*Africa*		*Asia*				*Oceania*	*Latin America and Caribbean*	*Commonwealth of Independent States*	
	Northern	*Sub-Saharan*	*Eastern*	*South-eastern*	*Southern*	*Western*			*Europe*	*Asia*
GOAL 1 : Eradicate Extreme Poverty and Hunger										
Reduce Extreme Poverty by Half	Low Poverty	Very High Poverty	Moderate Poverty	Moderate Poverty	High Poverty	Low Poverty	—	Moderate Poverty	Low Poverty	Low Poverty
Reduce Hunger by Half	Very Low Hunger	Very High Hunger	Moderate Hunger	Moderate Hunger	High Hunger	Moderate Hunger	Moderate Hunger	Moderate Hunger	Very Low Hunger	High Hunger
GOAL 2 : Achieve Universal Primary Education										
Universal Primary Schooling	High Enrolment	Low Enrolment	High Enrolment	High Enrolment	Moderate Enrolment	Moderate Enrolment	Moderate Enrolment	High Enrolment	Moderate Enrolment	High Enrolment

(*Contd.*)

Chart 1.1: *Contd.*

GOAL 3 : Promote Gender Equality and Empower Women										
Equal girl's enrolment in primary school	Close to parity	Far from parity	Parity	Parity	Far from parity	Nearly close to parity	Close to parity	Parity	Parity	Parity
Women's share of paid employment	Law share	Medium share	High share	Medium share	Low share	Low share	Medium share	High share	High share	High share
Women's equal representation in National Parliaments	Low representa-tion	Low representa-tion	Moderate representa-tion	Low representa-tion	Low representa-tion	Very low representa-tion	Very low repres-entation	Moderate representa-tion	Low repres-entation	Low repres-entation
GOAL 4 : Reduce Child Mortality										
Reduce Mortality of under five years old by two-thirds	Moderate Mortality	Very High Mortality	Moderate Mortality	Moderate Mortality	High Mortality	Moderate Mortality	High Morta-lity	Moderate Mortality	Low Morta-lity	High Morta-lity
Measles Immunization	High Coverage	Very Low Coverage	Moderate Coverage	Moderate Coverage	Low Coverage	Moderate Coverage	Very Low Cove-rage	High Coverage	High Cove-rage	High Cove-rage

(*Contd.*)

Chart 1.1: *Contd.*

GOAL 5 : Improve Maternal Health										
Reduce Maternal Mortality by Three Quarters	Moderate Mortality	Very High Mortality	Low Mortality	High Mortality	Very High Mortality	Moderate Mortality	High Mortality	Moderate Mortality	Low Mortality	Low Mortality
GOAL 6 : Combat HIV/AIDS, Malaria and other Diseases										
Halt and Reverse Spread of HIV/AIDS	—	Very High Prevalence	Low Prevalence	Moderate Prevalence	Moderate Prevalence	—	Moderate Prevalence	Moderate Prevalence	High Preva-lence	Low Prevalence
Halt and Reverse Spread of Malaria	Low Risk	High Risk	Moderate Risk	Moderate Risk	Moderate Risk	Low Risk	Low Risk	Moderate Risk	Low Risk	Low Risk
Halt and Spread of Tuberculosis	Low Mortality	High Mortality	Moderate Mortality	Moderate Mortality	Moderate Mortality	Low Mortality	Moderate Mortality	Low Mortality	Mode-rate Mortality	Moderate Mortality
GOAL 7 : Ensure Environmental Sustainability										
Reverse Loss of Forests	Small Area	Medium Area	Medium Area	Large Area	Medium Area	Small Area	Large Area	Large Area	Large Area	Small Area
Halve Proportion without Improved Drinking Water	High Coverage	Low Coverage	Moderate Coverage	Moderate Coverage	High Coverage	High Coverage	Low Coverage	High Coverage	High Cove-rage	Moderate Coverage

(*Contd.*)

Chart 1.1: *Contd.*

Halve Proportion without Sanitation	High Coverage	Very low Coverage	Low Coverage	Moderate Coverage	Very low Coverage	High Coverage	Moderate Coverage	High Coverage	High Cove-rage	Moderate Coverage
Improve the Lives of Slum Dwellers	Moderate Proportion of Slum Dwellers	Very High Proportion of Slum Dwellers	High Proportion of Slum Dwellers	Moderate Proportion of Slum Dwellers	Very High Proportion of Slum Dwellers	High Proportion of Slum Dwellers	—	High Proportion of Slum Dwellers	Low Propor-tion of Slum Dwellers	Moderate Proportion of Slum Dwellers

Note: Country experience in each region may differ significantly from the regional average. For the regional groupings and country data, see http://millenniumindicators.un.org.

Sources: United Nations, based on data and estimates provided by Food and Agriculture Organization; Inter-Parliamentary Union; International Labour Organization; UNESCO; UNICEF; World Health Organization; UNAIDS; UN-Habitat; World Bank—based on statistics available till September 2005.

Statistics Division, UNDESA.

Millennium Development Goals while also remaining cost-effective and friendly to the environment. Also, any FDI policy should stress on appropriate technology transfers and training of workers.

Information and Communication Revolutions (ICTs) across the globe and particularly in developing countries can also help achieve the Millennium Development Goals (MDGs), contribute to economic growth, productivity, and sustainable development and create jobs, and contribute to and improve the quality of life. The ICT sector is growing faster than the overall economy[6], and represents a substantial (and often increasing) share of GDP in India and some countries. However, the real potential of ICTs is not the direct impact of the ICT sector itself. The key economic impact of the spread and use of ICTs is indirect, by transforming the way individuals, businesses and other parts of the society work, communicate and interact. Information flows can help mobilize political action, build institutions, and foster accountability and governance. Of particular interest is the ability of ICTs to raise productivity. Through appropriate application, digital technologies might guide human capital accumulation, lower poverty, deliver information to schools and hospitals, improve public-services provision and make patterns of production more efficient. By increasing community outreach and enlarging the size and diversity of one's contact network, digital technologies might overcome obstacles to trade and thereby raise the degree of competition, making more efficient societies, not just individual workplace. Different macro-economic and firm-level studies confirm high potential productivity gains from ICTs but emphasize that the benefits of ICTs depend on a number of other factors. To maximize the effects of ICTs, other changes, including a new set of ICT skills, structural changes within business models and institutional and regulatory adjustments within the economy, must be made.

Furthermore, an interesting future area of research into this subject could examine if the growth of IT industry in India has ground level ramifications for India: drastic poverty, poor healthcare, providing quality education and access to books, national security and widespread hunger. If such growth is found to have positive effects, other countries would be well-advised to study the policies that the Government of India has undertaken and emulate them within the contexts of their own national goals.

The note suggests that the rhetoric on benefits and tensions of the globalization process often ignores the various complexities involved. More theoretical and empirical work is needed to examine the relationship between various macro- and micro-economic variables trade, poverty, unemployment, inequality, corporate governance, ICT technologies and national development, among others.

NOTES

1. This note draws heavily from Mathur, S.K. with S. Ashraf (2005), "Globalization and Development: Some Issues and Empirical Facts", in the felicitation volume of Professor Ashok Mathur (JNU) entitled "Industrialization, Economic Reforms and Regional Development", Shipra Publications, Delhi.
2. This forced many Indian Government politicians and officials at the time to propagate that India was relatively closed and so it survived the East Asian Crises. However, as mentioned later in the note that to deal with the banking and balance of payment crises country needs to curb speculative behaviour, reduce fiscal deficits of State and Central Governments, reduce its short-term debt to reserves ratio for reducing vulnerabilities, employ prudent supervision and regulations on movement of capital but making available adequate capital at the time of crisis to deal with the adverse impact of the crises. However, any solution needs to take into account that there is impossible trinity between monetary independence, full capital mobility and fixed exchange rate. It may be not out of place to also mention that there is a lot of discussion on movement of capital and policies to deal with the crises but with no commensurate discussion on movement of labour particularly from the developing countries to the developed world. This depicts the lack of focus of the international institutions to deal with core issues impacting the developing world.
3. While USA has approved 279 New Chemical Entities (NCEs) from 1995-2005, India faces the task of screening nearly 8000 applications for NCEs. Most of the applications its seems are for Incrementally Modified Medicines (IMM) and if we keep defining 'what is NCE' in a manner that we are doing right now there is a full possibility that patent may be granted to 'frivolous' or IMMs. The question is that why did we receive so many applications for NCEs knowing that there are only 25-30 new molecules founded every year.
4. Appendix Tables I and II give the Regional Breakdown of Poverty in Developing Countries ($ 1 a day) and Regional Breakdown of Poverty in Developing Countries ($ 2 a day) in 1990, 2002 and 2015.
5. The technology gap between and within nations is wide and substantial. It exists in all dimensions – from accessing knowledge to effective creation and use. Thus, the technology gap severely limits the efforts of developing countries in meeting the MDGs (Report of the Secretary General of the

United Nations to the Economic and Social Council. UN Commission on Science and Technology for Development (UNCSTD), UNCTAD, 30/03/06).

6. Access to information and communication technologies continues to grow at high speed and the digital divide—in terms of mobile subscribers, fixed telephone lines and Internet users—keeps getting smaller. International Telecommunication Union (ITU) statistics show that by the end of 2004, the telecommunication industry had experienced continuous growth, as well as rapid progress in policy and technology development, resulting in an increasingly competitive and networked world. There are more ICT users world-wide and more people communicating than at any other time in history. By the end of 2004, the world counted a total of three billion telephone subscribers, 1.8 billion mobile subscribers and 1.2 billion fixed lines. Both, the number of mobile subscribers and the number of Internet users more than doubled in just four years. By the end of 2004, the world had over 840 million Internet users, which means that on average 13 per cent of the world's population was online.

REFERENCES

Bardhan, Pranab (2006)," Globalization and the Limits to Poverty Alleviation", in Pranab Bardhan, Samuel Bowles and Micichael Wallerstein book entitled *Globalization and Egalitarian Redistribution*, OUP, India.

Bhagwati, Jagdish (1958)," Immiserizing Growth: A Geometric Note," Review of *Economic Studies*, June, Volume 25(3), pp. 201-205.

Crockett, A. (1997): "Why is Financial Stability a Goal of Public Policy?", Symposium on *Financial Stability in a Global Economy,* Federal Reserve Bank of Kansas City, Kansas, USA.

Harrison, A. and Hanson, Gordon, (1999), "Who Gains from Trade Reform? Some Remaining Puzzles", *Journal of Development Economics*, June.

Helpman, E. (1993),"Innovation, Imitation and Intellectual Property Rights", *Econometrica*, November.

Kumar, Nagesh (2006),"Emerging Multinationals: Trends, Patterns and Determinants of Outward Investment by Indian Enterprises", RIS Discussion Paper Number 117, RIS (www.ris.org.in)

Mathur, Somesh, K. (2001)," Domestic Challenges and the TRIPS Agreement: The Way forward for India", *Journal of World Intellectual Property Right*, Geneva, Vol. 4, No. 3, May.

Mathur, Somesh K. (2007)," TRIPS and Its Impact on Developing Countries including India, WIPO Round Table Conference Organized in Collaboration with I.I.T. Delhi and WIPO, March 6-7, 2007.

O'Rourke, K.H. and J.G. Williamson (1999), *Globalization and History: The Evolution of a Nineteenth Century Atlantic Economy* (Cambridge, MA: MIT Press).

O'Rourke, K.H. (2001), *Globalization and Inequality: Historical Trends,* Paper available at the ABCDE Europe Conference, 2001 web site.

Rodriguez, Francisco and Dani Rodrik (1999), *Trade Policy and Economic Growth: A Skeptic's View to Cross National Evidence*, NBER Working Paper No. W7081, April.

Reddy, Y.V. (1999): "Corporate Governance in Financial Sector", *RBI Bulletin*, August, pp. 993-1004.

Sachs, J., and A. Warner (1995), *Economic Reform and the Process of Global Integration*. Brooking Papers on Economic Activity 1995(1): 1-118.

Srinivasan, T.N. and Bhagwati, J. (1999),"Outward Orientation and Development: Are Revisionists Right? Paper available at J Bhagwati website.

The World Bank, *Global Economic Prospects, 2005*

UNDP (1999), *Human Development Report*, New York: Oxford University Press.

APPENDIX

Appendix Table 1.1: Regional Breakdown of Poverty in Developing Countries ($ 1 a Day) Poverty in Developing Countries ($ 1 Daily Income)

	1990	2002	2015
Millions of People Living on Less Than $1/day			
1. East Asia and Pacific	472.0	214.0	14.0
2. China	375.0	180.0	11.0
3. Rest of East Asia and Pacific	97.0	34.0	2.0
4. Europe and Central Asia	2.0	10.0	4.0
5. Latin America and Caribbean	49.0	42.0	29.0
6. Middle East and North Africa	6.0	5.0	3.0
7. South Asia	462.0	437.0	232.0
8. Sub-Saharan Africa	227.0	303.0	336.0
9. Total	1218.0	1011.0	617.0
10. Excluding China	844.0	831.0	606.0
Per cent of Population Living on less than $ 1/day			
1. East Asia and Pacific	29.6	14.9	0.9
2. China	33.0	16.6	1.2
3. Rest of East Asia and Pacific	21.1	10.8	0.4
4. Europe and Central Asia	0.5	3.6	0.4
5. Latin America and Caribbean	11.3	9.5	6.9
6. Middle East and North Africa	2.3	2.4	0.9
7. South Asia	41.3	31.3	12.8
8. Sub-Saharan Africa	44.6	46.4	38.4
9. Total	27.9	21.1	10.2
10. Excluding China	26.1	22.5	12.9

Source: The World Bank, Global Economic Prospects, 2005.

Appendix Table 1.2: Regional Breakdown of Poverty in Developing Countries ($ 2 a Day)

	1990	2002	2015
Millions of People Living on Less Than $ 2/day			
1. East Asia and Pacific	1116.0	748.0	260.0
2. China	825.0	533.0	181.0
3. Rest of East Asia and Pacific	292.0	215.0	78.0
4. Europe and Central Asia	23.0	76.0	39.0
5. Latin America and Caribbean	125.0	119.0	106.0
6. Middle East and North Africa	51.0	61.0	40.0
7. South Asia	958.0	1091.0	955.0
8. Sub-Saharan Africa	382.0	516.0	592.0
9. Total	2654.0	2611.0	1993.0
10. Excluding China	1829.0	2078.0	1811.0

(Contd.)

	1990	2002	2015
Per Cent of Population Living on Less Than $ 2/day			
1. East Asia and Pacific	69.9	40.7	12.7
2. China	72.6	41.6	13.1
3. Rest of East Asia and Pacific	63.2	38.6	11.9
4. Europe and Central Asia	4.9	16.1	8.2
5. Latin America and Caribbean	28.4	22.6	17.2
6. Middle East and North Africa	21.4	19.8	10.4
7. South Asia	85.5	77.8	56.7
8. Sub-Saharan Africa	75.0	74.9	67.1
9. Total	60.8	49.9	32.8
10. Excluding China	56.6	52.6	38.6

Source: The World Bank, *Global Economic Prospects*, 2005.

2

Moral Dilemmas in the Wake of Globalization: A Philosophical Reflection and Resolution

R.P. SINGH

The present millennium is different from all earlier such occasions. We have scientific knowledge which is the most delicate and advanced, technology which is the most capable and sophisticated, the fifth generation micro soft with knowledge and information; but do we have wisdom to make use of all these so that there is human face impressed on these achievements? One of the features of human history has been that people, resources, ideas and consciousness move from one place to another and in the wake of globalization these are moving all too fast and getting transformed gradually. The basic question arises what has been the role of values in such movements and transformations? Is our identity getting lost in the process of globalization? These are some of the most basic questions that I wish to address in this chapter.

As a matter of fact, the ancient world was finite in terms of its socio-economic conditions, scientific development, historical and cultural products. The modern world was infinite in terms of ideology, scientific and technological development, logocentrism, foundationalism, essentialism, and teleology, unified world-order, rationality, conceptions of morality and justice, etc. The post-modern world has again shrunk into finite propositions in terms of anti-foundationalism, anti-essentialism and anti-teleology, fragmentation, irrationality and plurality of ethnic identities, linguistic identities, etc. In the ancient world, different parts of the world, inhabited by different ethnic and linguistic groups had connectivity between them. There were numerous factors that made the interaction possible; such as, trade, travel, technology, conflict and war. It is in this process that there was contact, conflict and confluence of cultures and civilizations. The existential and spiritual features of culture get transformed into the material and instrumental features. The identity of culture is complex, plural and multilayered. Subtle relics of the human past underpin the visible parts of culture, ordinarily designated civilization. Comparative archaeologists and comparative philologists help us in discovering the vanished past marked by its ways of living, tools, utensils and other artifacts used by them. All these factors are interactive in character, paving the way to the emergence of new civilization and newer forms of culture. Even in the antiquity, the Indians, the Chinese, the Greeks lived with contact, though not much, with one another and in that sense there was pluralism. But each culture regarded its principles to be universally valid. **It is in this process that we come across moral dilemmas.** The need is to expose us to our own moral values in the wake of current development at the International scenario. It is urgent in view of the onslaught of Western Culture on our impressionistic minds, which creates a moral dilemma and leads to Cultural Amnesia.

The *Rta* of the *Vedas*, the Platonic *Forms*, the *Tao* of the Chinese—all claimed to be universal. Without their knowing it, they agreed that as in the cosmos, so in the human order *Yathâ pinde, tathâ Brahmânde*. Rightly understood, the emergence of the global society is not sudden. It has been in the making for a long time, perhaps very long time. History knows no hiatus in its course. The periodization of history under the labels of ancient, medieval, modern and post-modern has a liberal element of academic arbitrariness. Today the world is one; the Chinese, the Indians, the Europeans or the Americans mingle in academia and in the market place. The philosophical excursion into the emergence of global society requires us to undertake an exploration of many human horizons, proximate and distant, contemporaneous and historical. What is more, humans being essentially *Dasein*, projective in character, the fuller implications of emergence can be better understood if we look forward, more intensely and imaginatively, to the future which slowly, at times not so slowly, are coming up. Modern science and technology has played the most important role in bringing the people so close to one another. This is one of the most important features of globalization.

Moral Dilemma

A moral dilemma arises when we are confronted with equally valid moral alternatives. One faces a dilemma when one is committed to two or more moral obligations and one cannot fulfil one without violating one's duty to another. The choices that one makes test the moral fibre of one's character. These are dilemmas that are familiar to us being a part of our own experience and leave us grouping. What gives globalization its unending fascination and eternal relevance are the moral dilemmas that everybody faces, being constantly confronted by equally valid alternatives. It presents irreconcilable alternatives and the choice between them seems to be made irrationally or for reasons other than moral. The well-known example is that globalization is by no means uniform; it always means different things to different people. And there are sufficient moral grounds to justify or to reject certain choices. For some, globalization means media, rapid transmission of messages and symbols. For others, it is a deregulation of domestic as well as external markets—goods and services. It appreciates the total capital market with the need to promote investment. This is done with Cyber Space and the Internet. It can describe the expansion of economic activities across ethnicity and identity, values and practices and even beyond national boundaries. This later on is converted into trade and commerce, banking, rural institutions and so on. All these are necessary beyond the state because globalization means Global Banking, trade and commerce, Global migration of population, etc. All these require certain rules, institutions and the infrastructures, which can go beyond nation/state. So we have organizations like WTO, GATT, new definitions of the UNO and other UNO funded organizations. With these institutional mechanisms, global reality is regulated and managed. Globalization also has structural pre-requisites and imperatives. One such imperative is that people will 'move' and with them there will be a movement of consciousness and values.

Morals and conceptions of good are said to be relative to cultures, even large cultural identities have now disintegrated into smaller ones—cultural pluralism. Moral theories still oscillate between

Utilitarianism in so far as public policy, decisions of the emerging democracies are concerned, and Kantianism, in so far as individual moral life and principles are concerned. Both of these alternatives, however, appealing, are now seen to have a moral dilemma between personal and the public morality that cannot be resolved. More attractive today are Aristotelian *Ethics* expanded to include many present-day virtues and a communitarian ethics, which goes back to a sort of Hegelian *Sittlichkeit* as the basis of one's moral conceptions. It is here that the above moral dilemma can be resolved because both of these allow for pluralism and reject grand narratives. Pluralism and tolerance are the ethos of globalization. On the one hand, there are the pluralities of nation-states, of world-religions, of large cultural, ethnic, linguistic groups, with numerous internal differences; on the other hand, there is an overwhelming sense of One World i.e. the world coming together through technology. The idea of a Global Village, as an ideal, is widely valued.

Indian Perspectives

In the *Upanishads* alone for the first time from historical perspective, we come across a cognitive attempt to raise, discuss and resolve moral dilemmas pertaining to aim and ends of human life; i.e., *purushârthas*. The solution that the *Upanishads* provide is based on the eternal truths of *Âtmanic* experience and revelation. Its sources can be traced back to the *Vedas*, the first *Veda*, before it became totally distorted in the *Purva-Mimâmsâ*—with the noble actions of *Yajna* from which all creation originates *(Yajno bhuvanasya nâbhi*, Prajapati's sacrifice of oneself in order to engender the created order) and *Rta* which holds all things together in a transcendent, but comprehensive dynamic harmony, with enough room for creative disharmony within it. Then come back to the models of plurality in the *Vedas* and may include Jains and pick up their *Anekântavâda,* which can inoculate you against all dogmatisms including that of rationality. With this, we can now take up the moral insights from the *Upanishads.* The ethics of the *Upanishads* can be studied within the status of Being, Knowledge and Mysticism on the one hand and *Varnas, Âshramas* and *Purushârthas* on the other. This itself is a matter of debate how metaphysical issues like *Brahman* and *Âtman* could be related to ethics on the one hand and to mysticism on the other. Taking man's consciousness at the centre, we have to take a bold decision that it is the consciousness, which is at the centre of metaphysics, knowledge, mysticism and morality. It is on the basis of consciousness alone that the *Upanishads* present a synthesis of the four. Metaphysics without ethical backbone might only result in pure abstraction in as much as a mystic without ethical orientation might be a hideous creature who is a blot on spiritual evolution of man. In the same way ethics without metaphysics and mysticism will be unintelligible and without any goals. It would, therefore, be totally fruitless to develop the metaphysical problems reached in the *Upanishads* without the final mystical realization in the *Upanishads*. At the same time *Upanishadic* ethics is deeply rooted in the *Varnas, Purushârthas* and the *Âshramas*. The four *Purushârthas* can be broadly divided into two tier value systems; namely, *abhyudaya* consisting of *dharma, artha and kâma,* and *nihshreyas, i.e. moksha.* Ethics has perpetually been applied at every stage. Similarly the four *Âshramas* have the ethical orientation at every stage. Hence the *Upanishadic* ethical quest is at the centre of Being, Knowledge, Mysticism, *Purushârthas* and the *âshramas.*[1]

Plurality of Perspectives

The Vedic exhortation is *Ekam sat viprah bahudha vadanti.* This has been the fundamental act of philosophizing and ethicising in India. The Reality admits of alternative approaches in terms of thought constructions and linguistic expressions. It is pluralistic in its expression. The initial characteristics of Indian society are that it is diverse, liberal, democratic and pluralistic in regulating and restructuring the systems of Indian philosophy. Pluralism has been expressed in many ways in the later development of Indian philosophical systems; such as in the *Vedânta* philosophy, we go from one to many; in Vallabha *Vedânta,* we go from many to one; in *Sânkhya* and *Nyâya-Vaisesika* systems, we go from many to many and in *Buddhism*, we go from nothing, i.e. *svabhâva shunya* to many. The pluralistic nature of Indian society is manifested in various ethnic identities, community structure, linguistic identities, different nationalities, languages and so on. In search of our local identities, we have to go into the details of our tradition. Indian tradition could be divided into two kinds: namely, the *Brahminical* tradition and the *Shramana* tradition. The former is the textual, the written, the intellectual tradition or the *Sâstriya parampará* consisting of the *Dharma Sastras, Purusârthas, Asramas* etc. And the latter is the oral tradition, the folk tradition, the tradition of the people or the *Lokaparamparâ*. Fortunately we have had both the traditions as equally strong. However, it is the oral tradition, which has a stronger social basis. It consists of three pillars—family, community and the economy. Around these activities there developed idioms, symbols, proverbs, riddles and *sutras*. This was the corpus of knowledge. It is this oral tradition of our country that is the driving force behind our experience of democracy and secularism. Indians have always had political management at local level with consensus or the *Panchayat* tradition. In fact, in the last 51 years we have survived with democracy precisely because of consensus and the *Panchayat* tradition In India, there are 327 languages but more than 3000 communities out of 4000 in India speak in 33 languages. Despite these diversities, Indians have a participatory habit, we are not neutrals, we have audience participation. We are very talkative people. Traditional factor of India is its community structure. It is highly segmentary. It is a multiple society. Caste structure gives India regional identity from 20 miles to 300 miles. And there are above 4000 castes in India. So India is a land of very diversified and segmented social structure. It is in this rather complex situation that we have to assess our response to secularization. If we wish to secularize our religious institutions and ethnic identities, we will have problems. But at the level of our philosophic heritage, we are not so weakly placed. Our philosophy has always been conducive to secular ideas. I can illustrate this point with certain examples of Indian habits of mind different from European habits of mind. First of all Indian mind has perpetually been cosmo-centric. There is an organic unity between humanity and the rest of cosmic reality. And this is expressed in holistic values and attitudes of Indians. On the other hand, Europeans have an anthropocentric world-view. The early Greeks, particularly, Thales, Heraclitus, Democritus and others were cosmo-centric. With Sophists particularly with Protagoras the dictum came up—Man is the measure of all things. In modern times, particularly with liberal humanism, human being is regarded as 'given' and nature is regarded as another 'given' and nature is something for you to 'use'. One of the founders of modern thinking Immanuel Kant has said "The order and regularity in the appearances, which we entitle nature, we ourselves introduce. We could never find them in appearances, had not we ourselves, or the nature of our mind, originally set them there."[2] This was Kant's

Copernican Revolution, which quite literally shifted the direction of both epistemology and morality from the nature of reality, outside there, to the essential structure of human mind. Further, Indians have a cyclical perception. For them, the same divinity is born again and again or the concept of *avatar.* Europeans have a linear vision like premodern, modern and postmodern, etc. Indians are also idolatrous. We are idol worshippers. This approach differs radically from the Semitic religions—Judaism, Christianity and Islam who are bibliolatrous. In idol worshipping, what is so remarkable is the plurality of images taking place. Being imagistic, it has to have plurality. This is not possible in Semitic religions, which always emphasize on 'formlessness'. These are some of the ways of our thinking through which we fundamentally differ from Europeans.

European Enlightenment

Kant's principles of morality can give us insights into the Universality of Morality. Behind the notion of ought, there is a deeper philosophy and that is the philosophy of European Enlightenment. There is, however, a lack of sufficiently broad, accurate, comprehensible and useable definition of the early Enlightenment. Part of the reason of this lack is that during Enlightenment there have been complex and quite often contradictory views on such issues as democracy, modernity, secularism, religion and scientific knowledge etc. It is very difficult to provide one definition as the definition of the enlightenment, which fits all the men usually assumed to belong to it. Generally among the enlightenment thinkers we have Voltaire, Rousseau, Hume, Condercet and others. This is, however, not the occasion to go into the details of their specific philosophical systems, their mutual agreements and disagreements. I am basically concerned with the concept of freedom as the key concept of Enlightenment and as the ultimate source of Human Rights. Notwithstanding the mutual difference between one philosopher and another in the enlightenment, they have a fundamental preoccupation, i.e., freedom. It was Kant, one of its earliest prophets, who asked that question and answered it in his article in the *Berlinischer Monatsschrift,* December 1783 issue, entitled *Beanwortung der Frage: Was ist Aufklaerung? Or* "Answer to the Question: What is the Enlightenment"?

His answer is: "*Aufklaerung ist der Ausgang des Menschen aus seiner Selbst-verschuldeten Unmuendigkeit*". Let me give his full answer in

English; I confess my inability to give a totality word-to-word translation: "Enlightenment is coming out of man from his self-imposed immaturity. Immaturity is the incapacity to serve one's own understanding without direction (*Leitung*) from another. This immaturity is self-imposed; Reason itself languishes, not because it lacks understanding; what it lacks is resolution and courage; it is unwilling to serve itself (*Sapere Aude ! Hebe Mut).* Take courage to serve your own understanding! This is, therefore, the Motto *(Walspruch)* of the Enlightenment."[3] It is in this rather general framework of the Enlightenment rationality that the concept of humanity has evolved and it gets its elaborations in the categorical imperatives.

Kant is the first philosopher who has tried to give a definition of *how* a moral action *ought* to be in conformity with the Enlightenment rationality. These are the *principles* of human actions such as 'universality', 'end in itself' and 'kingdom of ends.' These principles could be prescribed to any study of morality anywhere. There have been certain attempts to define moral issues in terms of the constitution of nationality, ethnic, cultural and religious identities, etc. But if we wish to define morality in the most general sense of the terms inclusive of all specificities, Kant's categorical imperative is the only principle that could be taken into account. Kant has tried to give a definition of *how* a moral action *ought* to be *what* a moral action ought to be. These are the *principles* of human actions such as 'universality', 'end in itself' and 'kingdom of ends.' These principles could be prescribed to humanity as a whole in terms of maxims of the categorical imperative. The maxims, of course, go as follows:

- *The First Maxim*: "Act only on that maxim through which you can at the same time will so that it should become a Universal Law."[4]
- *The Second Maxim*: "Act in such a way that you always treat humanity, whether in your own person or in the person of any other, never simply as a means, but always at the same time as an end."[5]
- *The Third Maxim*: "So act as if you were through your maxim a law making member of a kingdom of ends"[6]

These maxims cannot be strange to any culture though they

could be naïve to every culture, they are universal and can be used to resolve moral dilemmas. One can easily imagine that the absence of any of these maxims could be tantamount to the denial of human dignity. But the basic question is—what is a moral right? The answer to this question is given by Kant in the treatise *Rechtslehre,* "The only original Right, belonging to each man in virtue of his humanity is Freedom..."[7] To elaborate this point, Kant says, "Every action is in accordance with Right which enables the freedom of each man's will to assist side by side with the freedom of very other man, according to an universal law."[8] We can then suppose that when Kant develops freedom as the only original moral right of man and proposes to limit that freedom in the case of each individual solely by the demand for an equal freedom on the part of all other individuals, it is evidently clear that for Kant an action would be contrary to morality if it interferes with the formal freedom of one's neighbour.

It may, however, be pointed out that Kant, in *Rechtslehre* has ruled out any distinction between laws imperative, *i.e.* moral laws and laws permissive, i.e., political rights. In that treatise the doctrine of the permissive nature of Right is silently dropped, the law of Right is definitely stated to be a special branch of moral law: its maxims, like the maxims of the moral law, are nothing if not imperative and universal, and it is of their essence to be enforced, when necessary by compulsion.[9]

It is in the light of the plurality of perspectives as envisaged in Indian tradition along with Kantian Categorical Imperatives as the necessary principles of morality that moral dilemmas in the wake of globalization can possibly be resolved. It is in this moral resolution of dilemmas that I wish to examine the moral dimensions of globalization.

Globalization

One of the major achievements of the last millennium is the emergence and development of Globalization. Globalization started during mid 70s in the developed countries in the last century and since 1990, the world has moved towards globalization in a big way. Globalization has evolved out of the golden period of capitalism; i.e.1940 to 1975. Globalization has challenged the nation/state territorial sovereignty, the institutional autonomy, shrinking the concepts of space and time. With the collapse of Socialism in the Central and East European countries during 1990s of which People's Republic of China just managed to escape, the world has moved towards defining values of universalism set out in "Universal Declaration of Human Rights" and in setting development goals in the United Nations conferences on environment, population, social development, women and human settlement.

As we know, in feudal society, there is land-based economy. Infrastructure like roads, transport, means of communications, etc. are not much developed. There is local production and local consumption. Religion has a rigid control over every walk of feudal life. Religion has three basic functions to perform in a feudal society; (i) it was a way of explaining the reality around us, of the natural reality, of life as such, of the relationship with other lives, and so on; (ii) it has given rise to highest virtues and value systems in the world like universal compassion, love, *ahimsâ*, sacrifice, etc.; and (iii) it has given rise to aesthetic experiences like music, dance, drama, composition of epics and so on. Technologically horse or bullock cart is the basis of the feudal society. The Centralized Government marks capitalist society. Infrastructure has to be developed; with constant renewal of technology and availability of markets. With secularization, the control of property and the ideas by the Church are given public openness. The dominant value of capitalist society is freedom with the developmentalist ideology. Steam engine is the basis of capitalism or industrial society. Electricity, nuclear energy and electronics lead to the advancement of capitalism towards post-industrial society. And subsequently, computer chips, micro technology of electronics and automations define the present phase, i.e., post-capitalist society. This is also called the 'Information society'. These three stages are generally characterized as industrial, technological and financing phases of capitalism. We know that today only Hong Kong Bank, Taipei Bank and Tokyo Bank alone possess world's 30 per cent of wealth.

Globalization is essentially a product of technological advancement. Origin of globalization involves economic factors with trade and finance liberalization; trade linked technology and political and moral situations helping it. It is a broad mindset that believes those world structures are possible. Globalization may be defined as Universalization, Internationalization, Liberalization, Westernization and Deterritorization. There are four dimensions involved in the formulation and implementation of the Policies towards globalization. The Neo-Liberals want that the market force should determine the course of globalization. The Reformists put the public policy whereas the Radicals want to deglobalize or to bring the society to pre-global *status quo ante.* Finally the Revolutionaries try to take globalization to the post-capitalist stage. There are certain imminent consequences of globalization, such as the end of state, the end of modernity and ideologies and the end of nationality, etc. It is in this context that moral dilemmas arise affecting both the aspects of moral values *i.e.* the relative and the universal. One of the features of globalization is that people, resources, knowledge, ideas and alongwith these the moral values move from one place to another. Globalization has the twin function to perform, *viz.* to enhance people's sensitivity to their moral values and to transform their attitudes to other values. Ronald Robertson argues that globalization is "the interpenetration of the Universalization of Particularization and the Particularization of Universalism".[10] Moral dilemmas arise only in this process of the fusion of the universal and the particular. It has created problems and a bit of it has gone towards fundamentalism and terrorism. This has led to a perception of globalization as an encroachment of the dominant moral values and culture of the West upon other cultures. The 'Theory of Clash of Civilizations' by Huntington is based upon the assumption that historically distinct cultural-religious traditions may not be able to arrive at reconciliation for degrees of inter-cultural interaction, dialogue and sharing, leading inevitably to larger conflicts in the future as the globalization process gains momentum.[11] Globalization carries the seeds of its own subversion. Multi-cultural paradigm of globalization hinges around the issues of encapsulated religious consciousness. This is an attempt to treat religion and culture as self-enclosing and self-delimiting phenomena contributing to the ideology of separateness and exclusiveness, with a negative value-load and an emotional-load in the perception of the "outsiders". This gives rise to the positive and the negative factors of globalization creating levels of moral dilemmas.

Positive and Negative Factors of Globalization

Globalization means liberalization and free movement of goods, services, capital and finance across national boundaries. In the world currency market more than $1.6 trillion is now exchanged each day and about 1/5 of the goods and services produced each year are traded; hence offering several opportunities for individual countries to achieve higher growth rates. In the last one decade, there have been several discussions on the implications with its positive and negative factors that globalization is going to have on development process particularly in developing and under-developed countries. In these countries, development is defined as a 'composite reality'; it is not only economic development but also cultural development, philosophical development, development of morals, ethos and values. In these developments local cultures and local identities are recognized as the valid elements of any design of human kind. So much so, the "'Copenhagen Summit on Development" which was held in the early 90s dealt very clearly on this theme that somehow the kind of change that is taking place in the world today is leading to massive mobility of human kinds, human resources, ideas and consciousness. There is a global worry on the process of globalization and the consequences that globalization will affect local cultures, local identities, the philosophical heritage and the very diversities that constitute the cultural matrix of human kind. I feel that globalization of technology, trade and commerce and the optimization of these factors may not be of much help unless we revitalize local identities. In fact, globalization, by its very process, enhances people's sensitivity to their local identities. There is the view that globalization triggers on the one hand massive movement of people, resources and values from one part of the globe to another part. To this extent there is interaction and homogenization between globalization and local cultures. On the other hand, the technology of globalization encourages and helps the formation of local cultures. This is an obvious fact. If we are on Cyber Space or on the Internet, we have teleconferencing. Even sitting in this hall, we can have dialogues with students and teachers in Europe and USA. But the question is—will this technology help preserve local identities? There is a feeling that local identities may not be 'real identities' but only 'virtual reality'. The Internet and Cyber Space have a different language. By computerization and digital system of Cyber processes, one can create such realities, which do not happen in real life. This, which does not happen in real life but by simple amalgamation of parameters, which are pre-structured and defined, you can create a 'virtual reality'. Thus technology can help in fostering local identities.

People who are in minority at one place can search for like-minded people throughout the globe. This way they can all come together through teleconferencing, without physical movement from one place to another. So globalization technologically does not prevent local identities.

The negative factors of globalization are at two different levels. It threatens the interests of the powerful and the weak nations along-with the corresponding notions of values and the morals. This is the dilemma of globalization. It is generally criticized in terms of Economic Darwinism implying survival of the fittest. Globalization is also the coming together of rich entrepreneurs of the whole world with the belief or rather make-belief that they do not need the poor. It threatens the power of those who are very strong specially those countries, which are totalitarian. We have examples of Soviet Union, Romania, Bulgaria, Poland, Czechoslovakia, Hungary and so on during late 80s and early 90s. I am not saying that media was totally responsible for the collapse of socialism. That will be too simplistic. There were many other factors involved. Like, Soviet Union was simply a Union of Republics but never a State. In the 70 years of socialist experience, socialism itself became vacuous, mechanical and undynamic. It may happen in anywhere. Even in India, democracy is getting vacuous. There are such signs. We have to be vigilant. But facts of the matter remain. Media did play an important role in shaping public opinion of the post second world war Soviets. People in these countries got exposed to new views, new value systems and new styles of life. People see what is happening around the world and State cannot control. So the powerful and vested interests are threatened. When this threat comes about, there is counter resurgence of ideas. All it does is to narrow down the process of globalization. It gives rise to different forms of fundamentalism. There may be ideological fundamentalism or cultural fundamentalism; even there will be fundamentalism of benign kinds, consumer fundamentalism, environmental fundamentalism, industrial fundamentalism and so on. This way globalization creates turmoil at the top.

Globalization also hurts the weak and the poor nations. They are hurt because they have no 'say' or 'share' in the process of globalization. This is what is the worry in the developing countries. There are many developing countries where political system is not conducive for encountering globalization. So there are examples of barring Disk Antenna, Transponders, Satellites, etc. And this is a very hopeless task. Many countries have tried it. But they have failed. So this is a losing game. The poorer countries which are not at all prepared to face globalization; they face problems in different ways. In such countries market is always restrained. If large number of people is illiterate and below the poverty line and have no access to new jobs and new way of understanding global situation, then they are out of market. So globalization, which brings market, creates this problem for the weaker people.

In the context of multi-culturalism, identity is a very important concept. Can globalization do away with local culture, local identity, and community identity? Looking at India, I can say that at the village level, the traditional social identity has weakened and most villages have become political communities. But the local culture survives. India is world's largest democracy and has a long history of democratic functioning with pluralistic values and philosophic universal concepts (holistic values included). India cannot remain indifferent to the development in terms of globalization and the New World Order, which has raised serious questions to the foundations of our traditionally established philosophic doctrines. The need is to expose us to our own Cultural Traditions in the wake of current development at the International Scenario. It is urgent in view of the onslaught of Western Culture on our impressionistic minds, which creates a cultural dilemma and leads to Cultural Amnesia. The new millennium is different from all earlier occasions. It has: New Markets—foreign exchange, capital markets linked globally; New Tools—Inter Net, Cyber Space; New Institutions—W.T.O., GATT, etc.; New Rules—multilateral agreements on trade, services, intellectual property rights, patenting rights, backed by strong enforcement mechanisms and binding on national governments, reducing the scope of national policies. Global markets, global technology, global ideas, global solidarity and above all global values can enrich the lives of the people everywhere expanding their choices.

Indian Response

For Indian minds, puzzled about the moral dilemmas in the wake of globalization, I will humbly recommend a change of perspective. Let us leave the moral issues raised by Aristotle, Kant, Hegel and even Marx, get out of the Enlightenment Frame of Mind and go to the *Upanishads.* There is no other way of detoxifying ourselves from the fumes of Enlightenment Rationality because the western way is not the only way of thinking and experiencing, let us as Indians emerge ourselves in our own rich Indian Heritage, especially before its breaking up into Buddhist, Jaina and Hindu—for example, the Samkhya-Yoga Heritage common to all three traditions—the great philosophical perspective that undergrades all *Upanisadic, Vedic, Buddhist, or Jaina* thought and experience. Keep your painfully acquired critical rationality from Kant and Hegel, but do get not tyrannized by it. Stay critical, but do not reject out of hand what seems strange at first. Expose yourself without hesitation to a system of thought and experience, which has endured for millennia and awarded us with freedom, autonomy and sovereignty.

To bring this chapter to a close, we cannot stop the process of globalization. But globalization is not forever; history has not come to an end. Despite the lofty claims that State has withered away in the era of globalization let me say it in very clear terms that State still exists and is accountable to the people. Where people are left out, they will not sit back quietly. There will be counter resurgence of struggles, which may take the shape of crimes like drug related crimes, ethnic struggles and so on. Therefore, State has to come forward to make strategic decisions. State can certainly and strongly find and frame rules and institutions for governance to provide enough space for local identities, communities and environmental resources to ensure globalization. Re-defining such values as in the adopting of Human Rights and setting development goals on Environment, Population, Social Development, etc., globalization should be with regard for pluralistic value systems without violation of human rights. Without marginalizing local identities, the reward of globalization should go towards creating equity between nations.

NOTES

1. Robert E. Hume, *The Thirteen Principal Upanishads,* Oxford University Press, 2002, p. 297.
2. Kant, Immanuel, *Critique of Pure Reason*, trans. N.K. Smith, London, The Macmillan Press Ltd., 1973, p. 147.
3. Kant, *Was ist Aufklaerung: Thesen und Definitionen,* Reclam, Stuttgart, 1986, p. 9. (translations mine).

4. Paton, H.J., *The Moral Law: Kant's Groundwork of Metaphysic of Morals,* London, Hutchinson University Library, 1969, p. 67.
5. *Ibid.*, p. 91.
6. *Ibid.*, p. 34.
7. Kant, *Rechtsleher Einleitung*, p.40, quotation taken from Vaughan, C.E., *Studies in the History of Political Philosophy before and after Rousseau*, Manchester University Press, 1939, p. 77.
8. *Ibid.*
9. *Ibid.* p.78.
10. Robertson, R., *Globalization: Social Theory and Global Culture,* (London, Sage, 1992), p. 100.
11. Huntington, S.P., *The Clash of Civilizations and the Remaking of the World Order,* Penguin Books, 1997.

3

Globalization, Economic Injustice and Health

LYNN ANNE MULROONEY and DEANE NEUBAUER

A front cover of *The Economist* has a malnourished African child wearing only jewellery reminiscent of shackles walking toward a luminescent cityscape on a hill under the headline: "A question of justice?" The inside editorial that once again reproduces this image acknowledges "the toll of global poverty is a scandal. But deploring economic 'injustice' is no answer". Injustice in quotation marks is trivialized and any linkages between the emiseration of the African child in the foreground and the wealth of the global city in the background are severed with reassurances that "the wealth of the wealthy is not part of the problem". This chapter will suggest a divergent interpretation of this arresting image that may be seen to connect globalization, economic injustice, and health with human security.

The March 13, 2004 front cover of *The Economist* featured an emaciated African child naked but for anklets and bracelets reminiscent of shackles walking toward a luminescent cityscape on a hill under the caption: "A question of justice?" The accompanying editorial to this image begins with the premise that "the toll of global poverty is a scandal. But deploring economic 'injustice' is no answer" (2004b: 13). Those who would discuss economic injustice or global inequality (without the sarcastic quotation marks) are associated with descriptors such as "debilitating preoccupation" and "obsession" situated "at gatherings of anti-globalists, in the corridors of aid agencies and in socialist redoubts in backward parts of the world". The premise of this article is "the wealth of the wealthy is not part of the problem" as "market economics is not a zero-sum game" (2004b: 13). It would seem then, that *The Economist's* preferred, if counterintuitive, interpretation of their arresting front cover is that the emiseration of the African child in the foreground is totally disconnected from the wealth of the global city in the background. More strongly, the authors argue that a perspective "that the rich enjoy their privileges at the expense of the poor—that poverty, in other words, is inseparable from a system, capitalism, that thrives on injustice" is not only wrong but harmful (2004b: 13). This chapter will suggest a divergent interpretation of this cover image in a narrative that argues that an ideology of neoliberalism does perpetuate injustice, which has profound implications for poverty, health, and security in an ever-globalizing world.

Suspending disbelief in the comfort provided by the text of the editorial, what if the visual image of the vulnerable child on the cover is indeed inviting us into a consideration of an issue that Nelson Mandela has compared with slavery and apartheid? (Cowell 2005)[1] The child in the foreground is naked, too much is visible, so our eyes slip off her bony protuberances and bare feet to the other major character in this tableau, the shining line of skyscrapers which seems to be her destination. The following section will suggest some of the context that helps make this symbolic representation intelligible as a compelling narrative of agency rather than a random juxtaposition of images devoid of meaning.

City on a Hill: Wealth and Neoliberalism

Ronald Reagan evoked John Winthrop's "shining city upon a hill" throughout his political career as a powerful metaphor celebrating American nationalism and commerce blessed by God.[2] If we ask how the wealth was created to build the shining city upon the hill, the regimes of Ronald Reagan and Margaret Thatcher in the 1980's will be found to be pivotal for privileging capital over all other considerations such as the environment or social relations. Reaganomics and the Thatcher Revolution were projects to dismantle the Welfare State by defining government as the problem as they implemented neoliberal reforms of privatization, deregulation, trade liberalization, and shrinking social programmes. As the underlying ideology of globalization (Steger 2000), neoliberalism asserts that market forces left unfettered lead to optimal societal outcomes. Its economic and moral presupposition is that economic and social aspects of life, including wealth and poverty, can be understood in terms of individual "choices" (Shakow and Irwin, 2000: 52-54).

Modern globalization has been characterized as an accelerated movement of information, goods, capital, and people across geographical and political borders (Daulaire 1999: 22). With neoliberalism as globalization's sustaining ideology, multinational and then Trans-National Corporations (TNCs) are "globalization's primary engine" (Neubauer, 2000: 16) (Barnet and Muller 1974; Barnet and Cavanagh 1994). Globalization has generated vast wealth through such mechanisms as the development of new manufacturing efficiencies, the creation of new markets, the invention of new technologies, and the creation of entirely new institutions such as global equity markets. Also at work, however, in corporate offices in global cities, is the "externalizing machine" or creation of externalities by "the legal rule that corporations must always act in ways that serve their own best interests, *i.e.* that maximize their shareholder's wealth" (Bakan 2004: 180). Social and ecological costs of corporations seeking to maximize their own economic fortunes become irrelevant to those most responsible for externalized harm in this legal construct and moral economy.[3]

A persistent outcome of the externalizing machine is that as the relative proportion of national wealth aggregated by TNCs grows, wages are constricted. Wages in the global North are reduced by three mechanisms. First is the actual loss of good paying jobs as TNCs move their physical plants or subcontract with local corporations in the global South or in "right to work" states in the U.S. south to chase lower labour costs. This trend in the decimated manufacturing sector is now of concern to other occupational groups as software development, data processing, call-centres, and radiology are among the tasks that may be technically done anywhere there is sufficient bandwidth. Second, as more service jobs are created by the older economies with the loss of manufacturing, there is a distributional shift: those at the top end require large amounts of technical skill and realize higher salary benefits; those at the lower end pay less, are likely to be non-unionized, and provide few or no benefits. Third, increasingly firms hire workers on contract, reducing corporate labour costs but also reducing the social value that workers gain from employment. Overall, economic growth is stimulated, resulting in the United States, for example, in job creation and high returns to capital. The results for labour, in general, are reduced wages and increased social cost.

Neoliberalism promotes this model as essential for "competitive economic growth." Translated, this means that nation states and their populations are urged to adopt political and economic policies that: reduce taxes (thus decreasing the relative burden on high income earners who can deploy their capital to investment); restructure taxes on income (shifting necessary taxation burdens to value added taxes, which tend to be more regressive than income taxes); open their borders to trade (which can undercut local labour and undermine efforts to sustain regulations to protect labour and consumers); pursue policies of deregulation of capital, labour and the environment (thereby permitting nations to be "more competitive" in open markets); and privatize many state functions (thereby permitting private capital to invest in markets that are highly profitable, e.g. telecommunications) (Kotz, 1999).

The result then of neoliberal ideologies and policies is "class-based production of inequalities" (Coburn, 2004: 41). The significance of this for health outcomes may be illustrated by a study looking at the impact of four major political traditions (Social Democratic, Christian Democratic, liberal, and ex-fascist) in the advanced OECD countries. Political traditions that were more committed to redistributive policies (both social and economic) and full-employment policies were generally more successful in improving the health of their populations (Navarro and Shi, 2001: 481). Labour-based social democratic, political economies in Sweden, Denmark, Norway, and Finland had lower poverty rates for the general population and for children, smaller household income inequalities, and the lowest infant mortality rates during the period 1960-1996 (Navarro and Shi, 2001). The most market-orientated of the liberal Anglo-Saxon countries in this study, the United States, had the highest poverty rates as percentage of the population (19.1% for the general population, 24.9% for children), highest household income inequality relative to national median incomes, and highest infant mortality rate of all the countries in this study (Navarro and Shi, 2001: 486-488). In 1996 the infant mortality rates for Sweden, Norway, and Finland were nearly double at 4.0 deaths per 1,000 live births of the 7.8 deaths per 1,000 live births for the United States (Navarro and Shi, 2001: 488).

The social costs of neoliberalism are of concern even for countries such as Ireland heralded as successful models of globalization. The Celtic Tiger economic boom has generated a growth in inequality and relative poverty as the share of national income has gone for profits to capital with a decrease of the national share going to wages (Kirby, 2004: 212-213). The Irish income tax system was found to be less progressive in the 1990's than in the 1980's and over the late 1990's, the poorest 20 per cent have seen a significant decrease in disposable income (Kirby, 2004: 217). Other social costs are a widening gap between the unskilled manual and the professional groups in their access to higher education, active support by the state for a two-tiered healthcare system, and widening inequalities as those who own property see its value ever increasing and those without property are left further behind (Kirby, 2004: 214-215).

Social costs of how we organize our societies are significant as they impact key determinants of health such as income and social status, social exclusion and social support, healthy child development, employment and working conditions, physical and social environments, education, food, transport, addiction, personal health practices and coping skills, and health services (Wilkinson and Marmot, 2003).[4] Or, in other words, "health is a measure of the degree to which the society delivers a good life to its citizens" (World Health Organization, 2005). The good life can vary tremendously, even within the most affluent country in the world, as Michael Marmot's example so clearly illustrates:

> *If you catch the metro train in downtown Washington, D.C., to suburbs in Maryland, life expectancy is 57 years at the beginning of the journey. At the end of the journey, it is 77 years. This means that there is 20-year life expectancy [gap] in the nation's capital, between the poor and predominantly African-American people who live downtown, and the richer and predominantly non-African American people who live in the suburbs (World Health Organization, 2005).*

This twenty-year difference in life expectancy is not random or accidental; it is a function of how this society is organized. "The pathologies that threaten 'inner city' neighbourhoods are the result of decades of political neglect, economic exploitation and resource withdrawal, which themselves stem directly from public and corporate sector strategies to facilitate capital accumulation and consolidation" (Whiteis, 1998: 795). When the New York City government closed fire stations in African-American and Hispanic communities in the Bronx in the 1970's, the "planed shrinkage" had repercussions that rippled out for decades:

> *As a result, uncontrolled fires destroyed many buildings. The social lives of building residents were severely traumatized. Great overcrowding took place in surrounding poor minority areas. Injection drug use (and later crack), alcoholism, sex trading, gangs and demoralization spread widely—followed later by outbreaks of STDs, HIV, tuberculosis and many other ills (Wallace 1990).*

A Zero-Sum That is No Game: Dying from Poverty in the Twenty-first Century

The emaciated, naked child in the foreground of *The Economist* cover gives only an understated hint of the plight of millions of people suffering and dying in Sub-Saharan Africa. To better appreciate the chasm between the shining city on the hill and the African child in the foreground, the following data are instructive. About 34 per cent of the population of this region are under-nourished and 42 per cent do not have access to clean water (Blair, 2005: 95). In Sub-Saharan Africa, 46.7 per cent or 300 million of the population fall within World Bank's category of extreme poverty as they tried to subsist on less than one dollar per day in 1999 (United Nations Development Programme, 2002: 18). This number of people living in extreme poverty is projected to rise to 404 million by 2015 (Blair, 2005: 95). In contrast to those in extreme poverty, "every cow in Europe has received almost US$ 2 a day in subsidies . . . . and Japanese cows nearly US $ 4" (Blair, 2005: 18).

The well-known relationship[5] between poverty and increased ill-health and death is evident in the mortality statistics. In 1990 the life expectancy at birth for Sub-Saharan Africa was 52 years and the median age of death was 5 years (World Bank, 1993: 200). In 2000 life expectancy at birth in this region had decreased to 48.7 years (United Nations Development Programme, 2002: 152) and by 2002 it had further shortened to 46.3 years (United Nations Development Programme, 2004: 142). South Africa and Zimbabwe both had a life expectancy at birth in 1990 of 62 years but this plummeted to 48.8 and 33.9 years respectively in 2002 (World Bank, 1993: 200; United Nations Development Programme, 2004: 141). There is now almost a fifty year difference between the country with the highest life expectancy at birth, Japan at 81.5 years, and the lowest, Zambia at 32.7 years (United Nations Development Programme, 2004: 139, 142). Of the estimated 10.8 million children under 5 years of age who died globally in 2000, 41 per cent of these child deaths occurred in sub-Saharan Africa (Black, Morris, and Bryce, 2003: 2226).[6] Disparities in child mortality between the global North and South are large and increasing. There was a 20-fold difference in 1990 between the 180 deaths per 1,000 live births in sub-Saharan Africa compared with only 9 deaths per 1,000 live births in the industrialized countries. This gap increased to a 29-fold difference in 2000 with mortality rates in sub-Saharan Africa of 175 deaths per 1,000 live births and 6 deaths per 1000 live births in the industrialized countries (Black, Morris, and Bryce, 2003: 2226).

The measurement of economic inequality and its consequences for health[7] are both sharply contested but it is clear that extreme poverty in the global South has increased as wealth in the global North has increased. Over the past 30 years, the poorest 20 per cent of the world's people saw their share of global income decline from 2.3 per cent to 1.4 per cent while the share of the richest 20 per cent rose from 70 per cent to 85 per cent (United Nations Development Programme, 1996). In 1960 the top fifth of income earners had 30 times the income of the poorest fifth—in 1997, 74 times as much (United Nations Development Programme, 1999: 36). Among the world's super-rich, the assets of the 200 richest people are more than the combined income of 41 per cent of the world's people (United Nations Development Programme, 1999: 38).

One of the most egregious examples of the poor subsidizing the wealthy is the direct result of predatory loans to impoverished countries by Western Banks seeking to invest a surplus of oil dollars after the 1973 OPEC oil embargo. In what Stephen Lewis has called "mathematics conceived by Dr. Strangelove," the poorest countries of Africa received $294 million U.S. in loans between 1970 and 2002. They have paid back $298 billion US in principal and interest and still owe more than $200 billion US (Manthorpe, 2005). African nations pay $1.51 in debt service for every $1 received in aid. All African countries are paying more on debt service than on health care—average spending per person on debt service is $14 per person while the average spending on health is less than $5 per person (Jubilee USA Network, 2005).

Harmful externalities that affect most those who have few choices in their implementation are a feature of Economic Structural Adjustment Programmes (ESAP) associated with the Washington Consensus. Reflecting the convergent interests of the United States Federal Government, the International Monetary Fund (IMF), and the World Bank as well as global capital, the Washington Consensus[8] advocates economic growth as the main goal of development. ESAP or conditionalities were initiated by the IMF and Word Bank in response to concern about debt repayment. In the 1980's as oil prices and interest rates rose dramatically, African export prices dropped and industrialized countries set up protectionist trade policies. While the North benefited from the export of cheap raw materials from the South, cash crops that generated foreign currency were grown at the expense of food for local sustenance. Countries being structurally adjusted were encouraged to devalue local currency to increase exports, which decreased the purchasing power for local citizens. In keeping with a neoliberal ideology of trade liberalization, subsidies or price control for basic food (sugar, bread, oil), fuel, water, public transportation, sanitation, housing, and medicines were reduced or eliminated.

Mandatory decreased spending in the public sector caused massive unemployment among public sector workers especially teachers and health care workers. Public services in education and health care were privatized as "cost recovery" programmes initiated user fees. Deregulation permitted increased foreign ownership, capital mobility, and liberalization of import controls (Gloyd, 2004; Logie and Woodroffe, 1993; Schoepf, Schoepf, and Millen, 2000). A review of IMF and World Bank loan conditionalities with 26 countries provided strong evidence of provisions that undermine labour rights, labour power, and conditions of living that include mandated wage reductions and pension reforms, including privatization, that cut social security benefits (Lloyd and Weissman, 2002).

This unjust economic system that has privileged the people of the North is directly connected to the suffering of people in the

South. Exploitation of labour for the accumulation of capital set-up the conditions of possibility for the 20,000 to 50,000 people across the globe who perish daily "because they are too poor to stay alive".[9] The 2.3 million adults and children who died of AIDS in 2004 in sub-Saharan Africa (UNAIDS/WHO, 2004: 19) contracted HIV during the late 1980's and 1990's as they were being structurally adjusted. The deleterious impacts of ESAP were clearly noted even as they were unfolding. Concerns about unprecedented inflation, lower real earnings, and increased malnutrition were documented only a few years after Nigeria's ESAP was started in 1986 (Igbedioh, 1990: 518). The social implications of reintroducing school fees in primary schools in Zimbabwe as a cost recovery measure were identified as increasing illiteracy, crime, prostitution, the number of street kids, the spread of diseases, and social discontent (Nyambuya, 1994: 14). ESAPs "undermine the social fabric" thereby potentially promoting behaviours which place people at risk for HIV disease while eroding health and social services that are needed for treatment (Lurie, Hintzen, and Lowe, 1995: 982).

Stephen Lewis, UN Special Envoy for HIV/AIDS in Africa, contends that "everything is related: it's a cyclical pattern of Western neglect and self-centredness, juxtaposed with African disasters and death" (Lewis, 2003). In this instance Lewis is describing the spiral between famine caused by drought caused by climate change caused by fossil fuels[10] exacerbated by the rapid onset of AIDS-related deaths as "the inescapable finale of a shortage of food" as he described below:

> *...the human toll is desolating. The immune systems of huge numbers of women farmers are desperately weak; seven million agricultural workers have died of AIDS since 1985, FAO estimates that another sixteen million may die by 2020; the household assets have been exhausted by attending to parental illness; children have been pulled out of school to care for sick and dying parents, losing, in the process, the one meal a day that might have been available from a school feeding programme; malnutrition is everywhere evident; fields are left untended; crops aren't grown; food isn't taken to market, and if it is, no one has money to pay for it...what we're talking about here is the way in which this virus—the cause of the most appalling communicable disease in human history—attacks the fabric of every sector, making the interplay of health and agriculture but one more*

shortcut to carnage. When the body has no food to consume, the virus consumes the body (Lewis, 2003).

Although AIDS does cause poverty, it is essential to understand that the causality arrow is bi-directional: the root cause of AIDS is poverty (Farmer, Connors, and Simmons, 1996). The synergistic effect of malnutrition and HIV is made possible by debilitating poverty that is generated by economic, social, and political choices made down the road and across the globe from the people dying in sub-Saharan Africa. Africa provides a dramatic illustration of webs of vulnerability but many more are at risk globally. There were 2.8 billion people living on less than two dollars a day in 1999 and of these people trying to survive at the economic margins, 1.2 billion were trying to do so on less than one dollar per day (United Nations Development Programme, 2002: 17).

HIV in Africa is a focus of concern as the magnitude of the suffering is compelling. There are 25.4 million people in sub-Saharan Africa who are living with HIV and of these 13.3 million are women (UNAIDS/WHO, 2004: 19). More than 60 per cent of all the people living with HIV in the world reside in sub-Saharan Africa, although the region has just over 10 per cent of the world's population (UNAIDS/WHO, 2004: 19). As Stephen Lewis described the desolating human toll, the winnowing of the adult population is stripping communities of their teachers, farmers, leaders, civil servants, health care workers, entrepreneurs, and scientists who make up the infrastructure of a society. Mothers and fathers die leaving 5.2 million newly created orphans in 2003 to join the ranks of 43 million orphans in sub-Saharan Africa (UNAIDS/UNICEF/USAID, 2004: 8-9). Gathered in by grandparents, extended family or neighbours, and too often by children only slightly older than themselves,[11] the care of these orphans threatens to topple already poor people into greater destitution. The physical and emotional trauma experienced by the orphans (and all those living in poverty) in their early years will have profound implications for their growth and development and the quality of their lives throughout their lifespan (Keating and Hertzman, 1999). Without sufficient nurturing and adult supervision and in a context of severe losses, people may be prone to engage in self-consoling behaviours such as sexual activity and drug use. Transactional or survival sex for food or money to support oneself and one's dependents is a reality rather than a choice. In Zambia 71 per cent of child sex workers are orphans (Blair, 2005: 42). Civil disorder and increased crime associated with AIDS orphans in South Africa "at greater than average risk of engaging in delinquent behaviour and exhibiting anti-social tendencies" has caused some to predict "widespread social anarchy within the next five to 20 years" (Brower and Chalk, 2003: 53-54). This new social anarchy on the continent will join old social anarchy as vestiges of colonialism and Cold War struggles for hegemony continue to fuel wars fought with arms from the global armament industry. Armed conflicts that displace civilian populations exacerbate the transmission of HIV disease through increasing poverty, food shortages, and sexual violence (Hankins *et al.*, 2002). International peace-keeping and national defense are compromised by HIV prevalence rates in militaries in sub-Sahara Africa that range from 80 per cent in Zimbabwe, 66 per cent in Uganda, to 10 per cent-20 per cent in Nigeria (Brower and Chalk, 2003: 50).

The last point to be mentioned in this web of inter-connected dynamics is the escalating loss of health care workers from sub-Saharan Africa, where there is high mortality and low density of health care workers, to areas in the North with low mortality and high density of health care workers (Joint Learning Initiative, 2004). Ghana, for example, has lost, over a decade, 50 per cent of its professional nurses to the United Kingdom, Canada, and the USA and there are more Ghanaian physicians working outside Ghana than in the country itself (Nullis-Kapp, 2005: 85). The "demand pull" of older populations in the North has created a health care "brain drain" that intersects with a flight from a health care sector decimated by two decades of ESAP that slashed expenditures on health (Neubauer, 2005). With a current global shortfall of approximately 4 million health care workers (Joint Learning Initiative 2004), wealthy countries in the North recruiting shell-shocked health care workers from the South, and wealthier African countries such as Botswana recruiting health care workers from poorer African countries with their own AIDS crisis (Dugger, 2003), this is a paradigmatic zero-sum game is in play. The poor are subsidizing the health care of the rich: South Africa alone has spent $1 billion educating health care workers who migrated abroad (Dugger, 2004).

Policy Options: Poverty is Not Natural

Like slavery and apartheid, poverty is not natural. It is man-made and it can be overcome and eradicated by the actions of human beings. And overcoming poverty is not a gesture of charity. It is an act of justice. It is the protection of a fundamental human right, the right to dignity and a decent life. (Nelson Mandela, February 4, 2005).

We know what we're doing, and we do it anyway. It's as though we have chosen to pursue and protect our own prosperity and comfort at all costs, and then have dehumanized Africa so that we can live with ourselves. It's as though the communities, families, women, children, orphans are figments, illusions, abstractions. We're not barbarians; we don't choose willfully to kill and to maim. But in watching and neglecting and allowing, and incredibly enough, abetting the cumulative loss of life in Africa, which we know we could bring to an end, we have become the latter day King Leopolds of the continent. Stephen Lewis, May 28, 2003.

If we don't want to channel King Leopold and if we are willing to believe that poverty is mutable, then there are a variety of policy options that may be explored:

1. *Social Determinants of Health*: The United Nations Commission on the Social Determinants of Health sees an "unprecedented opportunity" to improve health among the world's poorest by "tackling the root causes of disease and health inequalities" (Irwin and Scali, 2005: 4). Deepening understanding of the social determinants of health (Evans, Barer, and Marmor, 1994), working with civil society to make research relevant (Sanders *et al.*, 2004), and becoming informed about barriers to implementing multisectoral approaches to health (Lavis *et al.*, 2003; Irwin and Scali, 2005) are three complementary and preparatory trajectories to tackle root causes.
2. *Cancel the Debt*: Approximately US$600 billion in debt cancellation would be needed to ensure that debt repayment did not occur at the expense of essential social spending (Labonte and Schrecker, 2004: 1665).
3. *Fair Trade*: A few commodity crops such as coffee, cotton, and sugar account for 50 per cent of Africa's total agricultural exports. A decline in world coffee prices alone resulted in a decline of Ethiopia's GDP of about 6 per cent (Blair, 2005:

263). The link between commodity dependence and poverty is strengthened when a small number of corporations "capture most of the value of a product." An example of this is coffee where 90 per cent of value goes to retailers, processors, and traders (Blair, 2005: 268). Added to this is "while rich countries preach the benefits of free trade, they do not practice it" through protectionist trade policies (Blair 2005: 268-269).

4. *Official Development Assistance* (*ODA*): None of the G7[12] countries approach the goal of 0.7 per cent of GDP first proposed in 1969. In contrast with Denmark, Norway, and Sweden at 1.03, 0.83, and 0.81 respectively, Japan, Canada, and the United States contributions in 2001 were 0.23, 0.22, and 0.11 respectively (Labonte and Schrecker, 2004: 1671).
5. *Millennium Development Goals* (*MDGs*): In 2000, 147 heads of States adopted the MDGs "to address extreme poverty in its many dimensions—income poverty, hunger, disease, lack of adequate shelter, and exclusion—while promoting education, gender equality, and environmental sustainability, with quantitative targets set for the year 2015" (Sachs and McArthur, 2005: 347). These goals are a framework for action but they will be impossible to meet unless there is the political will from the North to cancel debt, trade fairly, and give ODA that is generous and without riders that benefit most the donor country.
6. *Governance and Accountability*: "Former Zairean dictator President Mobutu Sese Seko once reputedly said: 'It takes two to be corrupt—the corrupted and the corrupter.' And he should know" (Blair, 2005: 32). Laments about corruption in the South need to be accompanied by recognition of complicity by actors in the North. The Commission on Africa identified the need for assistance to develop capacity with prevention, identification of illicit funds, and freezing, confiscation, and repatriation of looted assets (Blair, 2005: 32).

NOTES

1. *The New York Times* reported: "'Do not delay while poor people continue to suffer,' said Mandela, who had compared the fight against poverty to the battles against slavery and apartheid" (Cowell, 2005). The fuller and

more political comparison is from Nelson Mandela's speech to 22,000 people attending the launch of the Make Poverty History Campaign in London: "Like slavery and apartheid, poverty is not natural. It is man-made and it can be overcome and eradicated by the actions of human beings. And overcoming poverty is not a gesture of charity. It is an act of justice. It is the protection of a fundamental human right, the right to dignity and a decent life" (Mandela, 2005).

2. See, for example, his Farewell Address to the Nation: "I've spoken of the shining city all my political life, but I don't know if I ever quite communicated what I saw when I said it. But in my mind it was a tall proud city built on rocks stronger than oceans, windswept, God-blessed, and teeming with people of all kinds living in harmony and peace; a city with free ports that hummed with commerce and creativity" (Reagan).
3. From an interview with Nobel Prize winning economist, Milton Friedman: "There is but one 'social responsibility' for corporate executives, Friedman believes: they must make as money as possible for their shareholders. This is a moral imperative. Executives who chose social and environmental goals over profits—who try to act morally—are, in fact, immoral" (Bakan, 2004: 34).
4. The key determinants of health listed are compiled from the World Health Organization, Regional Office for Europe, (Wilkinson and Marmot, 2003) and the Health Canada, Population Health Approach website, accessed October 28, 2003: http://www.hc-sc.gc.ca/hppb/phdd/determinants/determinants.html#income
5. Illustrative texts on poverty and health include scholarship by (Doyal and Pennell, 1981; Kim *et al.*, 2000; Leon and Walt, 2001; Farmer, 2003).
6. World-wide in 2000, six countries (India, Nigeria, China, Pakistan, Congo and Ethiopia) accounted for 50 per cent of the number of deaths in children under 5 years, and 42 countries for 90 per cent. Hidden in these statistics, once again, are large discrepancies even with nations. India, with the largest estimated number of child deaths at 2,402,000, had mortality rates for children under 5 years of age that varied from 18.8 per 1,000 births in Kerala to 137.6 per 1,000 in Madhya Pradesh. Countries in sub-Saharan Africa have relatively smaller populations but they dominate the highest ranks of mortality rates. Sierra Leone, Niger, and Angola, for example, had under five-year mortality rates of 316, 270, and 260 deaths per 1,000 respectively (Black, Morris, and Bryce, 2003: 2227). Most of the deaths in children under 5 years of age that occurred in these 42 countries are attributable to diarrhoea, pneumonia, measles, malaria, and HIV/AIDS, all exacerbated by undernutrition while asphyxia, pre-term delivery, sepsis, and tetanus lead the causes of death in the neonatal period (first 28 days of life) (Black, Morris, and Bryce, 2003).
7. See for example "More or Less Equal" in the March 14, 2004, *Economist* (2004a) as well as (Galbraith, 2002; Kawachi, Kennedy, and Wilkinson, 1999; Lynch *et al.*, 2004).

8. "John Williamson, who coined the term 'Washington consensus' to describe official wisdom on development policy *circa* 1989 has noted that in codifying the consensus he 'deliberately excluded from the list anything which was primarily redistributive, as opposed to having equitable consequences as a by-product of seeking efficiency objectives, because [he] felt the Washington of the 1980s to be a city that was essentially contemptuous of equity concerns'" (Labonte and Schrecker, 2004: 1672).
9. "Currently, more than 8 million people around the world die each year because they are too poor to stay alive. Every morning our newspapers could report, 'More than 20,000 people perished yesterday of extreme poverty'" (Sachs, 2005: 46). A figure used by Stephen Lewis, the United Nations' Special Envoy for HIV/AIDS in Africa is "50,000 people who starve each day" (Peplinskie, 2005).
10. In June of 1988 Stephen Lewis chaired the first International Conference on Climate Change, which pronounced: "Humanity is conducting an unintended, uncontrolled, globally pervasive experiment whose ultimate consequences could be second only to a global nuclear war." Lewis is unequivocal on the North's responsibility for climate change affecting Africa: "Our collective refusal, thus far, to significantly reduce our dependence on fossil fuels, and as a result of that refusal, to continue to blight the planet with carbon dioxide emissions, plays itself out, yet again, at the expense of Africa. We're responsible for climate change. We're responsible for the extremes of weather" (Lewis 2003).
11. "I was in Swaziland recently, meeting with the cabinet, we were discussing matters of public policy". The Minister of Labour jumped to his feet in a state of considerable agitation and said, "Mr. Lewis, enough of policy. Do you not understand we have wall-to-wall orphans in Swaziland? We have thousands of child-headed households where the age of the child heading the household is eight" (Lewis, 2005).
12. The six original countries that formed the G8 in 1975 after the oil crisis were France, the United States, Britain, Germany, Italy, and Japan. Canada joined in 1976 and Russia became a full member in 2003. The G8 account for 46.6 per cent of global GDP and 46.8 per cent of global exports. The G7 countries "dominate World Bank and IMF decision-making, and wield considerable power in the World Trade Organization" (Labonte and Schrecker, 2004: 1661).

REFERENCES

2004a. More or Less Equal? *Economist*, March 13, 2004, 69-71.
2004b. A Question of Justice? *The Economist*, March 13, 2004, 13.
Bakan, Joel, 2004. *The Corporation: The Pathological Pursuit of Profit and Power.* New York, Free Press.

Barnet, Richard, and John Cavanagh, 1994. *Global Dreams: Imperial Corporations and the New World Order*. New York: Simon and Schuster.

Barnet, Richard, and Ronald Muller, 1974. *Global Reach: The Power of Multinational Corporations*. New York: Simon and Schuster.

Black, Robert, Saul Morris, and Jennifer Bryce, 2003. Where and Why are 10 Million Children Dying Every Year? *Lancet* 361: 2226-2234.

Blair, Tony (chair), 2005. Our Common Interest: Report of the Commission for Africa. London: Commission for Africa.

Brower, Jennifer, and Peter Chalk, 2003. *The Global Threat of New and Emerging Infectious Diseases: Reconciling U.S. National Security and Public Health Policy*. Santa Monica: RAND.

Coburn, David, 2004. Beyond the Income Inequality Hypothesis: Class, Neo-liberalism, and Health Inequalities. *Social Science and Medicine,* 58: 41-56.

Cowell, Alan, 2005. Group of 7 Agrees to Ease Debt Burden of the Poor. *New York Times*, February 6, 2005.

Daulaire, Nils, 1999. Globalization and Health. *Development,* 42 (4): 22-24.

Doyal, Lesley, and Imogen Pennell, 1981. *The Political Economy of Health*. Boston, South End Press.

Dugger, Celia, 2003. Botswana's Brain Drain Cripples War on AIDS. *New York Times*, November 13, 2003.

——, 2004. An Exodus of African Nurses Puts Infants and the Ill in Peril. *New York Times*, July 12, 2004.

Evans, Robert, Morris Barer, and Theodore Marmor, (eds.), 1994. *Why Are Some People Healthy and Others Not? The Determinants of Health of Populations*. New York: Aldine De Gruyter.

Farmer, Paul, 2003. *Pathologies of Power: Health, Human Rights, and the New War on the Poor*. Berkeley, University of California Press.

Farmer, Paul, Margaret Connors, and Janie Simmons, (eds.), 1996. *Women, Poverty, and AIDS: Sex, Drugs, and Structural Violence*. Monroe, Maine: Common Courage Press.

Galbraith, James, 2002. A Perfect Crime: Global Inequality. *Daedalus* Winter 2002: 11-25.

Gloyd, Steve, 2004. Sapping the Poor: The Impact of Structural Adjustment Programmes. In *Sickness and Wealth: The Corporate Assault on Global Health*, edited by M. Fort, M.A. Mercer and O. Gish, Cambridge, South End Press.

Hankins, Catherine, Samuel Friedman, Tariq Zafar, and Steffanie Strathdee. 2002. Transmission and Prevention of HIV and Sexually Transmitted Infections in War Settings: Implications for Current and Future Armed Conflicts, *AIDS* 16: 2245-2252.

Igbedioh, S. 1990, Macroeconomic Adjustment, Food Availability and Nutrition Status in Nigeria. A Look at the 1990s. *Food Policy,* 15 (6): 518-524.

Irwin, Alec, and Elena Scali, 2005. Action on the Social Determinants of Health: Learning From Previous Experiences. Geneva: Commission on Social Determinants of Health, World Health Organization.

Joint Learning Initiative. 2004. *Human Resources for Health: Overcoming the Crisis*. Cambridge, Harvard University Press.

Jubilee USA Network. *Status of Debt in Africa: 2004* [cited April 7, 2005. Available from http://www.jubileeusa.org/jubilee.cgi?path=/learn_more/articles.

Kawachi, Ichiro, Bruce Kennedy, and Richard Wilkinson, (eds.), 1999. *The Society and Population Health Reader: Volume I Income Inequality and Health*. New York: The New Press.

Keating, Daniel, and Clyde Hertzman, 1999. *Developmental Health and the Wealth of Nations: Social, Biological, and Educational Dynamics*. New York, Guilford Press.

Kim, Jim Yong, Joyce Millen, Alec Irwin, and John Gershman, (eds.), 2000. *Dying for Growth: Global Inequality and the Health of the Poor*. Monroe, Maine, Common Courage Press.

Kirby, Peadar, 2004. Globalization, the Celtic Tiger and Social Outcomes: Is Ireland a Model or a Mirage? *Globalizations* 1 (2): 205-222.

Kotz, David, 1999. Neoliberalism and the Reproduction of Capitalism. Paper read at Union for Radical Political Economics at the Allied Social Science Associations Conference, January 3-5, 1999, at New York.

Labonte, Ronald, and Ted Schrecker. 2004. Committed to Health for All? How the G7/G8 Rate. *Social Science and Medicine* 59: 1661-1676.

Lavis, John; Suzanne Ross; Gregory Stoddart; Joanne Hohenadel; Christopher McLeod; and Robert Evans. 2003. Do Canadian Civil Servants Care about the Health of Populations. *American Journal of Public Health;* 93 (4): 658-663.

Leon, David, and Gill Walt, (eds.), 2001. *Poverty, Inequality, and Health: An International Perspective*. Oxford,Oxford University Press.

Lewis, Stephen, 2003. Africa Reaps What the World Sows—With a Vengeance. Paper read at Global Health Council's Annual Conference, May 28, 2003, at Washington, D.C.

——. 2005. Africa's AIDS Pandemic. *Toronto Star*, January 4, 2005.

Lloyd, Vincent, and Robert Weissman. 2002. How International Monetary Fund and World Bank Policies Undermine Labour Power and Rights, *International Journal of Health Services,* 32 (3): 433-442.

Logie, D., and J Woodroffe, 1993. Structural Adjustment: The Wrong Prescription for Africa? *British Medical Journal* 307 (6895), 41-44.

Lurie, P.; P. Hintzen; and R. Lowe, 1995. Socio-economic Obstacles to HIV Prevention and Treatment in Developing Countries: The Roles of the International Monetary Fund and the World Bank. *AIDS* 9 (6): 539-546.

Lynch, John; George Davey Smith; Sam Harper; Marianne Hillemeier; Nancy Ross; George Kaplan; and Michael Wolfson. 2004. Is Income Inequality a Determinant of Population Health? Part 1: A Systematic Review, *Milbank Quarterly,* 82 (1): 5-99.

Mandela, Nelson. *Make Poverty History: The Full Text of Nelson Mandela's Speech in Trafalgar Square*, February 4, 2005 [cited April 6, 2005. Available from http://www.ekklesia.co.uk/content/news_syndication/article_05024 mandelaspeech.shtml.

Manthorpe, Jonathan, 2005. UN Envoy Sees Hope in Africa's War on HIV/AIDS, *Vancouver Sun*, February 18, 2005.

Navarro, Vicente, and Leiyu Shi, 2001. The Political Context of Social Inequalities and Health, *Social Science and Medicine,* 52 (3): 481-491.

Neubauer, Deane, 2000. Assaying the Frontiers of Globalization: Explorations in the New Economy, *American Studies,* 41 (2/3): 13-32.

——. 2005. Global Stew: Poverty, Urbanization, Global Warming, Neoliberalism and Disease. Paper read at Ritsumeikan Asia Pacific Conference on the Limits of the Asia Pacific City in the 21st Century: The Intersection of Environmental, Social and Cultural Issues, January 29, 30, 2005, at Beppu, Japan.

Nullis-Kapp, Clare, 2005. Efforts Under Way to Stem 'Brain Drain' of Doctors and Nurses, *Bulletin of the World Health Organization,* 83 (2): 84-85.

Nyambuya, M. 1994. The Social Impact of Cost Recovery Measures in Zimbabwe, *South Africa Political Economy,* 7 (6): 14-15.

Peplinskie, Katy, 2005. Celebrities Join UN Envoy to Urge Action on Poverty. *Vancouver Sun*, February 12, 2005.

Reagan, Ronald. *Farewell Address to the Nation*, January 11, 1989 [cited April 4, 2005. Available from http://www.reaganlibrary.com/reagan/speeches/farewell.asp.

Sachs, Jeffrey, 2005. The End of Poverty, *Time*, March 14, 2005.

Sachs, Jeffrey, and J. McArthur, 2005. The Millennium Project: A Plan for Meeting the Millennium Development Goals, *Lancet* 365: 347-353.

Sanders, David; Ronald Labonte; Fran Baum; and Mickey Chopra, 2004. Making Research Matter: A Civil Society Perspective on Health Research. *Bulletin of the World Health Organization,* 82 (10): 757-763.

Schoepf, Brooke; Claude Schoepf; and Joyce Millen, 2000. Theoretical Therapies, Remote Remedies: SAPs and the Political Ecology of Poverty and Health in Africa. In *Dying for Growth: Global Inequality and the Health of the Poor*, edited by J.Y. Kim, J. Millen, A. Irwin and J. Gershman. Monroe, Maine: Common Courage Press.

Shakow, Aaron, and Alec Irwin, 2000. Terms Reconsidered: Decoding Development Discourse. In *Dying for Growth: Global Inequality and the Health of the Poor*, edited by J.Y. Kim, J. Millen, A. Irwin and J. Gershman. Monroe: Common Courage Press.

Steger, Manfred, 2000. Socialism and the Ideological Dimensions of Globalization. In *Culture and Politics: A Reader*, edited by L. Crothers and C. Lockhart, New York, St. Martin's Press.

UNAIDS/UNICEF/USAID, 2004. Children on the Brink 2004: A Joint Report of New Orphan Estimates and a Framework for Action. New York: Joint United Nations Programme on HIV/AIDS, the United Nations Children's Fund, and the United States Agency for International Development.

UNAIDS/WHO, 2004. AIDS Epidemic Update, 2004. Geneva: Joint United

Nations Programme on HIV/AIDS (UNAIDS) and World Health Organization (WHO).

United Nations Development Programme, 1996. *Human Development Report 1996*, New York: Oxford University Press.

——, 1999. *Human Development Report 1999.* New York: Oxford University Press.

——, 2002. *Human Development Report 2002.* New York: Oxford University Press.

——, 2004. *Human Development Report 2004.* New York: Oxford University Press.

Wallace, R., 1990. Urban Desertification, Public Health and Public Order: 'Planned Shrinkage', Violent Death, Substance Abuse and AIDS in the Bronx. *Social Science and Medicine,* 31 (7): 801-813.

Whiteis, David, 1998. Third World Medicine in First World Cities: Capital Accumulation, Uneven Development and Public Health, *Social Science and Medicine,* 47 (6): 795-808.

Wilkinson, Richard, and Michael Marmot, (eds.), 2003. *Social Determinants of Health: The Solid Facts*. second ed. Copenhagen: World Health Organization Regional Office for Europe.

World Bank, 1993. *World Development Report 1993: Investing in Health.* New York: Oxford University Press.

World Health Organization. *Interview with Professor Sir Michael Marmot.* Commission on Social Determinants of Health [cited March 31, 2005. Available from http://www.who.int/social_determinants/advocacy/interview_marmot.

4

Does Foreign Aid Ineffectiveness Cause Conflict and Instability?: A Case Study of Developing Country, Nepal

RAGHU BIR BISTA

Introduction

Recent version about Nepal is *armed conflict* country towards peace deal with Maoist[1], disarmament to Maoist and Constitutional Assembly (CA). It seems to be general but is specific and unique because the communist don't come in such democratic process. Therefore, this small Himalayan landscape is known for all these political issues and development, rather than its economic issue, poverty. Further, ethnic issues led *ethnic conflict* has also received specific attention of International arena because it has created *confusion and vacuum* to the political course towards *CA*.

If we talk about macro-economic indicators, all are in the shade of the political turmoil and constitutional vacuum. In other words, there are imbalance in political, economic and social sectors. Therefore, economic sectors have received *negligence and ignorance*, although foreign aid is focused more. It is very important because this chapter deals to foreign aid and its effectiveness. Concerning Macro-economic indicators and their trends, Nepalese economy has been in progressive character but it looks like stagnant.

Nepalese economy is called *agrarian*. Interestingly, the reports of World Bank and Asian Development Bank state agriculture traditionally subsistence. Statistics indicate stagnant. Surprisingly, it is a pioneering and foundation of non-agriculture development because its contribution is dominant. For example, in GDP, its contribution is 40 per cent. In Industrial Sector, its contribution is 50 per cent, like in export trade. In employment, its contribution is still 76 per cent. In simple, more than 50 per cent poverty is linked with this subsistence agriculture. Still, non-agriculture sector development is not sufficient to move forward Nepalese economy, although National Development Plan and Policy has been initiated since 1956. Trend analysis doesn't reflect on its growth and development. If we analyze in depth development plan and implementation and its external finance, there is vital backing of foreign aid. In addition, Nepal is categorized into the fragile states of different studies and reports of USAID. Therefore, aid's role is very significant for addressing chronic problems of this fragile state. Otherwise, it doesn't take more time to be changed into the failure state, despite the peace deal and disarmament if it revolts the ethnic conflict and destroys the foundations of nation and nation-building. Therefore, aid's performance and effectiveness are must. It is practically hard job. In this chapter, we try to find answers of the questions: what is its status and trend? Are their performance and effectiveness suspicious? If they are critical, what are reasons?

Status and Trend of Foreign Aid

In early 1950s, Rostow, Millikan, Rosentein-Rodan and P. Hoffman advocated foreign aid for economic development without empirically examining its impact on growth. Rosetein-Rodan (1968) the international aid would have two basic impacts: mobilization of domestic savings and interesting rate of investment. Griffin and Enos (1970) aid recipients appear to reduce domestic savings; thus, they don't add to investment. They argued that the inflow of foreign capital might reduce domestic savings in various ways. Therefore, developing countries have depended on foreign aid for meeting resource gap and development expenditure since 1950s.

Still, Nepal's development expenditure is based on foreign aid, although its trend is at fluctuation. Statistics reveals 60 per cent in development expenditure. However, grant ratio is significantly declining and is found small size. It means debt ratio is inclining and is found larger size. Therefore, Nepal bears 8-11 per cent of GDP for repayment and interest. Its share is 34 per cent in total expenditure and 60 per cent in development. Economist claims that it is a burden to the poor country; Nepal and its negative effects can be seen in development.

When we observe its trend, we can find fluctuation. The trend line was downturn till the fourth National Plan from the First National Plan. It was least foreign aid of all national plans from first to ninth that is 44.9 per cent. It restored its upturn but it couldn't reach of the First Plan. Foreign aid was 62.44 per cent in the Sixth Plan. Again, it was downward till the 1990s plan holiday. It got upturn in the Eighth Plan and downturn in the Ninth Plan. Therefore, its trend line is instable. Perhaps, there may be political reasons.

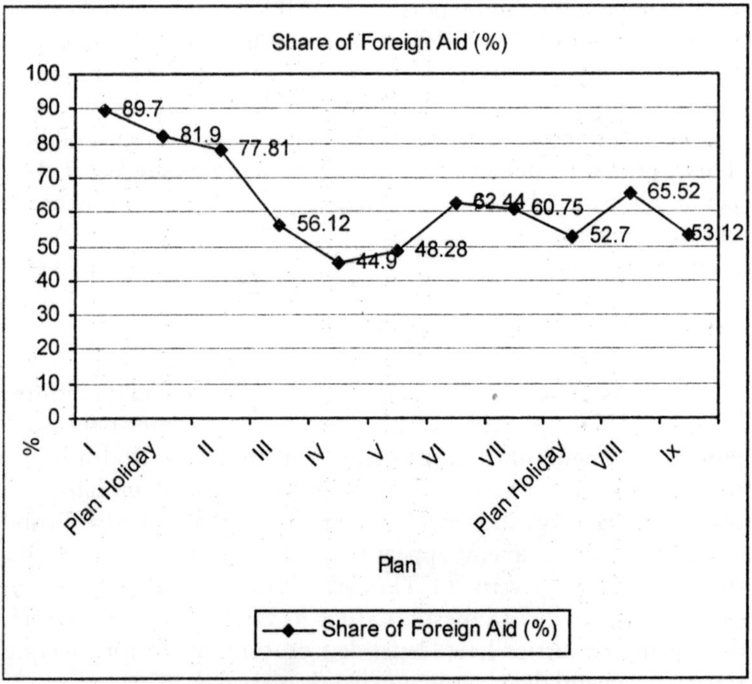

Source: *Economic Survey, 2006.*

Graph 4.1: Share of Foreign Aid Trend

Nepal is highly dependent economy on foreign aid for development. However, its regularity and uniformity are big issues to continue International agenda initiated by the donors. Development trap can be found as its negative consequences. In this context, development issues are generally found unsettled in the country. Therefore, vulnerability and fragility are found increasing trend.

Share of Grant and Debt in Foreign Aid

We cannot comment anything why grant ratio increase or decrease and why debt ratio increase or decrease. This is completely related to the supply side, the donors. It is evident that changing ratios of grant depends on political motives of donors. However, demand side, developing countries remain same.

Trend line of foreign aid is fluctuating and decreasing. Trend of share of grant and debt in foreign aid over 7 years period from 1998 to 2004 is discussed here. If we observe debt, the debt ratio in 1998 was 73 per cent but it was landslide declining at 29 per cent in 2002. Again, it dramatically inclined at 40 per cent in 2003. It slightly felt at 39 per cent in 2004.

Its reverse trend line can be found in grant ratio. The grant ratio in 1998 was 27 per cent but was dramatically and significantly inclining till 2002 in which it reached 71 per cent. However, it was instable and felt at 60 per cent in 2003. However, it slightly increased at 61 per cent in 2004.

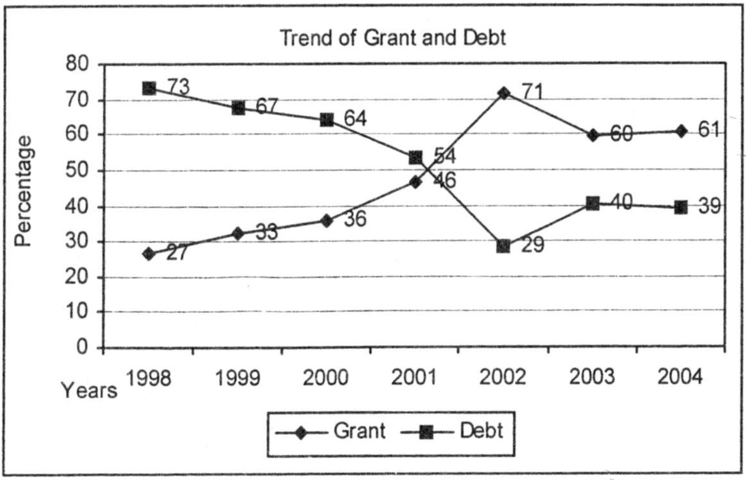

Source: *Economic Survey, 2006* and Series of Plan Development.

Graph 4.2: Share of Grant and Debt

Since 1996, Nepal has been under armed conflict after beginning Maoist's People's War. The State was fragile politically, constitutionally and socio-economically. For tackling and controlling Maoist's armed conflict, India, US and Britain have started to assist security hardware and logistic supports under bilateral grants. Therefore, grant ratio has been inclining till 2002. Accidentally, King did peaceful coup to democracy for addressing the conflict, political and constitutional deadlock. In the cost of democracy and human rights, India, US and Britain had suspended their security assistances on the request of democratic parties so that democracy would be restored.

Multilateral agencies provide preferential loan to Nepal. Since 1996, development projects in rural areas have been suspended one by one because of the growth of insecurity. Therefore, debt ratio was significantly decreasing till 2002. Then after, some suspended projects funded by World Bank and ADB were resumed but the existence of insecurity was key issues. Therefore, the State was very weak to deliver security, law and order, governance, development and human rights. Therefore, share of debt and grant depends on circumstances of developing countries and donors.

Performance and Effectiveness

For macro-economic stability and development and further policy implication, performance and effectiveness of Foreign Aid (FA) should be in depth studied minutely and timely at the Government and the non-governmental level. In developing countries, such practice is rare in the absence of resources. Therefore, its performance and effectiveness are rarely accounted. Its consequence is the formulation of weak and inappropriate policy. In other words, foreign aid, development and economic growth are not correlated.

In Nepal, 23 multilateral and 19 bilateral donors have been providing foreign aid for financing various developmental activities since 1956. In the foreign aid, they provide us most preferential assistance at 1 per cent interest rate for 10 years long time period in South Asia. Thus, debt ratio is dominant in foreign aid, instead of grant ratio. Therefore, Nepal bears 8-11 per cent of GDP for repayment and interest. Its share is 34 per cent in total expenditure and 60 per cent in development. If we observe characters of development projects, we can get that almost all rural intensive and related to infrastructure, agriculture, poverty alleviation etc. that are generally linkage with household livelihood improvements. Therefore, they have vital roles but its performance has been suspicious. It is verified the following studied at Government level, ADB and WB.

- National Planning Commission (NPC) is the central body of planning, allocation of resources and monitoring for overall development of the country. It has 50 years long plan development *experiences, knowledge and history*. When NPC conducted first time foreign aid funded projects in different sectors and areas, its finding was very surprising that 60 per cent proposed projects are classified not satisfactory and 50 per cent on-going projects are reported failure to address targets.
- Asian Development Bank (ADB) is major source of preferential development loans to assist development of Nepal. In Nepal, ADB assisted 89 projects. When 39 development projects were studied, its outcomes were also discouraging that 26 per cent of the projects were 100 per cent failure meanwhile 54 per cent projects were classified semi failures (Thapa, 2004).
- Another International Organization is World Bank. The World Bank conducted the study of the development projects. In the study, only 16 per cent projects were sustainable, although its rate is 55 per cent in South Asia (Thapa, 2004).
- Hegan (1993) evaluated 230 development projects, mostly rural funded by International Organization, bilateral aid and NGOs in 24 developing countries amounting to little over US $2 billion.
  Positive Projects 49.5 per cent (114 Projects)
  Cost of all positive projects 16 per cent
  Negative projects 50.5 per cent (116 Projects)
  Cost of all negative projects—84 per cent
  Average cost of positive projects US $15 million
  Proect-US $ 600 thousand
  Of each dollar of development aid, 84 cents is spent uselessly and wastefully causing harm to the receiving countries and its poor citizens.

Analyses and Lessons

Bad Intention of Donor Agencies

On the basis of these reports, development projects funded by donor agencies including multilateral (ADB and WB) and bilateral agencies are mostly just conducted not for development objectives and assistance to Nepal without logical and factual demand relevancy. It is blamed that the selection of the projects is error because donors select themselves in their national framework, although it is not relevant to local and national demand and circumstance. Therefore, more than 80 per cent foreign aid is misused for their own economic interest. For example: ADB provided US $15.0 million as technical assistance to Nepal in 2000. It was used 62 per cent for advisor's consultancy fee and 38 per cent for planning and preparation. Document development was done by ADB. It was completely white cheating and deceiving in the name of assistance and development. The project was dropped after spending US $15.0 million in the assistance to Nepal. In simple, its result was zero. It is just one story. There are many visible and invisible paper projects and paper development. In reality, development is zero. It seems to be pouring foreign aid in unproductive, unsustainable and non-relevant to national demand and goal. Its higher cost burden is paid annually in the budget. Its result is nothing. It raises a question, why we must use such valueless and useless assistance, except its cost burden?

Strategic Motives

Pearson Commission (1969: 4, quoted in Colaco 1973: 16)—A good deal of bilateral aid has been dispensed in order to achieve short-term political favours, gain strategic advantages or promotes exports from the donor. For example, much foreign aid was granted in the 1950's to enable some countries maintain large armed forces than to promote economic growth. In the none of these cases was the promotion of long-term development a dominant objective of the aid given. Milton Friedman (1958:24) the purpose of foreign aid was to win over to our side those uncommitted nations who are also under developed and poor. Otherwise, for example, El-Salvador is 3 times richer than Bangladesh but it gets 16 times more ODA from US than does Bangladesh. Therefore, developed countries are rarely good motive for development of developing countries. If not, Bangladesh gets more ODA from US. In reality, there are political, trade and security interest. In case of Nepal, we have three major bilateral donors: India, China and US. Their bilateral assistances are entirely of political nature. For example, in 1954, India decided to control the Koshi, which had perennially wreaked havoc in the Northern India and to a lesser extent in Southern Nepal. It was determined that India would pay all costs and that a barrage would be built partly in Nepalese territory (Mihaly, 1965:149). Another example of China: Mao Tse-Tung had described Nepal as part of the ancient Chinese empire and indicated that it should be restored and various Chinese Maps showed Nepal, along with much of South East Asia and the Himalayan region as the part of China (Mihaly, 1965:152). In these strategic bad motives, how Nepal can get development and stability?

Corruption

Resistance power and State will-power of developing countries are very weak with high-level political and bureaucratic corruption as well as resource gap. For example, a recent study estimates that between 40 and 50 per cent of total Food For Work (FFW) budget is believed to be siphoned off for personal gain by those implementing the programme. This black money is distributed among themselves in the following proportion (Meagher, *et. al.,* 1998, 8-9). Distribution of corruption amount was as follows: Entertainment cost 10 per cent, local audit cost 10 per cent, local politicians (if not thereto local engineers and overseas) 10 per cent, District engineer 15 per cent, District overseers 25 per cent, overseeing accountant and the Department, and Ministry in equal accounts 35 per cent. Foreign aid is responsible in developing economies for encouraging corruption, socio-economic discrimination and lebalism, aid dependency syndrome and lopsided development. Economic growth is occurring only in a few urban areas and has not led to automatic translation into growth for all. This is because the linkages between urban and rural areas are weak and there is a lack of sufficient roads, communications, infrastructure and appropriate skills among the rural poor. (World Bank, 1998) Therefore, despite unfruitful, wasteful and burdensome, foreign assistance is not rejected. Therefore, it is continuous; despite zero performance. But poverty, inequality and unemployment issues gradually grow towards complicated and complex. Hungriness, diseases and deprived will create a conflict and rebellion.

Serious and Sensitive Consequences to Nation-Building

Development delivery depends on the success of development projects. However, almost these are found failures but demand of population with higher population growth rate for basic utilities is reported increasing. The demand and supply gap between household, industry and the Government has become a big issue of poverty, inequality and unemployment which has created classes and castes divisions and struggle for survival. Invisible conflict and contradiction in the community has come into existence. It is blamed that all development are focused on urban areas. In addition, corruption culture of foreign aided projects has made neo-richer population. Interestingly, development projects, which are conducted in the areas, have exploited to the people. This is the negative feeling. Maoist cashed it for their political mileage in 1996. All know what happened from 1996 to 2006. The armed conflict has killed 13,000 people, displaced 2 million populations, damaged huge resources and suspended developmental activities. Thus, Nepal has been pushed 10 years back in development. Its by-product is ethnic conflict in terai. It has weakened the process of nationalism, nationality and nation-building towards peace, stability and prosperity. It has made confusion about Nepal. Therefore, foreign aid is attractive but dangerous matter to developing countries like Nepal.

Conclusions

In the context of globalization and regional integration, dependency of developing countries on developed countries and member countries has increased naturally for economic development and poverty alleviation (MDG target) on the basis of collectivism in cooperation and comparative benefits. How much developing countries seriously and attentively get benefits with ability and capacity may be a big curiosity. In general, capacity determines benefits from these opportunities. Otherwise, it may be risk to the economy. In the case of foreign aid, it is also State Will issue. If it is unfavourable to the nation-building, the State must reject it after convincing them. If it is favourable, the State must focus on its proper utilization through the implementation of projects. Its monitoring and regulatory mechanism should be made autonomous and strong for accountable, transparent and progressive for meeting targets at justified cost and benefit. In the supply side, ADB, WB and Bilateral Aid agencies should be clear about their assistance to developing countries whether their assistance is for proper development, rather than monopoly of international money-lender. They seem to be unclear when we remember paper project development, implementation, expenditure and completion without getting targets at huge resources expenses in the name of the country. Such a kind of corruption and deceives of international organization within the institution must be controlled. The selection of projects must be adjusted in accordance with National Plan and Development. The preconditions for aid must be related to project performance and effectiveness. Then, foreign aid will be beneficial to the poorest of the poor. Otherwise, this is development puzzle and legal exploitation. If it is not reviewed for stop, MDG will be highly talked gossip. Furthermore, foreign aid should be localized in the developing countries. It means utilization of local experts, labour, raw materials and local or modern technology. It helps to transfer the huge cost burden of consultancy services into the project field. Then, the project benefit will be greater than the project cost. Its benefits will help to achieve MDG. In case of this fragile state, donor's role should be specific and positive to improve its performance and effectiveness for making the successful State.

NOTE

1. Maoist is a term borrowed from "Great Philosopher and Leader Mao and his philosophy Maoism" in Nepal describes revolutionary forces with communist symbol. In Nepal, Jana Morcha, extreme revolutionary communist party, had participated in the general election 1992 in the multiparty system in Nepal with critically support and accept, although they had republican objectives like as United Marxism Leninism (UML), Nepal Majadur Kissan Party (NMKP), Nepal Communist Party (United) etc. They represented from 7 constitutional areas. In the mid-term general election, they defeated. Then, they went to Jungle with arm conflict. The conflict is called Maoist Conflict in Nepal.

REFERENCES

Asian Development Bank, 2000.
Economic Survey, 2005-06.
Griffin and Enos (1970).
Hegan, Tony (1993). *Bikas ka Lagi Budhi le Matra le Pugadina, Hatagoda Pani* Baliya Chahincha. *Himal,* p. 122.
Meagher *et al.*, 1998.
Milton Friedman (1958:24).
Mithley, Eugene Bramer (1965). Foreign Aid and Politics in Nepal (A Case Study). UK: Oxford University Press, p. 152.
Mithley, Eugene Bramer (1965). Foreign Aid and Politics in Nepal (A Case Study). UK: Oxford University Press, p.- 149.
Pearson Commission (1969:4, quoted in Colaco, 1973:16.)
Rosetein-Rodan (1968).
Thapa, Hari Bahadur (2004). *Malpractice of Foreign Aid*, Kathmandu, National Book Centre, p.140.
World Bank, 1998.
World Bank, 2000.

5

Technological Change and Growth of Indian Cement Industry under Globalization

P.R. BOSE

The process of liberalization opened by the Indian Government in July 1991 has translated the Indian economy from an inward looking and regulated economy to a market-oriented one with emphasis on private sector participation. Indian economy has emerged as the fifth largest economy in the world. India's GDP at factor cost has been rising steadily at about 6-7 per cent since 1990-91 with marginal fluctuations. The remarkable feature of India's growth is that it is the first time that the Indian economy has achieved a growth of this magnitude due to exceptional performance of sectors other than agriculture. GDP growth rate during Ninth Five Year Plan (1997-2002) has been estimated between 6.5 per cent to 7 per cent.

Cement is a core sector industry and its development is of vital importance to national growth. Government policies have affected the growth of cement industry in the country. It has passed through various stages and regimes, such as the regime of dominant imports 1914–24, regime of struggle and survival 1924–41, regime of price controls 1942–51, regime of planning and controls 1951–82, partial decontrol 1982–88 and then total decontrol from March 1989 (Chakravarty, 1989, p. 4). Currently it is passing through the phase of liberalization since July 1991. It aims at to accelerate the process of making Indian industry globally competitive. This thrust has increased the domestic and external competition through extensive application of market mechanisms and facilitating the relationship with foreign investors and suppliers of technology. In this chapter I have tried to focus on the impact of this new industrial policy on the R&D efforts and development of technological capability of our domestic industries with the example of cement industry.

Growth of Cement Industry

Cement industry in India has traditionally been in the heart of private sector. The all-round growth of the cement industry was seen in the decade of eighties. The impact of partial decontrol policy for cement industry in 1982 reflected in creation of new capacities and subsequently increased production. Installed capacity, which was 29 million tonnes in 1981 was doubled and reached to 58 million tonnes by 1990. Production also increased more than the double and rose from 21 million tonnes to 45 million tonnes during the same period. Again, in the decade of nineties, during the post-liberalization period, the existing capacity was doubled by another 58 million tonnes and reached to 116 million tonnes. The production went up from 45 million tonnes to 96 million tonnes with an increase of 51 million tonnes by the end of the decade *i.e.* the year 2000. It is interesting to note that Indian industry took 76 years to reach the capacity of 58 million tonnes beginning from 1914 to 1990 and the equal figure was achieved in next 10 years. In March 1999, there were 120 large plants belonging to 57 companies across the country with an installed capacity of 109 million tonnes. Of these, the private sector had domination in the industry and had capacity of 100.75 million tonnes, which was 91.6 per cent and the public sector had capacity of 9.22 million tonnes, which was 8.4 per cent of the total capacity in the country. The average capacity addition rose at 9.2 per cent in a decade period from 1989 to 1999. The all-India average capacity utilization of cement plants was at 82 per cent (CMA, 1999). Table 5.1 shows the growth of cement industry from 1985-86 to 1999-2000.

In India the concept of mini-cement plants, *i.e.* plants having one or more kilns with a total installed capacity not exceeding 200 tonnes per day, gained performance in the late seventies. In 1976 the Cement Research Institute (now known as National Council for Cement and Building Materials) commissioned the first

Table 5.1: Growth of Cement Industry (Large Plants)

(in million tonnes)

Year	*Capacity at the end of the Year*	*Cement Production*	*Production Growth (%)*
1981	28.93	20.77	–
1982	31.78	22.54	8.5
1983	33.86	25.41	12.7
1984	39.10	29.14	14.7
1985	41.85	25.11	6.8
1986	49.10	33.65	8.2
1987	54.51	36.97	9.9
1988	55.04	40.72	10.1
1989	56.36	42.07	3.3
1990	58.12	44.87	6.7
1991	60.61	49.47	10.3
1992	62.46	50.87	2.8
1993	66.90	52.78	3.8
1994	73.19	57.57	9.1
1995	82.06	62.08	7.8
1996	90.17	68.86	10.9
1997	99.92	74.75	8.6
1998	108.41	79.42	6.2
1999	109.44	91.72	15.5
2000	116.30	95.94	4.6

Source: CMA, (2001). Basic Data-2001, Indian Cement Industry, New Delhi.

20 tonnes per day cement plant at Madurathur in Tamil Nadu based on Vertical Shaft Kiln (VSK). The VSK mini-cement plants ranged in capacity between 50-100 tonnes per day. The rotary kiln mini-cement plants were normally of 200 tonnes per day or up to 66,000 tonnes per annum. Cement Corporation of India (CCI) in public sector was given responsibility to set up mini-cement plants to provide leadership. Mini-cement sector was banned for large houses and foreign majority companies. There was no government intervention in the choice of technology to be utilized in the setting up of the mini-cement plants. It was left to the choice of the entrepreneur. In March 1985, there were 25 mini-cements plants in operation with an installed capacity of 1.1 million tonnes. Mini-cement plants were completely free from price control and do not have to contribute to levy cement (BICP, 1987, p. 14-15). In August 1986, it was decided to include capacity up to 300 tonnes per day within the purview of mini-cement plants. By next year, it was further enhanced to capacity

up to 600 tonnes per day provided that this capacity was created by expansion of existing 300 tonnes per day mini-cement plants by installing pre-calcinator technology etc. Here, the Government had direct intervention to encourage and upgrade the better technology. By 1987, there were 118 mini-cement plants set up in the country with a capacity of 3 million tonnes and had contributed in production nearly 1.5 million tonnes. The number of mini-cement plants went up to 180 by the year 1992 and they together had contribution of 3 million tonnes in production, which was about 6 per cent of total cement production in country (Schumacher & Sathaye, 1999, p. 6). At present cement plants up to the capacity of 650 tonnes per day fall in the category of mini-cement plants. There are over 300 white and mini-cement plants having together an installed capacity of 9.0 million tonnes in addition to the production from large plants in the industry.

In 1982, among the different types of cement produced in the country the share of Portland Pozzolanic Cement (PPC) was the highest and accounted for about 60 per cent, followed by Ordinary Portland Cement (OPC), about 22 per cent, Portland Blast Furnace Slag Cement (PBFS), about 17 per cent and others less than one per cent. Altogether 11 different varieties of cement were produced in the country. The High Level Committee of 1981 reviewed the situation and recommended that the price of PPC should be lower than the price of OPC because PPC has limited application while OPC can be used for all purposes. The change in production trend was noteworthy and the increase in the share of OPC was three-fold, whereas the share of PPC decreased to about 22 per cent, and PBFS share was about 12 per cent in total production by 1988. At present the Indian cement industry produces 13 different varieties of cement. Among them OPC, PPC, and PBFS constitute the major share accounting for almost 99 per cent in total production. The production of OPC is about 63 per cent; PPC 25 per cent, PBFS about 11 per cent and others, such as oil-well cement and coloured cements are less than one per cent of the total. Table 5.2 shows trends in variety-wise cement production from 1986 to 2000.

In 1980, India was the eighth largest cement producing country in the world, with production of about 18 million tones. After a gap of one decade, in 1991, India was the fifth largest cement producing country after China, Russia, Japan and USA. World cement production was recorded 1164.2 million tonnes, China ranked first having production of 243.6 million tonnes, Russia ranked second having production of 122.4 million tonnes, Japan ranked third with production of 86.4 million tonnes, USA ranked fourth with production of 66.0 million tonnes and India ranked fifth with production of 52.5 million tonnes (Chakravarty, 1993, p. 4). They together produced 49 per cent of the total world cement production. Today, the Indian Cement business is the second largest in the world as well as in Asian continent after China and gives employment to 1.35 lakh people. India is however far behind from China, which is the world's largest producer with annual output of 573.0 million tonnes. The world's total cement production during 1999 was 1601.3 million tonnes, and China's share was 36 per cent followed by India 6 per cent, USA and Japan each having 5 per cent share (CMA, 2001, p. 2). These four countries together contributed 52 per cent in the world total cement production. Table 5.3 shows the performance of five world top cement producing countries for the period 1980-1999.

Cement Technology Development

The growth in the R&D expenditure of industrial sector in the country can be attributed to several factors including, increased awareness of the importance of the R&D activities, increase in the number of R&D units, introduction of several incentives for R&D by the Government, liberalized economic policies, international industrial competitiveness etc. The number of in-house R&D units for public and private sector during 1996-97 were 166 and 1270 respectively. In 1985-86 total national expenditure incurred on R&D was Rs. 2068.78 crore, out of which the share of private sector in the national expenditure on R&D was 12 per cent, it was 8 per cent of State Government sector and 80 per cent of Central Government sector. In the year 1997-98 the total expenditure incurred on R&D amounted to Rs. 9500.72 crore (GOI, 1997). The share of private sectors increased to the tune of 23 per cent, while the share of Central Government sector decreased to 69 per cent, and the share of State Government sector remained unchanged. The share of Government sector is constantly declining.

In the country, there are seven R&D units in public and private sectors in cement industry. It has 9 R&D personnel per thousand employees. The expenditure on R&D and development in cement

Table 5.2: Trends in Variety-wise Cement Production

(in million tonnes)

Year	*OPC*	*PPC*	*PBFS*	*Others*	*Total*
1986	16.50 (49.01)	12.87 (38.22)	4.08 (12.12)	0.22 (0.65)	33.67
1989	29.77 (70.76)	7.50 (17.83)	4.53 (10.77)	0.27 (0.64)	42.07
1992	36.48 (71.72)	8.46 (16.63)	5.49 (10.79)	0.44 (0.86)	50.87
1995	43.46 (70.01)	11.17 (17.99)	6.83 (11.00)	0.62 (1.00)	62.08
1996	47.57 (69.08)	13.39 (19.45)	7.26 (10.54)	0.64 (0.93)	68.86
1997	52.59 (70.36)	14.13 (18.90)	7.52 (10.06)	0.51 (0.68)	74.75
1998	56.52 (71.17)	14.83 (18.67)	7.58 (9.54)	0.49 (0.62)	79.42
1999	61.57 (67.13)	20.15 (21.97)	9.34 (10.18)	0.66 (0.72)	91.72
2000(P)	60.56 (63.13)	24.44 (25.47)	10.14 (10.57)	0.80 (0.83)	95.94

OPC : Ordinary Portland Cement.
PPC : Portland Pozzolanic Cement.
PBFS : Portland Blast Furnace Slag Cement.
Note : The figures in parenthesis show percentage.
Source : CMA, (2001). Basic Data 2001 Indian Cement Industry, New Delhi.

industry was Rs. 1046.27 lakh in 1994-95, Rs. 1058.15 lakh in 1995-96 and Rs. 1244.91 lakh in 1996-97. It accounted for 0.27 per cent in 1994-95; 0.23 per cent in 1995-96 and 0.25 per cent in 1996-97 of the total sales turnover in cement industry (GOI, 1999, p. 74, 75). In India, there are four organizations, which have developed the technology and have been successfully commercialized for mini cement plants. They are:

(i) NCB design, developed by the Cement Research Institute, which permits use of low-grade coals, which is the grade that the cement industry in the country gets.
(ii) RRL design, developed by Regional Research Laboratory, Jorhat of the Council of Scientific and Industrial Research (CSIR).

Table 5.3: World Cement Production

(Selected Years)

Country	*Export* Million tonnes*	*Cement production (Million tonnes) (%)*		
	1999	*1999*	*1991*	*1980*
China	6.3	573.0 (35.8)	243.6 (21.0)	n.a (—)
India	3.1	99.1 (6.2)	52.5 (4.5)	17.9 (2.0)
USA	0.3	85.0 (5.3)	66.0 (5.6)	68.2 (7.7)
Japan	7.7	83.5 (5.2)	86.4 (7.4)	87.4 (!0.0)
Korea	5.0	49.5 (3.0)	n.a (—)	15.6 (1.7)
Russia	0.8	25.5 (1.6)	122.4 (10.5)	124.8 (14.1)
Sub-Total	**23.2**	**915.6 (57.2)**	**570.9 (49.0)**	**312.9 (35.5)**
Other Countries	98.8	685.7 (42.8)	593.3 (51.0)	566.2 (64.5)
World Total	**122.0**	**1601.3**	**1164.2**	**881.1**

Sources: CMA, (2001, 1993,). Basic Data 2001, Indian Cement Industry, New Delhi.

(i) Chakravarty, S. M. (1989). *Indian Cement Industry from Control to Decontrol*. Wadhera Publications, Bombay.

(ii) JCA, (2001), *Cement in Japan-2001*, Tokyo.

(iii) The Saboo VSK technology, developed by Shri Saboo, Jodhpur.

(iv) The ATDA plant, developed by Appropriate Technology Development Association, Lucknow.

Worldwide, vertical shaft kiln, popularly known as, the VSK technology in mini-cement plants has been found to be feasible at lower production scales ranging from 1 tonne per day to 300 tonnes per day, while the rotary kiln is generally regarded efficient at higher capacities above 300 tonnes per day or 1 lakh tonnes per annum. R&D efforts abroad innovated the concept of precalcination in early seventies which enabled the higher capacity of a kiln up to the range of 9000 tpd. The precalcinator technology enables an increase in cement production of 2 to 2.5 times that of a kiln with only a suspension preheater. The precalcinating system developed till mid seventies used either oil or gas in the primary firing system as well as in the precalcinators. Very few systems like MFC and RSP systems developed in Japan, Polysius system developed in Germany and FLS system developed in Denmark experimented with coal for the secondary firing. At present the world over there are about 17 different precalcination systems including the CRI-Precal, developed in India, each claiming its own advantages. Of these, nine systems were developed in Japan alone, three in Germany and one each in Canada, Italy, France, Denmark and India (GOI, 1984, p. 296-98). Table 5.4 gives details of the different precalcination systems.

In India, the first dry process plant was commissioned in 1958 with a capacity below 500 tpd, and the industry was dominated by wet process capacity. During 1989 the average kiln capacity was 887 tpd. Process-wise, it was 393 tpd from wet process, 603 tpd from semi-dry, and 1472 tpd from dry process. After one decade by December 2000 the average kiln capacity was 1966 tpd and process-wise, it was 435 tpd from wet process, 657 tpd from semi-dry and 2471 tpd from dry process, mainly due to the application of latest and upgraded technologies. The average kiln capacity of dry process was only 3.6 fold higher than the wet process kiln capacity in 1989. In 2000 the dry kiln capacity was 5.7 fold higher than the wet process kiln. Process-wise kilns capacities during the year 1989 was 22 per cent from wet process, 75 per cent from dry process and 3 per cent from semi-dry process. This after a gap of a decade had remarkable technological changes and accounted for 4 per cent from wet process 94 per cent from dry process and 2 per cent from semi-dry process as on December 2000. Table 5.5 shows the comparative distribution of process-wise capacity in the country for the year 1989 and 2000. (See Fig. 5.2).

Technologically, there has been a major change in the size of kilns in cement industry. In 1960 kilns below 500 tpd capacity dominated the industry. In 1970, the regime of planning and controls, there were 119 kilns in total, out of which 55 kilns had capacities below 400 tpd, 63 kilns had capacities between 401-999 tpd and only one kiln had capacity above 1000 tpd. Its capacity was 1600 tpd.

Table 5.4: Precalcinators and New Suspension Preheater (NSP) Systems Developed

Abbreviation of the Process	*NSP Process*	*Process Developed by*
1. CSF	New Suspension Flash Calciner	Chichibu Cement Co. Ltd., **Japan**
2. DD	Dual Combustion and Denitration Calciner	Nihon Cement Co. Ltd., **Japan**
3. GG	Anti Pollution NSP Process	Mitsubishi Mining and Cement Co. Ltd., **Japan**
4. MFC	Mitsubishi Fludised	Mitsubishi Mining and Cement Co. Ltd., **Japan**
5. NKSV	New Kawasaki Spouted Bed and Vortex Chamber Process	Kawasaki Heavy Industries Ltd., **Japan**
6. NSF	New Suspension Flash Calciner	Ishikawajima Harima Heavy Ind. Co. Ltd. and Chichibu Cement Co. Ltd., **Japan**
7. RSP	Reinforced Suspension Preheater	Onoda Cement Co. Ltd., **Japan**
8. SCS	Sumitoma Cross Suspension Preheater and Spouted Furnace Process	Sumitom Cement Co. Ltd., **Japan**
9. TOKUJAMA	Tokujama Process	Tokujama Soda Co. Ltd., **Japan**
10. PREPOL	Polysius-Krupp Prepol System	Polysius, **Germany**
11. PYROCLON	Humboldt Wedgag System	Humboldt-Wedag, **Germany**
12. PREAXIAL	Preaxial Preheater System	Babcock Krauss Maffei Industri enanlagen GmbH, **Germany**
13. FCB	Fives Cail Babcok System	**France**
14. TOS-IT	Tos-It Calciner	Tosi-SPA Loganano **France and Italy Comonts, Italy**
15. FLS	FL Smidth System	F L Smidth, **Denmark**
16. AECO	Aeco Precalcining System	Abacus Industrial Equipment, Company, **Canada**
17. CRI-PRECAL	CRI Precalcinator System	Cement Research Institute of **India**

Source: Government of India, (1984). Government of India, Report of the working group on cement industry for 1985-90. Ministry of Industry, Department of Industrial Development, New Delhi, July.

Table 5.5: Process-wise Capacity

Process	*March 1989*			*December 2000*		
	Capacity (tpd)	*No. of Kilns*	*Average Kiln Capacity (tpd)*	*Capacity (tpd)*	*No. of Kilns*	*Average Kiln Capacity (tpd)*
Dry	116350 **(75)**	79 (45)	1472	291536 **(94)**	118 (75)	2471
Semi Dry	4830 **(3)**	8 (5)	603	5260 **(2)**	8 (5)	657
Wet	35033 **(22)**	89 (50)	393	13910 **(4)**	32 (20)	435
Total	156213	176	887	310706	158	1966

Note: Figures in parenthesis show percentage.

Sources: CMA, (1990). Structural changes in cement industry (large plants) 1989-90, New Delhi, January.
CMA, (2001). Basic data—Indian Cement Industry, New Delhi, March.

In 1988, there were 170 kilns in the industry and 54 kilns had capacities above 1000 tpd, with share contribution of 64.5 per cent in the total capacity. In 1993, there were 162 kilns in operation, out of which 18 kilns were in the highest range of 3000-4500 tpd and 53 kilns had capacities of above 1000-2999 tpd. All kilns of this range were in dry process including one in semi-dry. Between the range of 401-999 tpd capacity there were 48 kilns and below 400 tpd capacities the number of kilns was 43, mainly in wet process. During December 2000, there were 158 kilns, out of which only 25 kilns had capacities below 400 tpd, largely in wet process, 30 kilns were in the range of 400-999 tpd, 57 kilns were in the range of 1000-2999 tpd and 46 kilns were in the highest category of 3000-7500 tpd or above one million tpa, all in dry process. Table 5.6 shows size-wise distribution of kilns in the cement industry for the years 1988, 1993 and 2000.

Dry process kiln with suspension preheater and precalciner technology had steep rise in the country during post-new industrial policy regime. The number of cement plants having million tonnes and above capacity in the industry was two in 1982, eighteen in 1989 and this number rose to fifty-four in 2000. Thirty-six plants in the range of this capacity came up in nineties as the import of

Table 5.6: Range of Kilns Capacities (Selected Years) (Number of Kilns)

Size of Kiln (tpd)	1988				1993				2000			
	Dry	Semi-dry	Wet	**Total**	Dry	Semi-dry	Wet	**Total**	Dry	Semi-dry	Wet	**Total**
Below 400	5	1	49	**55**	5	1	37	**43**	3	1	21	**25**
401-999	19	6	34	**59**	13	6	29	**48**	11	6	13	**30**
1000-2999	42	1	2	**45**	52	1	–	**53**	56	1	–	**57**
Above 3000	11	–	–	**11**	18	–	–	**18**	46	–	–	**46**
Total	77	8	85	**170**	88	8	66	**162**	116	8	34	**158**

Source: Data worked out from:

CMA, (2001, 1993,). Indian Cement Industry-Basic Data 2001 and 1993. New Delhi.

Chakravarty, S M. (1989). Indian Cement Industry from Control to Decontrol.

Wadhera Publications, Bombay.

machinery became easier and liberal with the advent of new industrial policy. The installed capacity of these plants together accounts 87.31 million tonnes, which is 75 per cent of the total capacity of large plants. Larsen and Toubro (L&T), Gujarat is India's largest cement plant with the capacity of 4.20 million tonnes. L&T Gujarat, L&T ACW, L&T AP, together have capacity of about 11 million tonnes per annum. Other cement plants having largest capacity are ACC Gagal 2.7 million tonnes; Jaypee Rewa and Vikram Cement each having capacity of 2.5 million tonnes per annum.

Energy Consumption and R&D Efforts at Firms Level

Cement manufacturing industry being highly energy intensive, there is immense need for R&D in this area. During the last two decades and particularly with the advent of the Seventh Five Year Plan (1985-90), a real thrust had been given to technology upgradation, technology development and technology assimilation, whether by import of technology or developing indigenous technology through in-house R&D efforts. The energy alone accounts for more than 45 per cent share of the total cost of cement production in India. Considering the power consumption in various departments of the cement plant, three sections namely, raw mills, cement mills, and kiln and coal mills amount for 90-95 per cent of the total specific power consumption. The normal power consumption figures for wet plants is about 105 kWh/tonne of cement and varies 95-115 kWh/tonne of cement for dry plants. Fuel consumption varies between 15 to 25 per cent of coal/t of clinker in the case of dry plants and 30 to 40 per cent in case of wet process cement kilns. In the raw mill, use of Vertical Roller Mill (VRM) for cement grinding is very recent and the performance results are reported to be encouraging. The VRM has at least 30 per cent lesser power consumption, than the comparable ball mill system. Table 5.7 shows details of section-wise specific power consumption kWh/t of material from crusher stage to packing stage during 1995-96.

Table 5.7: Section-wise Specific Power Consumption

(kWh/t Material)

Sr. No.	*Section*	*Dry Process*		*Wet Process*	
		Range	*Average*	*Range*	*Average*
1.	Crusher	1.09-4.07	1.91	2.06-3.50	2.28
2.	Raw Grinding				
	(a) Ball Mill	17.79-28.40	23.03	12.20-20.79	17.21
	(b) VRM	14.02-24.50	18.61		
3.	Kiln Section	25.16-44.20	30.37	16.78-26.00	21.88
4.	Coal Grinding				
	(a) Ball mill	25.50-67.23	41.00	29.09-35.90	32.47
	(b) VRM	18.90-35.50	28.32		
5.	Cement Grinding	28.17-52.23	34.00	32.00-47.61	38.01
6.	Packing	0.94-3.38	1.96	0.80-1.52	1.32

Source: CMA, (1997). Energy efficiency improvement in Indian Cement Industry: National Council for Cement and Building Materials. Cement and Energy, New Delhi, Vol. 1(3).

Energy conservation was given highest priority in the overall cost reduction programme in cement manufacture. The cement plants have successfully adopted the various energy conservation measures and their specific energy consumption levels have reduced significantly over the years. It includes modernization and up-gradation of machinery and using-in-house expertise, modification and implementation of the relative measures using internal resources, and operating equipment efficiently and optimally. In this context the efforts and initiatives taken at Mysore Cements and Rajshree Cement are discussed in detail (CMA, 1999, p. 1-5).

Ammasandra unit of Mysore Cements in Karnataka,

commissioned in 1962, has at present a rated capacity of 5.70 lakh tonnes of cement per year based on dry process technology. Electrical and thermal energy form the major part of the cost of cement production, thermal energy accounting for 22 per cent and electrical energy about 20 per cent of the total. Hence, energy conservation has been accorded the highest priority to bring down the cost of production.

This plant comprising 4 kilns was initially designed and engineered to produce 5 lakh tonnes of cement per annum. A massive modernization and modifications programme was launched during 1987-88 to improve the operational efficiency and enhance productivity, with the result the power consumption per tonne of cement could be brought down from 143 units/tonne in 1986-87 (before modernization) to 129 units/tonne over a period of 7 years. In addition to this, several major modifications in the plant were also carried out, in-house, on a continuous basis from 1993-94 onwards as a result of which the power consumption could be further brought down from 129 units/tonne of cement to 112 units/tonne of cement at the end of 1997-98. Similarly, the fuel consumption could be brought down from 304 kg/tonne of clinker before modernization to 195 kg/tonne of clinker at the end of 1997-98. These efforts resulted in the plant winning the National Award for best improvement in thermal efficiency for 1994-95. The details of the modernization carried out and the results achieved are summarised in Table 5.8.

Table 5.8: Summary of R&D Results at Mysore Cements of Ammasandra Unit from 1986-97 to 1997-98

Stage	*Period*	*Fuel Consumption Kg/t of Clinker*	*Power Consumption Units/t of Cement*
1. Pre-modernization	1986-87	304	143
2. With technological up-gradation	1993-94	253	129
3. With in-house R&D major/ minor modifications and operational improvement	1994-95	215	126
	1995-96	229	125
	1996-97	239	124
	1997-98	195	112

Source: CMA, (1999). *Cement and Energy*, a Quarterly Newsletter. New Delhi, January.

Rajashree Cement, a unit of Indian Rayon and Industries was commissioned its first unit for cement in 1984. This unit is operating at present with 2200 tpd clnker capacity. In 1990, the plant went on to commission its second unit which is now operating at about 3300 tpd clinker. This in turn was followed by an expansion programme, with the commissioning of its third unit within a record time of 15 months in June 1995. With the most modern energy efficient equipment installed. This unit has a clinker production capacity of 3500 tpd or 12.8 lakh tonnes per annum.

This plant has utmost priority to energy conservation and has constantly been making focused efforts to achieve optimum energy consumption levels. In this context various means adopted include recourse to latest technology, modifications and design change and installation of latest energy saving equipment in consultation with machinery manufacturers, minor modifications and design changes, and implementation of innovative ideas.

Under its vision-2002, the plant has drawn up an action plan for second unit based on the experiences of its third unit for achieving benefits of increase in production, reduction in power and thermal consumption. It was worked out that a total reduction of 8.75 kWh/t of cement in power and 42 kcal/kg of clinker in thermal energy can be achieved. Thus the overall power consumption will ultimately reduce from 104 to 95.25 kWh/t of cement and thermal energy consumption from 742 to 700 kcal/kg of clinker. Table 5.9 shows the details of energy conservation implemented and proposed at Rajshree Cement.

During the year 1986 the Inter-Sectoral Science and Technology Advisory Committee (ISSTAC) constituted in Department of Science and Technology, New Delhi. It identified energy management in cement industry among several new and selective areas for taking up as multi-partnership Research Development and Demonstration (RD&D) projects (DST, 1996-97, p. 30). NCB a research organization in cement, carried out a study in a large number of cement plants in the area of energy conservation, which shows that the average specific heat consumption level of dry process plants was 780.12 kcal/kg clinker in 1995-96. As compared to 1992-93, there was a reduction of 1.6 per cent in the specific heat consumption. The study indicated that 55 per cent plants were operating below 800 kcal/kg clinker, 40 per cent plants were operating at 800 to 900 kcal/kg clinker production, whereas 5 per cent were operating above

Table 5.9: Energy Conservation Measures Implemented and Proposed at Rajshree Cement

S. No.	A. Section-wise Measure(s) Adopted	Potential Energy Saving	
		Power kWh/t of Cement	Thermal kcal/kg of Clinker
1.	**Raw Mill** Bucket elevator in place of air lift for raw meal feeding to silo	2.00	–
2.	**Kiln**		
	(a) Retrofit of one grate cooler with project grate	0.50	30
	(b) Installation of variable speed drives in all grate cooler fans (ACFC)	1.00	–
	(c) Installation of variable speed drives like GRR in kiln ESP fans, cooler ESP fans, PH fans	1.15	–
	(d) Pfister pump (Pyro)	0.25	3
3.	**Cement Mill** Bucket elevator in place of air lift for cement feeding to silo	1.85	
	Total ....A	6.75	33
	B. Further Energy Conservation Measures Proposed		
1.	Installation of bucket elevator in place of air lift in kiln feed of preheater	2.00	3
2.	Installation of high efficiency/low primary air (project) burner in kiln	–	6
	Total............ B	2.00	9
	Grand Total (A+B)	**8.75**	**42**

Source: CMA, (1999). *Cement and Energy*, a Quarterly Newsletter. New Delhi, January.

900 kcal/kg clinker. In case of electrical energy consumption the average specific power consumption level in dry process plants was 104.35 kWh/t cement in 1995-96. As compared to 1992-93, there was a reduction of 7.01 per cent in specific power consumption. It was seen that 30 per cent of plants were operating in the range of 105 to 115 kWh/t of cement and 43 per cent plants were operating in the range of 95 to 105 kWh/t, while only 13 per cent plants had achieved the target of operating below 95 kWh/t of cement (CMA, 1997).

In the year 1991-92, RRL Jorhat rendered extension services to M/s Udayana Cement Pvt. Ltd., Lanka; M/s Prag Shiva Cement Pvt. Ltd., Guwahati; M/s Bomber Cement Plant Pvt. Ltd.,

Meghalaya; M/S Karbi Anglong Chemicals, Diphu for the setting up to mini/tiny VSK cement plants. During that period 36 VSK mini cement plants were in commercial production based on RRL technology and they produced cement worth of Rs. 20 crore during the year 1991-92 (CSIR, 1993, p. 29).

Dalmia Cement through its own R&D has successfully developed oil-well cement class 'G' in 1985-86, an import substitution for use by ONGC etc. and had been the first company in India to receive the rights or use of the prestigious API (American Petroleum Institute) monogram for this. The company proved its technical capability in development of this cement know-how, without any foreign collaboration/know-how. Associated Cement Company's R&D efforts in technology assimilation and absorption of MFC technology had led to improvement of Mitsubishi Fluidised Calciner (MFC) to New Mitsubishi Fluidised Calciner (NMFC). The company has been operating for the past 19 years and the cements plants owned by Yanbu Cement Company, Saudi Arabia. The company has earned the highest bonus of Rs. 17.1 million during the year 1998. The contract has been renewed further up to 2002. New in-house R&D Centres in the area of cement are coming up. Recently, L&T has set up new R&D Centres in Bangalore and Chennai. Grasim Industries has instituted a central R&D laboratory at Jawad in Madhya Pradesh. R&D efforts in this laboratory have resulted in converting industrial waste into fuel. Research to explore non-conventional energy sources is claimed in progress. Still R&D opportunities lie in utilising different cement replacement materials such as peanut shell ash, rice husk ash, silica fume, fly-ash, red mud etc.

Environmental Issues

All new capacities which have come in operation during 80's were fitted with pollution control equipments such as, electrostatic precipitators (ESPs), bag filters, cyclones etc. Dust is generated at all steps in the cement manufacturing, from quarrying through the crushing, burning, grinding, handling and storing to the final distribution. The major source of air pollution is of course the cement kilns. The operating efficiency of the ESPs are normally around 99.5 per cent. The operation of ESP also depends on the CO content of the fuel gas. Whenever the CO content goes beyond

0.6 per cent the ESP trips. As far as kilns are concerned, 132 out of 151 kilns in the country were fitted with ESPs/other pollution control equipments during 1988-89. Other 19 kilns were not in operation. The industry in its comprehensive modernization and expansion programme had given priority to the pollution control and had incurred capital expenditure of around Rs. 200 crore up to March 1991. Over 90 per cent of the capacity was pollution free.

The present trend has been to install bag houses for the kiln and raw mill exhaust. The comparison of the ESP and bag house are as below:

(i) The ESP trips, whenever the CO content goes beyond 0.6 per cent, while the operation of the bag house is not dependent upon the CO value.
(ii) The collection efficiency of the bag house is much higher at 99.9 per cent, while that of ESP is marginally lower. However, presently ESP's with efficiencies of 99.9 per cent require higher investments.
(iii) The ESP requires conditioning with power consumption for the GCT pump and screw conveyors.
(iv) The GCT in the ESP system needs water for conditioning, while the bag house does not need water.

Almost all cement plants in the country are equipped with high efficiency dust collection systems. A very important development in cement technology is in the field of rational utilization of cement, which directly or indirectly have positive impact on environment and contribute in maintaining ecological balance. Use of blended cement, utilization of waste heat in cement plant to generate electrical energy and use of alternate fuels have helped cement industry in promoting healthy environment as well as ecological balancing.

Foreign Collaborations and Technology Acquisitions

The collaboration agreements signed in the 1950s and the 1960s covered almost all aspects of production technology. The designing and the production capabilities of the Indian firms were weak and their dependence on their collaborations was very large. Four designs of precalciner, which are available from various machinery suppliers all over the world, were manufactured in India with foreign collaborations. They were Larson & Toubro, Bombay, developed the design in collaboration of F.L. Smidth, Denmark; Backau Wolf, Pune, in collaboration of Krupp Polysius, West Germany: Central Indian Machinery Manufacturing Company, Delhi in collaboration of Klockner Humboldt Deutsche, West Germany; and KCP Madras, in collaboration of Fuller Company, USA (DSIR, 1990, p. 69). In 1960-61, India produced cement machinery of the value of Rs. 0.6 crore. In 1970-71, it produced the cement machinery of the value of Rs. 4.2 crore, which was higher by seven-times. In 1980-81, the capability of machinery making in the country went up to the value of Rs. 33.6 crore, higher by eight-times. In 1990-91, the production touched the figure of Rs. 276.1 crore, and this increase is over eight times. By 1996-97, the cement machinery produced in the country was of the value of Rs. 455.3 crore, which is almost double of the figure in 1990-91 (GOI, 1998, p. 259). Table 5.10 shows the production of cement machinery in India from 1970-71 to 1996-97.

Table 5.10: Production of Cement Machinery in India

Years	*Rs. in crores*
1970-71	4.2
1980-81	33.6
1985-86	95.4
1990-91	276.1
1991-92	224.6
1992-93	169.5
1993-94	371.5
1994-95	295.2
1995-96	365.5
1996-97	455.3
1997-98	351.4
1998-99	183.0
1999-2000	133.0

Sources: GOI, (1998). Government of India, Handbook of Industrial Policy and Statistics. Office of the Economic Adviser, Ministry of Industry, New Delhi, p. 259.

CMIE, (2001). Industry market size and shares-cement machinery. Economic Intelligence Service, Mumbai, August, p. 323.

F.L. Smith & Co., Denmark; ONODA, Japan; Polysius, West Germany; and KHD Humboldt, France had been the major cement machinery suppliers to Indian cement companies. It may be noted that in most cases Indian firms claimed to have been able to import the latest technology without difficulty. The intense competition in the international market had increased the willingness of foreign firms to enter the Indian market through collaborations. A number of new firms from Spain and Greece had set up very large cement plants, as a result of which, the industry in developed countries was facing a serious problem of excess capacity. On average, the capacity utilization in most plants in developed countries was only between 50-70 per cent during sixties and seventies. Accordingly, the demand for cement machinery in developed countries was very small and the plant manufacturers were keen to export machinery and technology to developing countries. In view of India's large potential demand, they had been particularly keen to enter the Indian market. Their keenness was shown by the fact that they have been willing to transfer their latest technologies, such as NMFC of Mitsubishi, without equity participation. Except for the KCP—Fuller collaboration, in which the latter had an equity of 40 per cent. All the collaborations signed in the 1980s were purely technical in nature.

Indian cement industry had 69 foreign collaborations during the period 1951-87. Country-wise it had 12 collaborations with U.K. 11 each from Germany and USA, and 10 from Japan. These four countries together accounted for 64 per cent of the total collaborations. The collaborations during the period 1951–80 were 39 (56.5 %), whereas, it was 30 during the period 1981-87 (43.5%). During the period 1971-76 there was not a single collaboration with any firm abroad. The four companies namely, ACC, Bombay; Walchandnagar, Bombay; KCP Limited, Madras; and L&T; Bombay entered in collaborations for about 43.5 per cent of the total collaborations during this period. The highest number of collaboration was of the nature of machinery making (22), followed by product related (16), process related (6), complete plant making and consultancy related each (5), and 15 collaborations were of miscellaneous nature. Some important foreign collaborations were as under (Bose, 1990; Alam, 1988).

Today, L&T Gujarat, the largest cement plant in India has the capacity of 4.20 million tonnes a year whereas, Mitsubishi Materials at Kyushu, the largest cement plant in Japan, has a capacity of more than eight million tonnes a year. It is a model of environmental friendly production. The plant employs a fluidized bed kiln for calcinations in the preheater, which raises energy efficiency and productivity greatly. It has licensed the calcination technology used

Indian Firm	*Foreign Collaborator*	*Duration*
ACC, Bombay	Polysius (FRG)	1955–60
	Vickers Armstrong (UK)	1958
	Fullers (USA)	1962–72
	Mitsubishi (Japan)	1977
	Lafarge Coope (France)	1985
ABL	Vickers (UK)	1958
	KHD Humboldt (FRG)	1961–71
	Fives-Lille-Cail (France)	1981–91
KCP, Madras	Fives-Lille-Cail (France)	1963–73
	Prerov (Czech)	1976
	Fullers (USA)	1983–88
Walchandnagar Ind., Bombay	Prerov (Czech)	1966
	Polysius (FRG)	1968–78
	Allis Chambers (USA)	1981
	Onoda (Japan)	1982–87
L & T, Bombay	F.L. Smith (Denmark)	1959–94
Buckau Wolf, Pune	Polysius (FRG)	1981–88
CIMMCO	Humboldt (FRG)	1981–90

at the plant to other producers around the world. Its global network of cement plants and distribution channels serve needs for cement in nations throughout the Pacific Rim.

So far, in India the market has seen only two major international players, Lafarge SA (formerly known as Lafarge Coppee SA) and Cements Francais, in action. Lafarge has already taken over two marginal Indian players, Tisco and Raymond, for Rs. 5.5 bn and Rs. 7.85 bn respectively. It produces and distributes cement, lime, concrete, gypsum and speciality products. The company has 57 cement plants in 15 countries. It has operations in 70 countries and has 70,946 employees. Cements Francais, an Italcementi group company has inked a strategic 50 : 50 joint venture with KK Birla Group's Zuari Industry. Cemex S.A. is the largest cement company in the Americas and one of the three largest in the world. It operates subsidiaries in the USA, Spain, Panama, Venezuela, Colombia, the Philippines and the Caribbean. It markets its products in 60 countries and has 20,902 manpower. The takeovers in the last two years culminating in Gujarat Ambuja taking a stake in ACC, the second largest cement company in India bears ample testimony to this fact. Till now, over 12 million tonnes has changed hands, excluding Indian Rayon's transfer of 3 million tonnes to group company. The other multinational corporations, such as Cemex, Blue Circle, The Big Daddy, Holders Bank are in the race. Cementia Holding AG, Switzerland is another biggest cement manufacturers in the world, with operations in Switzerland, Czech Republic, Spain, Austria, America, Turkey, Kenya and around the Indian ocean (Corp. Inf.). Table 5.11 shows the mergers and acquisitions of Indian cement companies, which took place after liberalization policy in the country especially during late nineties (INFAC, 2000, p. 24).

Table 5.11: Cement Companies: Mergers and Acquisitions

Acquirer	*Acquired Company*	*Capa-city Mn.tpa*	*Location*	*Year of Acqui-sition*
ACC	CCI-Damodhar	0.27	West Bengal	1996
Grasim	Dharani Cement	0.07	Tamil Nadu	1998
Grasim	Shree Digvijay	1.23	Gujarat	1998
Gujarat Ambuja	DLF Cement	1.40	Rajasthan	1999
Gujarat Ambuja	Modi Cement	1.80	Madhya Pradesh	1997
Hyderabad Botting Co.	Suvama Cement	0.15	Andhra Pradesh	1999
India Cements	CCI-Yerraguntla	0.40	Andhra Pradesh	1997
India Cements	Rassi Cement	1.80	Andhra Pradesh	1998
India Cements	Sri Vishnu Cement	1.00	Andhra Pradesh	1999
India Cements	Visakha Cement	0.90	Andhra Pradesh	1997
Lafarge	TISCO	1.73	Madhya Pradesh	1998
Larsen & Toubro	Narmada Cement	1.40	Maharashtra,Gujarat	1999

Source: INFAC, (2000). *Cement Industry Review and Outlook: 1999-2000.* January, p. 24.

Cement and Gypsum products was one of the five sectors attracting the highest foreign direct investment inflows in the country during the month of March 2000. Its share was 1.48 per cent having actual inflow of Rs. 211.9 million (GOI, 2000, p. 3). Then again, it was one of the five sectors having the highest foreign direct investment approvals during the month of January 2001, sharing 7.72 per cent with approvals of Rs. 759.8 million, equivalent to 16.9 million US $ (GOI, 2001, p. 2). So far foreign direct investment and technical collaborations approved during the post-policy period from August 1991 to December 2000 in cement industry in India account for Rs. 16839.38 million, which is 0.68 per cent to the total approved amount during this period. It has total 97 foreign collaborations, 57 financial and 40 technical (GOI, 2001, p. 17).

International Market

There has been no major export of Indian Cement Plant and Machinery except for dry process cement projects at P.T. Semen Padang, Indonesia and Nepal and a wet process plant at Bangladesh. The various machinery suppliers have been trying hard for entering the export market. L&T was able to export packing machines to Italy, Mexico, Kuwait and Iraq. One of the reasons for failure to export is attributed to the high cost of Indian machinery. Also lack of confidence by the potential importers in the Indian cement machinery manufacturing capability was reported another major reason (DSIR, b 1990, p. 38).

In the changing scenario, the export of cement depends on the competitiveness of the Indian product *vis-à-vis* major cement producing countries in the world as well as in Asia such as China, Korea, Indonesia, Japan, Thailand etc. Our ex-factory price should reach a level of their FOB price and only then our product would be competitive worldwide. In Asian Continent China, Japan, Thailand and India are the major exporters of cement. Per capita consumption of cement in India is very low, at about 79 kg. This reflects the relatively low rate of infrastructural growth in the country, especially housing. Urbanization, which is one of the large determinants of use of cement is currently at 27 per cent and is expected to go up significantly in the next two decades. This will increase per capita consumption of cement. Our neighbour countries such as Taiwan has 1004 kg. per capita cement consumption with 69 per cent urbanization, Thailand 600 kg. per capita cement consumption with 21 per cent urbanization, China 410 kg. per capita cement consumption with 32 per cent urbanization in the country. Though China's rate of urbanization is comparable to India, is much higher cement consumption reflects its greater investment in public infrastructure such as dams, roads, bridges and fly-overs etc. In Japan per capita cement consumption is 603 kg. with 78 per cent urbanization, South Korea has 1391 kg. per capita cement consumption having 62 per cent urbanization (World Bank, 1999, p. 156-158 and Cement Co). India exported 1.95 million tonnes of cement and 1.19 million tonnes of clinker in 1999-2000, which is over 3 per cent of the total cement production in the country. The cement exported to Nepal, Bangladesh and South Africa together constitute 93 per cent of the total export during this period. The clinker exported to Bangladesh, Bhutan, and Nepal together account for 6.6 per cent. Table 5.12 shows country-wise export of cement and clinker from 1992-93 to 1999-2000.

Conclusion

Though, India is second largest in world as well as in Asia, after China in cement manufacturing but the R&D support in cement sector has been very low. A few designs for mini-cement plants were developed indigenously and they are capable to consume raw materials of low quality, locally available in the country. The constant efforts of in-house R&D Centres in cement industry have successfully brought down the level of energy consumption and consequently brought down the production cost. Control technology have brought additional benefits. In the era of liberalization less R&D expenditure from Government sources was compensated by constantly increasing number of in-house R&D Centres and their initiatives in the private sector. This resulted to successful development and productionisation of energy saving and cost saving technologies. Overall, it appears that liberalization, privatization and globalization has beneficial effect on R&D, technological capability and competitiveness of the cement industry of India. The growth of cement industry in the country took a quantum jump with the beginning of decontrol era in cement sector in 1989 and then in nineties, with the introduction of New Industry Policy in 1991. This step in the industrial sector gave further boost to this industry being already in control of the private sector. A large number of large plants, having capacities of million tonnes and above came up during this period as the import of machinery became easier and liberal. At present more than 46 per cent cement plants in the country are in the category of having attained the capacities of over one million tonnes per annum and goes up to over four million tonnes per annum. Now, Lafarge SA and Cements Francais, the world well known multinational corporations, in cement industry are in existence in the country. Foreign collaborations are turning into acquisitions and consolidations, which will put India in the global network. Cement industry has shown overall growth during the liberalization, privatization and globalization regime.

Table 5.12: Country-wise Cement and Clinker Exports

('000 tonnes)

Country	*1999-00*	*1998-99*	*1997-98*	*1996-97*	*1995-96*	*1994-95*	*1993-94*	*1992-93*
Bangladesh	522.33 (60.58)	534.01 (32.30)	921.98 (97.94)	463.48	516.66 (8.71)	458.04 (92.40)	470.08 (135.16)	304.74 (57.00)
Maldives	10.81	40.86	54.78	34.11	41.67	24.89	24.67	3.67
Nepal	816.90 (12.79)	824.32 (1.18)	588.59 (1.27)	620.01	498.62	409.65	352.41	293.27
Sri Lanka	0.40	81.83 (20.46)	442.63 (78.84)	308.78 (198.97)	352.88 (350.57)	409.68 (344.21)	117.33 (295.98)	5.64 (53.00)
UAE	5.31	6.18 (64.72)	19.20 (705.97)	(565.30)	6.14 (507.88)	(870.99)	7.45 (548.69)	6.43 (163.00)
South Africa	475.47	314.00	93.48	17.48	3.76	36.14		
Burma			37.25	22.56	11.98	74.78	81.87	
Mauritius		4.56	204.51	154.15	40.09			
Bhutan	(5.41)	(1.18)	(0.10)					
Pakistan					17.28	129.44	89.90	
Qatar						(25.54)	(86.06)	14.61
Yemen						14.13	79.46	52.86
Saudi Arabia						(13.71)	(76.30)	
Baharain					(5.57)			

(Contd.)

TABEL 5.12—*Contd.*

Country	*1999-00*	*1998-99*	*1997-98*	*1996-97*	*1995-96*	*1994-95*	*1993-94*	*1992-93*
Egypt		62.79						
Germany							0.33	
indonesia							6.50	
Kenya				(56.08)				
Kuwait			(42.57)					
Moroni						8.39		
Medagascar				9.00				
Philippines								11.49
Seychelles			15.79					
Singapore			9.00					
Sudan						23.35		
Others	117.66 (1113.75)	189.16 (1334.93)	296.26 (795.56)	79.96 (115.53)	16.60 (23.68)	46.27 (184.00)	80.21 (397.39)	140.96 (86.00)
Total Cement	1948.88	2057.70	2683.46	1709.54	1505.67	1634.76	1310.20	833.67
Total Clinker	(1192.53)	(1453.58)	(1722.24)	(935.88)	(896.41)	(1530.84)	(1539.58)	(359.00)
Total Cement	3141.41	3511.28	4405.70	2645.42	2402.09	3165.60	2849.78	1192.67

Notes: Figures in parenthesis show clinker.
Source: CMA, (2000). Meeting of the CMA Committee Export Agenda, May.

REFERENCES

Alam, G. (1988). *Technology Acquisition Activities by India's Cement Machinery Manufacturing Industry*. Prepared for DSIR, National Council for Applied Economic Research, New Delhi. December.

BICP, (1987). *Studies on the Structure of the Industrial Economy—Cement Industry*. Bureau of Industrial Costs and Prices, Ministry of Industry, Government of India, New Delhi, Vol. III, pp. 67.

Bose, P.R. (1990). *An Analytically Study of Foreign Collaborations in Cement Industry in India*. National Institute of Science & Technology and Development Studies, New Delhi.

*Cement co.http:www.cement co.uk/gcr/top*15

Chakravarty, S.M., (1989). *Indian Cement Industry from Control to Decontrol*. Wadhera, Bombay, pp. 587.

CMA, (1990). *Structural Changes in Cement Industry—Large Plants 1982–89*. Cement Manufacturers' Association, New Delhi, January.

CMA, (1993). *Indian Cement Industry–Basic Data 1993*. Cement Manufacturers' Association, New Delhi.

CMA, (1997). *NCB Energy Efficiency Improvement in Indian Cement Industry, Cement and Energy,* Cement Manufacturers' Association, issue no. 1(3).

CMA, (1999). *Basic Data–Indian Cement Industry-1999*. Cement Manufacturers' Association, New Delhi, June.

CMA, (1999). *Cement and Energy*, a quarterly newsletter. Cement Manufacturers' Association, issue no. 3(1).

CMA, (2000). Meeting of the CMA Committee Export Agenda. New Delhi, May.

CMA, (2001). *Indian Cement Industry: Basic Data-2001*. Cement Manufacturers' Association, New Delhi.

Corporate Information, *http://profiles.wisi.com*

CSIR, (1993). *Annual Report 1991-92*. Council of Scientific and Industrial Research, New Delhi, February.

DSIR, (1990). *Technology in Indian Dry Process Cement Plants*—a study prepared under the national register of foreign collaborations. Department. of Scientific and Industrial Research, Ministry of Science and Technology, New Delhi, July.

DST, (1996-97). *Annual Report 1996-97*. Department of Science and Technology, New Delhi.

GOI, (1984). *Report of the Working Group of Cement Industry for 1985–90*. Government of India, Ministry of Industry, Department of Industrial Development, New Delhi, July.

GOI, (1997). *R&D in Industry 1996-97*. Government of India, Ministry of Science and Technology, New Delhi, October.

GOI, (1998). *Handbook of Industrial Policy and Statistics*. Government of India, Office of the Economic Adviser, Ministry of Industry, New Delhi.

GOI, (1999). *Research and Development Statistics 1996-97*. Government of India, Ministry of Science and Technology, Department of Science and Technology, New Delhi. June.

GOI, (2000). *SIA Newsletter*. Government of India, Department of Industrial Policy and Promotion, Ministry of Commerce and Industry, New Delhi, April.

GOI, (2001). *SIA Newsletter*. Government of India, Department of Industrial Policy and Promotion, Ministry of Commerce and Industry, New Delhi, January.

GOI, (2001). *SIA Newsletter*. Government of India, Department. of Industrial Policy and Promotion, Ministry of Commerce and Industry, New Delhi, February.

INFAC, (2000). *Cement industry review and outlook:1999-2000*. January.

Schumacher, K.; and Sathaye, J, (1999). *India's Cement Industry: Productivity, Energy Efficiency and Carbon Emissions*. Environmental Science Division, Office of Biological and Environmental Research, U.S. Department of Energy, July 1999.

World Bank, (1999). *World development indicators–1999*. Washington, March.

6

Terrorism in Kashmir: Origin and Growth

SHIBEN KRISHEN RAINA

Broadly speaking, when justice and right are denied to a person over a longer period of time, the person is left with two options: bear the situation patiently, or the reaction is anguish, and that reaction, in the process culminates into terrorism. Besides other things, spreading of communal hatred, religious frenzy, separatist tendency etc. are the tools which terrorists generally use. Guns too are used to achieve the so-called specified mission. Fanaticism, extremism, radicalism, separatism, militancy, activism etc. are its other names or manifestations. This is one side of the picture of terrorism. (Terrorists fighting for a genuine cause *i.e.* liberating themselves, their society/country from the oppressor/perpetrator). Another side of the picture is disgusting and questionable. Over the years terrorism has emerged as a systematic use or threatened use of violence to intimidate a population, community or government and thereby effect political, religious or ideological change just to achieve personal gains. Modern terrorism has resorted to other option of intimidation, *i.e.* influence the mass–media, in an effort to amplify and broadcast feelings of intense fear and anger among the people. Needless to mention here that acts of terror are carried out by people who are indoctrinated to the extent of following a strategy of dying to kill. They are the ones who have become pawns in the hands of their masters who direct their paths, sitting in the comforts of far off places with all the facilities available to them. Masters have their vested political interests while as pawns seemingly have nothing to gain except suffer for a cause about which they themselves don't know or know very little.

Terrorism in Kashmir is almost 18 years old now and has likeness to the second side of the picture. It has a history long enough to be traced from the date when partition was forced resulting in the emergence of two nations—India and Pakistan—after the sub-continent freed itself from the colonial rule of the British Empire. It may not be out of context here to probe into the consequences in detail that gave rise to terrorism in Kashmir. But again, before that, giving a brief introduction of this widely known beautiful valley would be too apt.

Kashmir—Paradise on Earth—(Switzerland of Asia) Nature's grand finale of beauty is a masterpiece of earth's creation of charm and loveliness. Famous for its beauty and natural scenery throughout the world and for its high snow-clad mountains, scenic spots, beautiful valleys, rivers with ice-cold water, attractive lakes and springs and ever-green fields, dense forests and beautiful health resorts, enhance its grandeur and are a source of great attraction for tourists. It is also widely known for its different kinds of agricultural products, fruit, vegetables, saffron, herbs, and minerals, precious stones, handicrafts like woollen carpets, shawls and finest kind of embroidery on clothes. During summer, one can enjoy the beauty of nature, trout fishing, big and small game hunting etc.; during winter climbing mountain peaks and sports like skating and skiing on snow slopes are commonly enjoyed. In addition to the above, pilgrimage to famous religious shrines of the Hindus and the Muslims make Kashmir a great tourist attraction. About Kashmir Sheikh Sadie a great Persian poet is believed to have said, "If there is any heaven on earth, it is here in Kashmir, in Kashmir in Kashmir only." Apart from natural beauty, Jammu and Kashmir has a unique cultural blend which makes it different from the rest of the country (India). It is not only distinct in cultural forms and heritage, but in geographical, demographical, ethnical, social entities, forming a distinct spectrum of diversity. The people of Kashmir, Jammu and Ladakh, all follow diverse religion, language and culture, but continuously intermingling which symbolizes Indian Unity amidst diversity. Its different cultural forms like art and architecture, fair and festivals, rites and rituals, seers and sagas, languages and literatures, embedded in ageless period of history, speak of endless unity and diversity with unparalleled cultural cohesion and amicability. Kashmir has been a great centre of learning. A treasure of rich Sanskrit literature is to be found here. Early Indo-Aryanic civilization has originated and flourished in this land. It has also been embracing point of advent of Islam bringing its traditions of Persian civilization, tolerance, brotherhood and sacrifice.

After the British withdrew from the Indian subcontinent in 1947 and India and Pakistan emerged as two separate countries, princely states were given an option to choose the country they wanted to stay on. Obviously, the states falling geographically within had no other option but to merge with the country they were situated. Border States like Kashmir, Jodhpur etc. took time to come out with their firm decisions probably because they wanted to enjoy the status of an independent Statehood. In the case of Kashmir, where Maharaja (King) Hari Singh was the ruler, situation worsened considerably. Territorial disputes over Kashmir had already started brewing-Pakistan claiming that Kashmir should go to his side since Muslims were in majority there. Apprehending that Maharaja might opt for an accession to India, Pakistan prepared for an aggression in a bid to capture the State forcibly hoping that masses, mainly Muslims, would support its mission but that didn't happen. Secular forces headed by the then popular mass leader Sheikh Mohammad Abdullah fondly known as Sher-i-Kashmir motivated the Kashmiri people (Hindus, Muslims and Sikhs) to rise to the occasion and stand united to counter and frustrate the evil designs of the enemy who was marching to the capital city Srinagar indulging in bloodshed and mayhem. A new slogan echoed the entire valley: *"Hamlavar khabardaar, hum Kashmiri hai tayaar—Hindu Muslim Sikh Ithaad, Naya Kashmir Zindabaad—"* Beware you attackers ! We Kashmiris are ready to counter you—Long live the Unity of Hindus, Muslims and Sikhs !! At Hazuri Bagh, Srinagar before a large crowd on October 1, 1947, Sher-i-Kashmir proclaimed: "Till the last drop of my blood, I will not believe in two-nation theory." It was a rebuff to Mr. Jinnah—father of the nation of Pakistan—who was watching the developments so closely from his country side. Finding their designs on Kashmir not fructifying, Pakistan rulers launched an armed attack on Jammu and Kashmir to annex it. Tribes in thousands along with Pak regular troops entered the State on October 22, 1947 from several points and indulged in loot, arson, rape, bloodshed and mayhem. Bowing before the wishes of the people and seeing his own regular army being outnumbered and to push back the invaders, the Maharaja signed the Instrument of Accession in favour of India on October 26, 1947 on the prescribed terms and conditions. This was accepted by the Governor-General of India, Lord Mountbatten the next day. The Instrument of Accession executed by Maharaja Hari Singh was the same which was signed by other rulers of the other princely States. Similarly, the acceptance of the Instrument of Accession by the Governor-General was also identical in respect of all such instruments.

With J&K becoming legal and constitutional part of Union of India, Indian army rushed to the State to push back the invaders and vacate aggression from the territory of the State. The first batch of Indian Army troops arrived at Srinagar airport immediately after the Accession was signed. On October 30, 1947 an Emergency Government was formed in the State with Sheikh Mohammad Abdullah as its head. The Army fought sustained battle with the tribals/Kabayilies and after several sacrifices pushed them out of the Valley and other areas in the Jammu region. (Earlier Brigadier Rajendra Singh, Chief of State Forces, with a small number of soldiers at his disposal fought valiantly with the enemy and laid down his life in the process.)

Meanwhile, the people of Kashmir under the towering leadership of Sher-I-Kashmir were mobilised and they resisted the marching columns of the enemy. Till the arrival of Indian troops, it was mainly the Muslim volunteers under the command of Sheikh Mohammad Abdullah who braved death to push back invaders. While the army pushed back the invaders, there were several instances where people put up a gallant resistance and stopped the advancing invaders. The most glaring examples of people's resistance were the martyrdom of Mohammad Maqbool Sherwani and Master Abdul Aziz both staunch followers of Sher-i-Kashmir Sheikh Abdullah. Sherwani did not oblige the invaders when they enquired from him the route to Srinagar. Instead, he put them on a wrong track gaining time for troops to reach Srinagar from New Delhi. Somehow the tribesmen came to know about his tactics and nailed him at a Baramulla crossing and asked him to raise pro-Pakistan slogans. He did raise slogans but these were different. These were pro-Hindu-Muslim unity and in favour of Sher-i-Kashmir. Enraged by this, the ruthless tribesmen emptied their guns on him. The sacrifice of Master Abdul Aziz too was exemplary. The invaders who raped the nuns and wanted other non-Muslim women to be handed over to them, Master Abdul Aziz, a tailor by profession, held the holy Quran in his hand and said that they can touch the women only after they pass over his dead body and the holy Quran. The brutal killers did not spare him either.

On January 1, 1948 India took up the issue of Pak aggression in Jammu and Kashmir to UNO under Article 35 of its Charter. The Government of India in its letter to the Security Council said, "...Such a situation now exists between India and Pakistan owing to the aid which invaders, consisting of nationals of Pakistan and tribesmen... are drawing from Pakistan for operations against Jammu and Kashmir, a State which has acceded legally to the Dominion of India and is part of India. The Government of India requests the Security Council to call upon Pakistan to put an end immediately to the giving of such assistance which is an act of aggression against India. If Pakistan does not do so, the Government of India may be compelled, in self defense, to enter into Pakistan territory to take military action against the invaders." After long debates, cease-fire came into operation on the midnight of January 1, 1949. Eventually, India filed a complaint with the UN Security Council, which established the United Nations Commission for India and Pakistan (UNCIP). Pakistan was accused of invading the region, and was asked to withdraw its forces from Jammu and Kashmir. The UNCIP also passed a resolution stating: "The question of accession of the State of Jammu and Kashmir to India or Pakistan will be decided through the democratic method of free and impartial plebiscite". However, this could not take place because Pakistan did not comply with the UN resolution and refused to withdraw from the State. The international community failed to play a decisive role in the matter saying that Jammu and Kashmir is a "disputed territory". In 1949, with the intervention of the United Nations, India and Pakistan defined a ceasefire line ("Line of Control") that divided the two countries. This has left Kashmir a divided and disturbed territory up till now.

In September 1951, free and fair elections, as per the Constitutional modalities, were held in Jammu and Kashmir, and National Conference party under the leadership of Sheikh Abdullah came into power. With the advent of the Constituent Assembly of the State of Jammu and Kashmir representing the aspirations of the people of Jammu and Kashmir, the State became an integral part of India constitutionally. After Sheikh Abdullah; Bakshi Gulam Mohamad, G.M. Sadiq, Mir Qasim, Gul Shah, Mufti Sayed and

Dr. Farooq Abdullah ruled the State as Chief Ministers. Mr. Gulam Nabi Azad is the current Chief Minister of the J&K State.

Though the governments ran smoothly over the years, continued instigations and arousing religious frenzy by Pakistan did not stop. The year 1965 saw a war between India and Pakistan claiming so many lives on either side. A cease-fire was established and the two countries signed an agreement at Tashkent (Uzbekistan) in 1966, pledging to end the dispute by peaceful means. Five years later, the two again went to war that resulted in the creation of Bangladesh. Another accord was signed in 1972 between the two Prime Ministers—Indira Gandhi and Zulfiqar Ali Bhutto—in Simla. After Bhutto was executed in 1979, the Kashmir issue once again flared up.

During the 1980s, massive infiltrations from Pakistan were detected in the region, and India has since then maintained a strong military presence in Jammu and Kashmir to check these movements along the cease-fire line. India says that Pakistan has been stirring up violence in its part of Kashmir by training and funding "Islamic Guerrillas" that have waged a separatist war since 1989 killing tens of thousands of people. Pakistan has always denied the charge, calling it an indigenous "freedom struggle."

In 1999, intense fighting ensued between the infiltrators and the Indian army in the Kargil area of the western part of the State, which lasted for more than two months. The battle ended with India managing to reclaim most of the area on its side that had been seized by the infiltrators.

In 2001, Pakistan-backed terrorists waged violent attacks on the Kashmir Assembly and the Indian Parliament in New Delhi. This has resulted in a war-like situation between the two countries, with Pakistani President General Pervez Musharraf asking his army to be "fully prepared and capable of defeating all challenges," and the then Indian Prime Minister Atal Bihari Vajpayee saying, "We don't want war but war is being thrust upon us, and we will have to face it."

Plight of Pandits (Hindus)

The Pandits, who are the Hindu community of Kashmir and have an ancient and a proud culture, have been amongst the most afflicted victims of the Pakistani-supported campaign of terrorism in Jammu and Kashmir. Their roots in the Kashmir Valley run very deep. They are the original inhabitants of this beautiful valley. Their number being small and peace-loving by nature, they have been the soft targets of terrorists. Virtually the entire population of 300,000 Kashmiri Pandits have been forced to leave their ancestral homes and property. Threatened with violence and intimidation by Muslim fundamentalists, they have been turned into refugees in their own country leaving behind their shops, farms, cattle and age-old memories. As a matter of fact, Jammu and Kashmir has become a target of Pakistan, sponsored by religion-based terrorism. The persecution by Muslim extremists of the Hindu minority and the systematic religion-based extremism of terrorist elements has resulted in the exodus of these Hindu/Pandits and other minorities from the Kashmir Valley to other parts of India. Fundamentalists and terrorists have also targeted and assassinated Muslim intellectuals and liberal Muslim leaders too, who spoke of Hindu-Muslim unity and brotherhood. Terrorist acts by Kashmiri militant groups have also taken place outside Jammu and Kashmir.

India claims most of the separatist militant groups are based in Pakistan and Pakistan-administered Kashmir (also known as Azad Kashmir). Some like the All Parties Hurriyat Conference and the Jammu and Kashmir Liberation Front (JKLF), demand an independent Kashmir. Other groups such as Lashkar-e-Toiba and Jaish-e-Mohammed favour a Pakistani-Kashmir. Of the larger militant groups, the Hizbul Mujahideen, a militant organisation is based in Pakistan-administered Kashmir. Sources reveal that Al-Qaeda too has a base in Pakistani Kashmir and helping to foment terrorism in Jammu and Kashmir.

India is unwilling to lose even one additional inch of his land. New Delhi is also concerned that Kashmiri autonomy would set a precedent for breakaway movements in other Indian States (e.g., Punjab or Assam). To Pakistan, Kashmir is symbolic of its national ethos and commitment to protect Muslim interests against Indian encroachment. It believes that the creation of a separate, strongly sectarian nation is incomplete without contiguous Kashmir. *In brief, Kashmir is a target of externally sponsored religion-based terrorism. The aim is to divide people on the basis of sectarian affiliation and undermine/weaken the secular fabric and territorial integrity of India.*

However, as and now with the passage of time, the passion of the Jehad/movement which once had the mass public support has started declining since it has turned out to be a movement run by those who are more interested in their own personal gains. Confusion within the separatist groups too has weakened the movement. The hard liners led by Jamat-e-Islami advocate total merger of Jammu and Kashmir, with Pakistan whereas the soft liners led by J.K.L.F. (Jammu and Kashmir Liberation Front) stands for total independence of J&K. *This has given rise to a totally confusing and conflicting situation resulting in disillusionment, disarray and disinterest of the common man in Kashmir who has suffered a lot for the past 18 years and is not prepared to suffer any more.*

7

Participation and Partnership for Change: Economic Empowerment and Social Engagement (Case Study of Two Women's Organizations in Mumbai)

SUDHA MOHAN

Empowerment is the process of enabling an individual to think, behave, take action, and control work and decision-making in autonomous ways. It is the state of feeling self-empowered to take control of one's own destiny.

Empowerment is defined as a process of making people animators, change-agents, by awakening them to their potential—to develop fully and to experience humanness—in the sense of being (politically) aware of the root causes of marginalisation, of being confident, autonomous and capable of undertaking action to redress human rights violations.

Although empowerment has, in the recent years, become a buzzword, the concept has been used in many different ways. Definitions of what constitutes empowerment have ranged from the development of personal instrumental competencies and skill, to the process of challenging existing power relations, to household decision-making, to gaining access and control over resources like credit, income, land knowledge, etc, as well as to subjective variables like the sense of personal power or self-efficacy.

In an interesting analysis of Empowerment Naila Kabeer (1994), draws on Lukes' (1986) three-dimensional views of power to discuss this issue. The first dimension relates with the *power to.* This is associated with decision-making over issues where there are observable conflicts. In this dimension power is seen as the capacity to affect outcomes. The second dimension relates with *power over,* whereby one group manages to suppress certain conflicts by denying their validity. The third dimension of power recognises that conflicts of interest may be suppressed not only from the decision-making agenda, but also from consciousness of the parties involved. Here both the dominant and the subordinate parties subscribe to accounts of social reality that deny that any inequality exists.

This chapter makes an attempt to examine (a) the ways in which the urban informal sector has 'opened up' new space for women in employment; (b) how women have been able to use this opportunity to enhance their economic position and social status; (c) the manner in which economic participation and community partnership have led to enhancement of social capital and political empowerment. With this as the conceptual basis this chapter will contextually locate it by studying Lijjat and Annapurna, two exclusive women's organizations in Mumbai, to analyze the above-mentioned objectives.

Women and the Informal Sector

The meaning of the term "informal sector" has remained somewhat elusive in spite the voluminous research and literature. It has been the subject of controversy despite the fact that it has gained wide currency during the last two decades. It is important to point out that first; this sector is heterogeneous in terms of actors and activities; scale and scope. In order to develop a strategy for the sector one however does require a practical meaning and interpretation. This is possible if we examine women in community-based organisational structures that contribute immensely to not only to economic independence but also to empowerment of a kind that is essential.

Thus, lack of access to productive resources due to discriminations in property ownership and in employment; lack of time because of unequal gender division in unpaid productive and reproductive activities; lack of skills due to lower levels of literacy and formal education; lack of access to labour as a result of norms of gender hierarchy and separation; and lack of access to markets due to their exclusion from the most lucrative markets have left women in the margins of the employment scene. The lack of access to informal and formal credit by women micro and small entrepreneurs has been identified by numerous studies as a major constraint. Formal financial institutions are even less receptive and welcoming to female entrepreneurs. Their collateral requirements, bureaucratic loan application, disbursement procedures, the time and resources necessary to visit the banks and discriminatory banking culture virtually exclude poor women as clients. (Sethuraman, S.V. 1981).

Since the focus of this study relates specifically to the women employed in this sector it is essential to state that there are many areas where the women have created new employment opportunities for women themselves without displacing anyone else. Self-employment opportunities increase when there is opening of a new market or expansion of an existing market. This was exactly the case way back in the late 1950s, when a small but very committed group of women realised the potential for market in the food sector. This saw the emergence of Lijjat, which is officially called Shri Mahila Griha Udyog Lijjat Papad. *Mahila* (in Hindi) means women, *griha* is house, *udyog* is work/industry, *lijjat* is tasty (in Gujarati) and *papad* is a flat, thin, dried roll of kneaded flour mixed with spicy ingredients. *Papad* has a reasonably long shelf life, can be toasted or fried in oil and it serves as a snack or is taken along with food. This particular item is an integral part of a meal amongst almost all communities in India. The women, therefore, capitalising on the expanding market entered into this enterprise that saw them take the business opportunities as well as their own choice and avenues for enhancement, both economic and political.

Lijjat: Collective Ownership and Entrepreneurship

The exciting journey of the united effort by seven women at making papad began on 15 March, 1959, on the terrace of their flat in an old, residential building, in Girgaum, a thickly populated area in South Bombay. Only women can become the members of the organisation. All members are also the owners of the organisation and are fondly referred to as 'sisters'

Lijjat grew as a concept and the reason for its rapid growth was due to its basic philosophy and pragmatic approach. It was a voluntary organization of the small select group of committed women. From its inception, these member-sisters (as they were and still are referred to) had started sharing the profits or losses among themselves. It was realized by these member-sisters that in their interest to strive for the growth of production and sale and to run the business wisely. Thus, the organization grew on the basis of collective ownership. Its essence was to provide for self-employment, dignity of labour and earning capacity for women, working from their homes. The organisation started with 'what they know, build on what they have, teaching by showing, learning by doing and by not conforming but to transforming, not relief but release women's potential and capabilities—has been the motto, signpost for success and triumphs.

This woman's entrepreneurial organisation applied the Gandhian Philosophy of trusteeship—where the member-sisters were all owners of the organisation—and hence shared in both its profits and losses. In order to facilitate travel, transportation was/is provided. The women arrive at their specific branches by the institution's transport. Everyday, a bus does the rounds, picking up women from different areas and bringing them to the centres, so that they don't spend their earnings on transport. This novel method (of being picked-up and dropped) provided the much-required mobility to these women, who otherwise may not be in a position to either get out of their homes or even have the resources to spend on transportation. The whole point is that women can fit papad-rolling around the demands of family life.

Small Beginnings with Humungous Results

The organisation has expanded significantly with its Central Office at Mumbai and its 60 centres and 40 divisions in different States across the country. Though the organisation started of with a paltry sum of Rs. 80 (1.7 million with conversion rate of Rs. 47) it has achieved incredible sales of over Rs. 300 crore (.21 million) with exports itself exceeding Rs. 10 crore. Besides this commercial expansion, its membership has also grown from an initial number of 7 member-sisters to over 40,000 members throughout India !

Lijjat follows an 'open' policy in employment. They believe that as long as women are capable of rolling dough into circles, they can certainly be part of the organisation. They are another important distinction of this group. They don't believe in taking any donation or amount from anyone. They pride on the fact that Lijjat has a 'no gifts' policy. It is a fact that Lijjat has never accepted, nor is it ever going to accept, any charity, donation, gift or grant from any quarter," says the mission statement. On the contrary, Lijjat members donate collectively from time to time. (e.g., it has adopted a quake-affected village, where the money could help rebuild housing). In fact, Lijjat prides itself on uniquely bringing socio-economic empowerment to women without using aid of any sort.

It is hardly surprising that Lijjat's logo says 'Symbol of Women's Strength', a logo that is emblazoned proudly on every bit of Lijjat packaging. Every time any restaurant, hotel, shop or individual buys a packet of 32 Lijjat Papads—flavoured with pepper, green and red chillies, masala or garlic—they are reminded that this household name is a product of female endeavour.

It is this commitment and tremendous concern for women that got Jashwantiben Popat, this humble grandmother from one of Bombay's impoverished neighbourhood, in September, to collect India's top business award for women. The Businesswoman of the Year, 2002, was awarded to Jashwantiben Popat who proudly claimed the prize not for her but for the 41,000 mostly illiterate women who co-own this co-operative enterprise. Spelling out and impressing upon Lijjat's achievements—that it employs 40,000 women and has opened operations in Kashmir—the astute CEO Jashwantiben Popat, seized the moment to pitch the Finance Minister (sitting five feet away) for tax concessions ! (*Financial Times*, December 29, 2002).

Lijjat Papad works because there are no barriers to entry such as skills; making papad is like a birthright to the Indian woman. And the model is scaleable unlike a crafts-based cottage industry, says Haresh Shah of the Khadi and Village Industries Commission, a Government agency that supports job creation projects. Co-operatives historically have symbolised a third way between State ownership and the markets in India. Their value has extended beyond jobs; by being inclusive they have cultivated an ethos of democratic participation.

The President of the Lijjat Mrs. Jyoti Naik said the institution has recently initiated Papad Unit in Jammu and Kashmir, which will be a step towards self-reliance for the ladies of the State. The new Unit will cater to the needs of Jammu district initially. Towards this endeavour, exports to countries and regions that most women can barely place on a map, such as the US, UK and the Middle East, generate 4 per cent of sales. Jashwantiben Popat reiterates this ambition by always making it a point to state that she wants more sales abroad and to double the size of "the sisterhood" in five years! Besides, this expansion will invariably provide more opportunities to more women being employed that would in some way alleviate their economic condition. As was pointed out by Popat, "the women are poor and often the sole earners in their household. If they don't earn here, they won't eat at home." (*Financial Times*, December 29, 2002).

Annapurna Mahila Mandal (AMM): Mobilising Women for Joint Economic and Social Action

Working class women's grassroots organisation was formed in 1975 as a result of the textile strike of 1974 in Mumbai. The women displayed tremendous will to tackle both their economic conditions and the treatment meted out to them by the textile mill-owners. Prior to the formation of the Unions, if and when women were employed in the mill they were given a poor salary with absolutely no facilities at all. The union made several demands on behalf of all employees and some specific demands were made for women workers such as maternity leave with pay, crèche and nursery for children. But the simpler way out that was sought by the mill-owner was to stop employing women in mills rendering about 45,000 women jobless. Thus, the jobless women workers problems compounded when their men folk went on an indefinite strike to press for their demands. Unable to cope with the deteriorating position economically, most of the women decided to do what they could do well, depending on their skill and resources *i.e.*, cook and provide food to the mill-workers, who had migrated to Mumbai leaving behind their families and could not afford to eat in a hotel on a daily basis. Thus began the history of Annapurna Mahila Mandal (AMM).

The AMM began with the following objectives: first, for the official recognition of their business; second, recognition of the income earning capacity of woman working in the *Khanawali* (cooking/catering) occupation and more importantly their credit worthiness; third, to strengthen women's economic position by providing support to their existing occupation; fourth, to mobilise women for joint economic and social action by using group pressure;

and fifth, to organise them for social education. Their endeavours during the past two decades show that most of these objectives have been fulfilled.

AMM: Constructive Engagement and the Participatory Development Process

Since its formation, the AMM has progressed successfully from using credit as a strategy to build a grassroot organisation, develop local leaders and neighbourhood groups. Later it expanded its activities to conducting health programmes, legal aid service and also providing short-term shelter for battered women. Vocational training programmes in tailoring and catering were also set up. Since 1985, AMM has expanded its catering programme and has set up different canteens, women's hostels, hospitals and housing society. AMM operates in seven working class areas in Central Mumbai that include forty sub-areas. The catering scheme of AMM is an employment generation programme. It is interesting to note that two of the schemes started by the Government namely, the Rashtriya Mahila Kosh (RMK) that provided an alternate source of credit for poor women and the Indira Mahila Yojana (IMY) that offers schemes to women were inspired by NGOs like AMM. (*Annapurna Mahila Mandal, 22nd Annual Report 1996-1998, 1999-2004)*.

The story of AMM is one of constructive engagement in the mainstream of planned development process, for facilitating access and rights to the poor women. It is one of the few NGOs in Mumbai or even India that opted to work as an intermediary between the formal banking system and the women micro-entrepreneurs in the informal banking sector. From facilitating access to institutional credit, it has now set up its own Credit and Co-operative Society with flexible and member-friendly procedures and system. (Sudha Mohan, 2002).

It is also a success story of sensitising the formal institutional system that had failed to accommodate or be responsive to the needs of the disadvantaged section of society. The organisation has worked both towards an enabling and sensitising process, bringing the women and the formal structures to operate and co-operate closely. This process of enabling of women to become micro-entrepreneurs and self-employed workers has helped the women in discovering their innate strength. It has also enabled them to collectively work towards solving any problem. Most important, it has empowered the women involved with this organisation to articulate their aspirations for their children. The continued effort and diverse activities of this organisation is a testimonial to the fact that poor people are willing to pull themselves out of their poverty, if they are given access to basic economic inputs and the right kind of support, assistance and help at the right time.

Since its formation the AMM has progressed successfully from using credit as a strategy to building a grassroot organisation, develop local leadership and neighbourhood groups. AMM has expanded its activities to conducting health programmes, legal aid service and also providing short-term shelter for battered women. Vocational training programmes in tailoring and catering were also organised. Since 1985, AMM has expanded its catering programme and has set up canteens, women's hostels, hospitals and housing society. Thus the AMM's novel and very innovative strategies adopted to alleviate the problems and poverty that women undergo has resulted in provision of self-employment and generation of individual enterprises of all which bestow on women much dignity and self-respect.

Lessons in Economic Empowerment and Social Engagement from the Two Case Studies

- The story of these two organisations is one of constructive engagement with the mainstream development process by facilitating access and rights to poor women to envisaged resources.
- It is also about sensitising the formal institutional system that had failed to accommodate the needs of the disadvantaged section of our society.
- This process of enabling women to become micro entrepreneurs and self-employed workers has helped women in discovering their innate strength, the vigour of social capital in joint action and to collectively work towards solving their myriad problems.
- This awareness is what has actually motivated them to continue with the organisation, to be financially self-sufficient, contribute substantially to the family income, realise the importance of education and thereby translating their aspiration to their children.

- ❖ It has become a symbol of women's economic enfranchisement in Mumbai, in particular and also in India. It is a reenforcement of the Gandhian principles of self-help and trusteeship.
- ❖ These principles have not only enabled women to overcome their economic hardships, but also in the long run helped them become conscious of their rights and most importantly it has helped women to live with dignity and self-respect. (Sudha Mohan, 2005)

Participation, Partnership, Empowerment and Sustainability

The forty-seven years of Lijjat's life and the 32 years of AMM have synchronised with the drawing up of the theoretical framework of empowerment, along with its practical implications. The rights of women and questions of equality in the personal and public domain have for too long been compounded by factors like poverty, social disruptions and patriarchal biases in the Government policies as well as in the society. The primary need was a spontaneous grassroots movement by women that, however small in its origin, was capable of self-sustaining and self-propelling growth. Moreover, it is also critically important to point out that the women belonged to the disadvantaged section of the society, and the driving force came not from above, but from below.

The grassroots organisations grew out of this need felt by women to become active agents of change in their lives. The aim was to support the efforts of people in finding their own solutions to poverty, rather than imposing solutions from above or outside. When communities work together to improve their own lives, the result is a permanent strengthening of the community and renewed hope for the future. With this as the backdrop the main objectives of the organisations apart from making women economically self-sufficient, is to promote the principles of Participation, Empowerment and Sustainability.

Participation

The organisations help those who are striving to help themselves. Participation means that the poor people themselves are involved in identifying the problems they face, determining ways to overcome them, designing realistic plans to achieve these goals, and carrying them out. Solutions devised and fulfilled by the people in need are far more likely to prove successful than those imposed from outside.

Partnership

Another important component has the potential of generating change that is self-enforcing. Interestingly partnerships are viewed as "instruments of governance" by Jon Pierre. (Jon Pierre: 1998). Governance especially since the nineties has come to refer to self-organisation, inter-organisational networks characterised by a shared set of goals, interdependence and interfacing with the state a manner that is both beneficial in (the short run) and empowering (in the long run) for the members concerned. (Sudha Mohan: 2006).

Empowerment

From participation grows empowerment. People who truly participate in their own development are permanently strengthened. This helps build up more self-confidence and hope in the participants—confidence that they can make a difference and that they can improve their lives. If organisations can give poor people confidence, hope, dignity and strength, they will strengthen women people more than any short term financial help could ever do.

Sustainability

Participation and empowerment seek to ensure that lasting change which will strengthen women's ability and belief on their own strengths. Sustainability is a long term approach that seeks to understand and respect women's conditions, which give a voice to all members, which ensure that the women continue with such activities and sustain them economically, and otherwise.

A Continuum (Not Conclusion) in the Trajectory of Empowerment

This study proves that first and foremost, the overall improvement of women's status in the household is mainly due to their role as financial mediators, by easing cash flow bottlenecks in the household. Besides, it can be argued that such economic participation of women in the informal sector in the long run leads to empowerment of the kind that is both enabling and conducive to women's over all enhancement. Secondly, women employed in the informal employment sectors like the LIJJAT and AMM have been functioning, as 'agents of change' in opening up space that are both necessary and beneficial to women.

Thirdly, this study provides evidence that women participation in decision-making increased, particularly in the important areas of family planning, household nutrition and raises aspirations for children's education. (As was pointed out to this researcher by the women who were interviewed). Besides, participation of other family members also increased in the housework significantly, as women spent more time on their work, which in turn contribute more to the household income.

Fourth, this study elucidates a number of interesting issues raised way back in a seminal work of Theodore Mills (1967:21), The Sociology of Small Groups, where it was argued that small groups increase the capabilities for meeting a wider range of possible demands. Its *adaptation* (*i.e.* openness, capacity, and accommodation) *goal-attainment* (*i.e.* shift or add new goals) *integration* (*i.e.* capacity to differentiate into sub-parts while maintaining collective unity) and *Pattern Maintenance* (capacity for involvement and the ability to convey experience, learning and capabilities to others.

Women's employed in such organisations like Lijjat and AMM, it could be argued, address the issue of poverty with some measure of success. If it has been able to address the issue of poverty (albeit in a small but certainly in a significant manner), there is a need to both, turn to, and actively encourage such entrepreneurial enterprises. There is growing evidence of a significant relationship between entrepreneurship, and poverty reduction. Frequently, Small, Micro and Medium-sized Enterprises (SMMEs) offer the only employment available to millions of poor people in the developing countries. According to the Global Entrepreneurship Monitor (GEM), in the 29 countries surveyed in 2001, almost 150 million people are engaged in some form of entrepreneurial activity. There is no doubt that entrepreneurs create jobs. In India itself, the Lijjat Group and AMM have empowered over 10,000 women to lead a life of dignity.

If we mean empowerment as to increasing the strength of individuals in their personal, economic, political and social interaction and involving the empowered developing confidence in their own capacities, it is easy to discern how women themselves have contributed most to alleviate their condition. In fact, the Lijjat and AMM experience clearly is indicative of the fact that the lead taken by the modest entrepreneurs has facilitated other such women. More importantly, it has also created conditions under which women have become more aware of the opportunities and thereby able to organize themselves more effectively, face challenges and oppositions and finally to transform and triumph. The positive consequence of these developments is the kind of change that is experienced by women or in other words 'empowerment' that is essentially and by its very nature, a process aimed at transformation.

This is an abridged but updated version of the project entitled "Empowerment and through participation: A case study of women employed in the informal sector."
It was a small research project awarded by the University of Mumbai in July 2003.

REFERENCES

Access to research information and material for this work is procured from annual reports and monthly newsletter published in English and Marathi by concerned organisations, alongwith their official files and newspaper reporting. These provided interesting information about the changing role and functions, landmarks and achievements of organisation and the women working there. Besides, the researcher also had conducted and undertaken unstructured interviews of women working in the organisations that provided insightful inputs to the study.

Annapurna Mahila Mandal, 22nd Annual Report (1996-1998, 1999-2004), Mumbai,

Journal Lijjat Patrika, Annual Report (1996-2005), Mumbai.

Jon Pierre (1967), *Partnerships in Urban Governance*, London, Macmillan, p. 20.

Kabeer, Naila (1994), Reversed Realities: Gender Hierarchies in Developmental Thought, Kali for Women, New Delhi.

Lukes, S. (1986), *Power: A Radical View,* Macmillan, London.

Mills Theodore, *The Sociology of Small Groups,* New Delhi, Prentice-Hall, p. 46.

Sethuraman, S.V. (1985) *Habitat International,* Vol. 9, No. 3/4, pp. 299-316.

Sethuraman, S.V. (1981) *The Urban Informal Sector in Developing Countries.* Geneva: ILO.

Sudha Mohan. (2002), "Role and Relevance of Civil Society Organisations in Mumbai", *Indian Journal of Political Science,* (Special Issue on Civil Society) Vol. 63, Nos. 2 and 3, June-September, pp. 193-211.

Sudha Mohan, (2005), *Urban Development and New Localism,* Rawat Publishers, Mumbai, New Delhi and Jaipur.

Sudha Mohan, (2006), Issues, Challenges and the Changing Sites of Governance: Self-Organising Networks in Mumbai, *Journal of Governance and Public Policy*, Vol. 1, No. 1, June, pp. 25-40.

8

Family Owned Enterprises in Global Competitive Era

TAPOMOY DEB

Introduction

All these years family owned enterprises has been under criticism for altruism, nepotism and weak risk bearing attributes, which is believed to harm the efficiency and long term sustainability of these enterprises in a fast changing dynamic global business scenario. However, most of the business houses across the world are family owned or controlled. For instance, Shanker and Astrachan (1996) estimated that about 22 million businesses in USA were family owned or controlled, accounting for approximately 92 per cent of all businesses and about half of the gross domestic product. Neubauer and Lank (1998) estimated that in Europe the percentage of family owned enterprises ranges from 70 per cent in Portugal to more than 95 per cent in Italy, with other European countries between 80-95 per cent. In the Middle East, it is more than 95 per cent. Excluding government owned enterprises would increase the percentage even more thereby highlighting the important role played by family owned enterprises in the context of business and economic development.

Family Owned Enterprises

Family owned enterprises refers to those businesses in which the family either owns the business outright or if they have gone to the markets for capital, still hold enough of the stock that they can retain management control without fear of being replaced or voted out. Recently the way these family owned enterprises are viewed is increasingly changing. Their economic importance and ubiquity are now routinely emphasized and the way family owned enterprises accumulate and utilize their resources are now assuming paramount importance.

To understand what makes family owned enterprises gain and/ or sustain competitive advantage, we need to refer agency theory. The agency theory suggests that owing to unification of ownership and control, these enterprises tend to have low agency costs because they, in order to retain ownership, pay premium to minority shareholders. In this process, the value of these enterprises depresses thereby inhibiting its growth due to capital constraint. Consequently, heirs to large family fortunes are less likely to fund innovative ventures, more likely to entrench their management, and more likely to seek to preserve their wealth through political lobbying. But as we have seen above that family owned enterprises enjoy a numerically dominant position in most of the economies and have been so for centuries. It may, therefore, be argued that social cohesion of the family provides it distinct advantages in business landscape fraught with uncertainty and high risks. However, there is growing evidence that family owned enterprises retain their advantages in more developed economies and in highly codified legal environments.

A key strategic advantage for family owned enterprises lies in its ability to foresee market, product and service that may not be profitable today or may not exist at all but in the long term it can prove highly beneficial to the enterprise. This implies that these enterprises have long term visibility of business for making appropriate decisions; even they make evolve unconventional strategies to realize their foresightedness. This is because family owned enterprises have personal interest and have fewer committees, hierarchies, and other constituencies with which management must deal with, which makes decision making faster. Given that family controls ownership in such enterprises and have day to day involvement in business, therefore, communications amongst themselves, being part of the family, is a routine practice in order to solve problems and make managerial decisions for effective running and management of such enterprises. Such communications amongst family members results in consensus building which makes decision-making easy to take and implement.

Generally, people are more prudent with their own, as opposed to "other peoples", money. Family owned enterprises take more personal interest in their business as compared to professional managers since family's personal fortune and reputation shall always be at stake. This does not mean that family owned enterprises do not hire professional managers, they do. These enterprises hire professional managers for their functional competencies in order to advise the family in making appropriate business decisions. Such managers are not expected to make their own decisions as family being the 'owner manager' takes their own decisions which extends their managerial authority.

Since family owned enterprises do not have to grapple with managerial aspirations of increasing span of control so that his resume looks attractive for the next job at other company, therefore, these enterprises can easily engage in cautious growth and reasonable diversification that can build wealth and strength for the family. To assure accountability, managers in public enterprises are subject to a set of organizational rules, policies and formal planning procedures that fragment authority in a bureaucratic system of checks and balances, which is missing in family owned enterprises. Therefore, the alignment of interest between senior management and family in family owned enterprises is stronger and strategic which reduces chances of failure to a substantial extent.

Since family is the key to success of businesses and it will be prudent to assert that trust is the foundation of the family. Trust forms the basis on which these enterprises function well, anywhere in the world. At the same time differences among family members can prove fatal for these enterprises as well. Family businesses have a different relationship where management and ownership overlap even in large family owned or controlled 'public' enterprises. The key decision-makers are nevertheless the family only. This implies that with such sweeping powers, family sometimes bypasses board of directors for certain key decision including differences in appointment of CEO.

Perhaps more importantly shareholders and family are the same entity. Therefore, working for the best interest of shareholders is the same as working in the best interest of the family and *vice versa*. The key trust relationships on which these enterprises must work are those between generations, between family branches when the enterprises grows bigger and survives long enough that more than the entrepreneurial members are involved, and between key non-family managers and family employees as well as management. For instance, in a large family owned and controlled diversified business house, there is a practice that every audit process involves a person, known as "Babu Auditor" who has been directly engaged by the family to oversee the entire audit process for best possible results. It is not that the family does not believe the capability of the auditors they have engaged, but the purpose of deputation of Babu Auditor is to facilitate the process of audit so as to gain deeper insight into accounting/organizational processes and practices. Such audit of auditor concept is neither thinkable nor practiced even in large public or state owned enterprises. Thus, trust between these constituencies of family owned enterprises is vital to its survival and sustenance.

Trust is a crucial component of all business transactions all over the globe. Family owned enterprises have distinctive advantages in terms of their holistic understanding of dynamics. Because in a public owned enterprise, professional managers are accountable to shareholders and, therefore, they cannot justify business relationship based solely on personal criteria, otherwise such professional managers might be under scanner for violating codes of conduct of the enterprise. Under the circumstances, business partner/s understand that future of their association is uncertain and accordingly they tend to always seek newer principals or move to more profit generating existing principals in order to continue their business venture successfully.

However, in the context of family owned enterprises, the situation is just the reverse, that is, these enterprises can justify relationships based on compassionate and personal criteria and, therefore, they are able to seek and sustain the commitment of other partner for a longer period. Formal contracting with a few preferred partners exists which depends upon the personal and particularistic values of the family, whereas the efficacy of such contracting processes is critically dependent upon the acuity and business sense of the family, which varies from enterprise to enterprise and across generations. This results in better understanding between the partners to a business transaction and each potential partner looks upon the other as 'someone like us'.

A key factor in building and maintaining trust is communication.

It is, therefore, important for family members to consciously and deliberately plan how to communicate about business in addition to whatever informal communication takes place between them. Most successful family businesses have specific family council meetings about the business that include all family members. They may be annual or more frequent depending on geographical spread of business and other pertinent factors. In addition, family members can be invited to observe board meetings on a regular or periodic basis. One of the established practices of family owned enterprises to groom younger family members for key leadership positions is by the way of assigning them some operational management responsibilities in the enterprise. These younger members are often briefed by the professional managers and they in turn discuss with some of their elder family members who acts as mentor to develop entrepreneurial skills amongst the new generation.

Competitive Advantage

Hence, these particularistic and personalistic characteristics of family owned enterprises generate competitive advantage. As Michael Porter (1980) says competitive advantage is at the heart of a firm's performance in competitive markets and goes on to say that competitive advantage means having low costs, differentiation advantage, or a successful focus strategy. Competitive advanatge grows fundamentally out of a value a firm is able to create for its buyers that exceeds the firm's cost of creating it. Competitive advantage shall accrue to an enterprise if it is able to produce and market its products and services at a lower cost (cost leadership) or delivers such benefit or value which justifies a higher price (differentiation leadership). In order to realize competitive strategy, competent personnel are required to man the operations of the enterprise. However, in family owned enterprises, key managerial personnel are selected not for their professional abilities, but based on family ties. This implies that fewer number of professional managers are hired and family members occupies key leadership positions and their performance, contribution and remuneration are monitored and controlled by family through its own (informal) code of discipline, passed from one generation to another. Given the scenario, top managerial talents are less likely to be attracted to such family owned enterprises for jobs and even those chosen few who joins, their compensation does not include stock options; in order to prevent dilution of family control of their enterprises. Hence, family owned enterprises tend to employ fewer professional managers and those employed are concerned with day-to-day operating details to the detriment of strategic planning. With shortage of managerial talent (human capital) amidst competitive threat, family owned enterprises tend to rely more upon financial capital to succeed and generally have tight financial monitoring and control measures in place to evaluate performance of various work units and the enterprise itself. This kind of system is likely to work successfully in labour intensive industries where the competitive strategy revolves around primarily cost leadership. This type of approach and planning system is ill suited to knowledge-intensive and technologically dynamic industries.

With lower capital base (closely held business) and shortage of managerial talents, the ability of family owned enterprises in acquiring resources and strategic capability is highly limited which restricts their competitiveness in capital and knowledge-based industries. Moreover, decision-making is restricted to a few insiders which results in speedy decision-making yet such decision structures inhibit accumulation of intangible skills and organizing systems necessary to coordinate varied functions and large number of people. All these imperatives implies that family owned enterprises shall be less able to invest heavily in research and developmental activities, innovative business modeling, new experimentation, newer product development and design, etc. which disqualifies them from attaining differentiation advantage especially at global scale.

Therefore, family owned enterprises have cost leadership advantages and shall be more successful in local markets. With closer family ties based on trust, family owned enterprises tends to develop a series of advantages with regard to creation and using of social capital, both within the enterprises and in its environment. Nahapiet and Ghoshal (1998) defines social capital as 'the sum of the actual and potential resources embedded within, available through, and derived from the network of relationships possessed by an individual or social unit'. Therefore, family owned enterprises enjoy advantages in forming and sustaining personal business contacts and networks given dense concentration of property rights, authority and decision making power. Social capital so generated helps family owned enterprises to access and screen strategic information that enhances bargaining and lobbying power for venturing into new business opportunities for personal interests. In the Indian context, such social capital has been instrumental in forging alliance with politicians and bureaucrats for securing personal favours in business especially in tendering processes. Moreover, intuitiveness acts as strategic tools in the hands of these family owned enterprises as they are responsible to themselves only and hence possess immense freedom to allocate and use their resources under different market conditions.

Conclusion

Regardless of many managerial and capital constraints, family owned enterprises has been growing and expanding even in this global economic era. The superior performance of family owned enterprises is even more evident in emerging markets where they are viewed as 'engines' of the economy (Whyte, 1996). This implies that these enterprises have inherent strength in terms of speedy decision-making, absence of bureaucratic procedures, effective communication and most importantly trust—the key ingredient of social capital which appears to be a driver of competitive advantage in family owned enterprises.

REFERENCES

Biggart, N.W., and Delbridge, R., 2004. *Systems of Exchange*, Academy of Management Review, 29(1). pp. 28-38.

Barclay, M., and Holderness, C., 1989. Private Benefits from Control of Public Corporations, *Journal of Financial Economics,* 25. pp. 371-396.

Fama, E.F., and Jensen, M.C. 1983. Separation of Ownership and Control. *Journal of Law and Economics,* 26. pp. 301-326.

Fukuyama, F. 1995. *Trust: The Social Virtues and the Creation of Prosperity*, New York: Free Press.

Kogut, B., and Zander, U. 1992. Knowledge of the Firm, Combinative Capabilities, and the Replication of Technology, *Organization Science, 3.* pp. 383-397.

Lovett, S.; Simmons, L.C.; and Kali, R., 1999. Guanxi *versus* the Market: Ethics and Efficiency, *Journal of International Business Studies,* 30. pp. 231-248.

Mintzberg, H., 1994. *The Rise and Fall of Strategic Planning*, Englewood Cliffs: Prentice Hall.

Neubauer, F. and Lank, A.G., 1998. The Family Business: It's Governance for Sustainability, New York: Routledge.

Nahapiet, J. and Ghoshal, S., 1998. *Social Capital, Intellectual Capital, and the Organizational Advantage*, Academy of Management Review, 23(2). pp. 242-266.

Porter, M.E. (1985). *Competitive Advantage*, New York: Free Press.

Porter, M.E. (1998). Capital Disadvantage: America's Failing Capital Investment System. In M.E. Porter (Ed.), *On Competition* (pp. 431-467). Boston: Harvard Business Review Book.

Schulze, W.S.; Lubatkin, M.H.; Dino, R.N.; and Buchholtz, A.K., 2001. Agency Relationships in Family Firms: Theory and Evidence, *Organization Science,* 12(2). pp. 99-116.

Shanker, M.C. and Astrachan, J.H., 1996. Myths and Realities: Family Businesses's Contribution to the US Economy—A Framework for Assessing Family Business Statistics, *Family Business Review*, 9(2). pp. 107-124.

Useem, M., 1993. *Executive Defense: Shareholder Power and Corporate Reorganization*, Cambridge MA: Harvard University Press.

Uzzi, B., 1997. Social Structure and Competition in Inter-firm Networks: The Paradox of Embeddedness, *Administrative Science Quarterly,* 42(1). pp. 35-67.

Whyte, M.K., 1996. The Chinese Family and Economic Development: Obstacle or Engine? *Economic Development and Cultural Change,* 45(1). pp. 1-30.

Williamson, P., 1999. *Asia's Emerging Competitors. Global Finance*, 13(12).

9

Key Concepts of Social Impact Assessment and Resettlement Action Plan for Infrastructure Development Projects

PRASENJIT MAITI

Introduction

Resettlement of affected persons and rehabilitation of their lost assets (land and/or structures) and livelihood are critical yet imperative social development exercises of linear road projects that require displacement of individuals and groups in order to either upgrade/ widen existing road networks or else to construct new road systems for better transport facilities and streamlined movement of vehicular traffic essential for economies undergoing reforms. Involuntary resettlement caused by road projects should be informed by comprehensive mitigation measures in order to reduce adverse impacts on the existing social fabric of Project Affected Persons.

Resettlement Action Plan

One of the most crucial aspects of implementing infrastructure development projects (such as roads and highways projects) is acquisition of land and/or properties and resettlement thereof of Project Affected Persons and their families/households.

Land Acquisition Act 1984

The Land Acquisition Act I of 1984 (along with its modifications) usually forms the basis of the land acquisition process in India. [The National Highways (Amendment) Act 1997 may be applied if the project road is declared as a National Highway.] The value of land depends upon its area and location along with its type that is classified as residential, agricultural, ponds, barren etc. besides Government Land being used for railways, roads, canals, public utilities etc.

National Policy on Resettlement and Rehabilitation 2003

In case of projects relating to Railway Lines, Highways, Transmission Lines and laying pipelines wherein only a narrow stretch of land extending over several kilometres is being acquired, the Project Affected Families will be offered an *ex gratia* amount of Rs. 10,000 per family, and no other Resettlement and Rehabilitation benefits shall be available to them.[1]

The system of extending cash compensation does not, by itself, in most cases, enable the affected families to obtain cultivable agricultural land, homestead and other resources, which they have to surrender to the State. The difficulties are more acute for persons who are critically dependent on the acquired assets for their subsistence/livelihoods, such as landless agricultural workers, forest dwellers, tenants and artisans, as their distress and destitution is more severe, and yet they are not eligible for cash compensation.[2]

Project Affected Family means a family/person whose place of residence or other properties or source of livelihood are substantially affected by the process of acquisition of land for the project and who has been residing continuously for a period of not less than three years preceding the date of declaration of the affected zone or practicing any trade, occupation or vocation continuously for a period of not less than three years in the affected zone, preceding the date of declaration of the affected zone.[3]

Affected zone, in relation to a project, means declaration . . . by the appropriate Government area of villages or locality under a project for which the land is being acquired under Land Acquisition Act 1894 or any other Act in force . . . [4]

The National R&R Policy displays concern for the more vulnerable sections of society that may be unevenly impacted by project interventions. It is to be realized that R&R is centrally about securing justice in nearly all its forms to Project Affected Persons. The unique feature that sets R&R apart is its attempt to explore new institutional mechanisms outside the scope of the conventional legal framework.

National Policy Guidelines

The Government of India has prepared an R&R Policy that strives to standardize the good practices related to involuntary displacement of persons and their assets in the national context. State Governments as well as Central Government Agencies more or less adhere to this policy in the case of development projects. This is evident from the review of different Entitlement Matrices of road projects spread across the country.

It is imperative that best practices and lessons learnt continuously evolve during the preparatory and operational phases of development projects so that change management in difficult situations may be efficaciously handled by the concerned project authorities. So information dissemination and knowledge-sharing exercises have to be constantly upgraded with regard to the problems as well as the solutions in the context of projects involving R&R.

The National Policy on Resettlement and Rehabilitation for Project Affected Families (2003) prepared by the Ministry of Rural Development (Department of Land Resources) of the Government of India states that "Compulsory acquisition of land for public purpose including infrastructure projects displaces people, forcing them to give up their homes, assets and means of livelihood. Apart from depriving them of their lands, livelihoods and resource-base, displacement has other traumatic psychological and socio-cultural consequences. The Government of India recognizes the need to minimize large scale displacement to the extent possible and, where displacement is inevitable, the need to handle with utmost care and forethought issues relating to Resettlement and Rehabilitation of Project Affected Families. Such an approach is especially necessary in respect of tribals, small and marginal farmers and women."

"The system of extending cash compensation does not, by itself, in most cases enable the affected families to obtain cultivable agricultural land, homestead and other resources which they have to surrender to the State. The difficulties are more acute for persons who are critically dependent on the acquired assets for their subsistence/livelihoods such as landless agricultural workers, forest dwellers, tenants and artisans, as their distress and destitution is more severe, and yet they are not eligible for cash compensation."

This is a limitation of the National R&R Policy. The primary stakeholders who are not entitled to any cash compensation from the project can subsequently become a social problem in terms of their relative deprivation.

"... The Policy essentially addresses the need to provide succour to the assetless rural poor, support the rehabilitation efforts of the resource poor sections, namely, small and marginal farmers, SCs/STs and women who have been displaced. Besides, it seeks to provide a broad canvas for an effective dialogue between the Project Affected Families and the Administration for Resettlement and Rehabilitation. Such a dialogue is expected to enable timely completion of projects with a sense of definiteness as regards costs and adequate attention to the needs of the displaced persons, especially the resource poor sections. The intention is to impart greater flexibility for interaction and negotiation so that the resultant (Compensation/Support/Assistance). Package gains all-round acceptability in the shape of a workable instrument providing satisfaction to all stakeholders/Requiring Bodies."

Dialogues in the context of involuntary resettlement of Project Affected Persons is essential in order to provide the necessary interactive space within the framework of entitlements and benefits designed for PAPs. This dialogue must continue throughout and even beyond the project cycle in order to ensure that PAPs have secured adequate representation during the policy formulation stage and comprehensive participation during the project implementation stage.

This policy further states that "In case of projects relating to Railway Lines, Highways, Transmission Lines and laying pipelines wherein only a narrow stretch of land extending over several kilometres is being acquired, the Project Affected Families will be offered an *ex gratia* amount of Rs. 10,000 per family, and *no other Resettlement and Rehabilitation benefits shall be available to them*" (emphasis added). This contradicts the long term income/livelihood restoration objective of development projects that induce displacement as per the World Bank's policy guidelines.

"The National Policy on the Resettlement and Rehabilitation of Project Affected Families will be in the form of broad guidelines and executive instructions for guidance of all concerned and will be applicable to Projects *displacing 500 families or more en masse* in plain areas and *250 families en masse* in hilly areas, Desert Development Programme (DDP) blocks, areas mentioned in Schedule V and Schedule VI of the Constitution of India" (emphasis added).

This is another limitation of the National R&R Policy due to its mentioning of the specific number of Project Affected Families. It implies that development projects displacing less number of families would not be covered by this policy. This shortcoming may be corrected in the future to ensure social safeguards. It is essential to impart social and economic justice to Project Affected Persons. It is also imperative to ensure that their community fabric and kinship ties and cultural identities are not destroyed by way of project interventions.

World Bank Policy Guidelines

The World Bank has extended different categories of bilateral support to facilitate implementation of development projects since its inception. It also simultaneously ensures that Structural Adjustment Programmes are duly implemented by the countries receiving monetary support (loans/credit/grant) as a condition attached to such financial assistance. So adherence to the World Bank's R&R Policy Guidelines on the part of national and/or State Governments is imperative in order to be eligible for any project support.

"The World Bank's involuntary resettlement policy states that project planning must avoid and minimize involuntary resettlement, and that if people lose their homes or livelihoods as a result of Bank-financed projects, they should have their standard of living improved, or at least restored."[5]

Project implementing authorities who seek World Bank funding must ensure proper adherence to the Bank's Policy Guidelines in order to qualify for long term financial support and assistance. Comprehensive R&R policy frameworks must be prepared in this connection as one of the preliminary tasks during the project preparatory phase.

"Involuntary resettlement may cause severe long term hardship, impoverishment and environmental damage unless appropriate measures are carefully planned and carried out. For these reasons, the overall objectives of the (World) Bank's Policy on involuntary resettlement are the following:

- Involuntary resettlement should be avoided where feasible, or minimized, exploring all viable alternative project designs.
- Where it is not feasible to avoid resettlement, resettlement

activities should be conceived and executed as sustainable development programmes, providing sufficient investment resources to enable the persons displaced by the project to share in project benefits. Displaced persons should be meaningfully consulted and should have opportunities to participate in planning and implementing resettlement programmes.

- ❖ Displaced persons should be assisted in their efforts to improve their livelihoods and standards of living or at least to restore them, in real terms, to pre-displacement levels or to levels prevailing prior to the beginning of project implementation, whichever is higher."[6]

It is evident that the World Bank intends to maintain all possible social safeguards in order to mitigate/reduce negative impacts caused by development project interventions. So policy-planners of the concerned implementing agencies who accept World Bank funding should prepare their R&R guidelines in accordance with the Bank's social and environmental prescriptions. Such guidelines must also be in tune with the national context and ground realities of specific projects.

World Bank Funded Road Projects

Several State Governments in India such as Andhra Pradesh, Gujarat, Karnataka, Kerala, Uttar Pradesh, Mizoram and Tamil Nadu and Government Agencies like the National Highways Authority of India have in recent times undertaken road improvement projects funded by the World Bank.

R&R Policy Guidelines were prepared by the concerned implementing agencies in accordance with the World Bank's Operational Directive 4.30/Operational Policy 4.12 related to involuntary resettlement. A few road projects can be cited in this regard such as:

1. Third National Highway Project (TNHP),
2. Grand Trunk Road Improvement Project (GTRIP),
3. Allahabad Bypass Project (NHAI Project),
4. Lucknow-Muzaffarpur National Highway Project (NHAI Project),

5. Andhra Pradesh State Highways Project (APSHP),
6. Karnataka State Highways Improvement Project (KSHIP),
7. Tamil Nadu Road Sector Project; and
8. Uttar Pradesh State Roads Project.

Certain changes have taken place over time in the policy formulation stage of different road projects funded by the World Bank. Such moderate policy shifts indicate that road or any other development projects require streamlining in accordance with the local-level situation and ground realities although the general policy framework with regard to involuntary resettlement of Project Affected Persons remains almost the same.

This is a lesson learnt *i.e.* specific projects require specific planning attuned to the ground realities in order to ensure that R&R policy guidelines are properly followed as mandated by the World Bank. Lacunae identified in earlier road projects can be addressed in subsequent projects (especially with regard to the entitlements of PAPs) in this process that strategizes continuous knowledge upgradation underpinned by change management mechanisms.

Case Studies

For instance: The Entitlement Matrix of the Allahabad Bypass Project mentions that "PAPs will be explained the process (of acquisition of land and assets and compensation against such acquisition at replacement cost or actual market value) and their views will be taken into consideration while determining the market value."

This concern was not reflected in similar terms in the Entitlement Matrix of the Lucknow-Muzaffarpur National Highway Project. But it was duly reflected in the case of the Kerala State Highways Project. The National Highways Authority of India's Detailed Entitlement Matrix for the National Highway Corridor (Public-Private Partnership Project) also includes this people's participation factor in its design (2002).

The provision of verification of mortgage clearance by the Project Authority is included in the Allahabad Bypass Project while it is not included in the Lucknow-Muzaffarpur Project. Categories of land loss were included in the Entitlement Matrix of the Andhra Pradesh State Highways Project (1996). This was a novel approach to identify the types of land loss in terms of magnitude (>25% and <25%).

The provision of "Unforeseen impacts shall be documented and mitigated based on the principles agreed upon in this policy framework" was absent in the Andhra Pradesh State Highways Project. This provision is essential to address new factors that may emerge at different points of the project cycle.

The Kerala State Highways Project (2000) provided "For those who choose self-relocation, the Project Displaced Persons will be entitled to plots . . . even if they do not opt for resettlement sites." This was a unique effort to incorporate an adequate social space required for Project Affected Persons in their pursuit of alternative places of residence and/or work.

This project also mentioned that "Easily replaced resources such as cultural properties will be conserved (by means of special protection, relocation, replacement etc.) in consultation with the community." This provision respects the cultural identities of Project Affected Persons and ensures that participatory development is safeguarded under the project so that the primary stakeholders are properly benefited from the positive impacts of the civil works undertaken in connection with the project. It is also reflected in the Entitlement Matrix of the Uttar Pradesh State Roads Project Phase I (2002).

The Tamil Nadu Road Sector Project (2003) remarked in its Detailed Entitlement Matrix that "The land (agricultural or otherwise) purchase grant will be available if alternative land is purchased and registered within one year of receiving the compensation amount. The grant will be released on the submission of copy of registered sale deed".

This provision (available to those Project Affected Persons who lost more than 25 per cent of their land-holding and were left with less than the minimum economic land-holding) is a good practice as it considerably streamlined the land compensation mechanism and ensured social safeguard for PAPs. This project also included the option of built houses depending on the size of houses lost. This may be replicated elsewhere if practicable.

The Karnataka State Highways Improvement Project (Raichur and Bijapur Bypasses) pinpointed the budgetary provisions for implementation of the Resettlement Action Plan by mentioning that "All the costs calculated will be pegged to the inflation costs after 2 years from the Cut-Off Date". It also proposed in its Entitlement Matrix that "The maintenance of common property resources and infrastructure will be handed to the Local Authority."

This provision ensures that the benefits of the project percolate to the grassroots as a result of decentralization of power and devolution of resources. The project also included a "Scope for making amendments in the R&R Policy." This is critical in order to accommodate any factor(s) not conceived during the project preparatory stage.

The Detailed Entitlement Matrix of the Gujarat State Highways Project (Phase IIB) included the institutional arrangement of an Independent Committee entrusted to decide the replacement cost or actual market price of agricultural land and assets of private property owners. This was a good practice and can be emulated elsewhere. This provision made the assessment procedure of land and assets transparent and also made this committee accountable to the Project Affected Persons.

The organizational structure of the R&R Cell has been mentioned in the Assam State Roads Resettlement and Rehabilitation Policy (2004). This is important because such organizational structures and institutional arrangements ultimately help implement the Resettlement Action Plan and facilitate entrenchment of good practices as per World Bank Guidelines.

Review of different project policies reveal that a uniform set of guidelines apply to the Detailed Entitlement Matrices with minor inclusion and exclusion of certain provisions. The key beneficiaries have already been identified and the principal entitlements have been decided upon. Such policy continuity is essential for the long term sustainability of benefits accruing from road projects funded by the World Bank.

Legal Framework

The Land Acquisition Act I of 1984 allows Government Agencies to expropriate any private land for a public purpose (by exercising Eminent Domain), provided the owners in possession of legal titles to occupy the land and structures are duly compensated. Current land acquisition compensation packages include the following:

1. Market value of the land.
2. A solatium of 30 per cent on the market value of land.
3. An interest of 12 per cent on the market value of land from the Date of Notification to the Date of Declaration of Award.

4. Additional compensation is also allowed for loss of trees, crops, houses and other immovable assets.
5. The compensation for loss of earning to the sharecropper would be not more than six times of net average annual income derived during the three years immediately preceding the Date of Acquisition.
6. Damage due to severing of the land-holding from adjoining land.
7. Damage due to land acquisition leading to change of residence or place of business.

Whenever it appears to the appropriate Government that the land in any locality (is needed or) is likely to be needed for any public purpose (or for a company), a Notification to that effect shall be published in the Official Gazette (and in two daily newspapers circulating in that locality of which at least one shall be in the regional language), and the District Collector shall cause public notice of the substance of such Notification to be given at convenient places in the said locality.[7]

Where land acquisition is required the practice is to refer to the Date of Notification under law as the Cut-Off Date. Compensation is paid on the basis of value of the land at the time of Notification. The District Collector would issue a Notification announcing the public purpose for which the land or property is to be acquired. This would be followed by a period of one month during which objections may be filed by concerned persons with an interest in the land/property to be acquired. Hearing of objections and the award of compensation by the District Collector would follow subsequently. All legal procedures would be meticulously followed while awarding compensation packages to Project Affected Persons in possession of legal titles to the land and (residential/commercial) structures to be acquired for the project.[8]

Resettlement and Rehabilitation Guidelines

Every conceivable effort should be made during the project design and preparation stages to minimize acquisition of land and other assets in order to reduce adverse socio-economic impacts. The structures/assets falling outside the Right of Way/Corridor of Impact should be left undisturbed as far as practicable. Road and/or flyover projects may have to deal with Project Affected Persons who fall under the following categories:

1. Legal owners and/or tenants getting adversely affected due to the acquisition of their land and assets or due to the fact that such land or assets so acquired are their sources of livelihood; and
2. Encroachers and/or squatters who are the illegal occupants/ users of public property/land/structures falling within the Right of Way and accordingly live and/or earn their livelihood by operating within the Right of Way.[9]

The Project Authority would take final decision with regard to compensation and/or Resettlement and Rehabilitation assistance. No compensation for land may be provided to the encroachers and squatters keeping in mind their illegal status. R&R assistance may be provided to encroachers and squatters who belong to the disadvantaged and vulnerable groups. Compensation for structures and other lost assets (required for the project) may be paid at the replacement value[10] to encroachers/squatters who belong to the vulnerable groups.[11] The Project Authority would take final decision in this regard.

R&R Compensation

Legal owners of land and property shall be entitled to compensation. Squatters and encroachers who are not ordinarily entitled for compensation may receive certain benefits as per their respective entitlements if they belong to vulnerable groups. The compensation for land and buildings shall be provided within the ambit of the Land Acquisition Act 1894 and assistance would be provided to meet the replacement value. All losses, including loss of income, should be compensated within the overall Resettlement and Rehabilitation package as per the (proposed) Entitlement Framework. The Project Authority shall take the final decision in this regard.

Compensation and assistance would be extended to Project Affected Persons who were identified on or prior to the Cut-Off Date. Where land acquisition is required, the practice is to refer to the Date of Notification under law as the Cut-Off Date. Compensation is paid on the basis of value of the land during

Notification. The Project Authority would ensure that a Notification is issued by announcing the public purpose for which private land and/or property are to be acquired. This would be followed by a period of one month during which concerned persons may file objections with an interest in the land/property to be acquired. The Grievance Redress Committee would deal with claims regarding assistance.

Payment of compensation against land acquired by the Project Authority may be made on the basis of updated official records and ground-level information. Land records of title/classification/current land use may be updated to ensure adequate cost compensation and allotment of land to the Entitled Persons/Project Displaced Persons. Official records as they are on the Cut-Off Date may be consulted in order to determine the classification and current use of land. If 75 per cent or more land-holding of a Project Affected Person/Project Displaced Person is acquired or when the part of a plot of land remaining after acquisition becomes economically unviable after acquisition, the owner of such land/property shall have the right to seek acquisition of his/her entire contiguous land-holding/property provided the residual land is less than the Minimum Economic Holding.[12]

The compensation amount for the land and properties to be acquired by the Project Authority shall be paid according to the provisions of the Land Acquisition Act. The Project Authority shall pay the difference as assistance if the provisions are less than the replacement value. The Project Authority may decide on the magnitude of loss to structures (in terms of percentage of the existing area or otherwise) in order to consider the owners of such affected structures to be Project Displaced Persons.

The Project Authority shall determine the possible replacement cost of land and assets to be acquired. Land rate surveys may be carried out by the Project Authority for this purpose in association with representatives of Project Affected Persons and external assessment agencies. The Project Authority may utilize the following system of assessment while determining the replacement cost of land:

1. Taking into account such prescribed rates or the average of the actual transaction rates of similar lands for contemporary years for which sale deeds are registered.

2. Taking into consideration twenty times of the annual value of gross production of the concerned land averaged over the preceding five years.
3. Fixing up market value of land equal to the minimum land value if so prescribed by the State Government under the Indian Stamp Act for the purpose of registration of sale deeds under the Indian Registration Act of 1908.

The replacement cost of land to be fixed by the Project Authority would be the amount that shall be the highest among the three amounts arrived at by the aforesaid three alternative methods. The difference shall be paid in the form of assistance in case the replacement cost is higher than the market value determined by the Project Authority.

The value of the houses, buildings and other immovable properties of the Project Affected Persons (including the Project Displaced Persons) shall be determined for the purpose of payment of compensation without depreciation.

Compensation for properties belonging to the Project Affected Community or for common places of religious worship that would be acquired for the project shall be provided to enable construction of the same at the relocation site(s) (if any) through the offices of the concerned local self-governing bodies in accordance with the modalities determined by such bodies to ensure proper utilization of the compensation amount.[13]

Persons (belonging to the vulnerable groups) who derive their livelihood from the common places of religious worship may be supported by the project's special assistance scheme (if any).

Compensation for trees would be based on their market value in case of timber bearing trees and replacement cost in case of fruit bearing trees as per the rates decided by the Project Authority in consultation with the concerned Government Departments. Loss of income may also be considered when assessing the compensation amount.

Compensation shall be paid and efforts would be made to complete the Resettlement and Rehabilitation of Project Affected Persons/Project Displaced Persons before taking possession of their land and/or properties. The Project Affected Persons/Project Displaced Persons shall hand over their land and properties to the Project Authority free from all encumbrances such as mortgage, debt etc. for the purpose of acquisition.

In the case of any loan on such acquired land and properties extended to the Project Affected Persons by any Government Agency remaining unadjusted as per the information furnished by the Project Affected Persons or by the loaner agency such amounts shall be deducted from their total compensation.

All transaction costs (including transportation costs/wages lost due to the project) shall be assessed and compensated for. The payment of this amount shall be made in accordance with the relevant clauses of the Land Acquisition Act.

All payments shall be made into the joint bank accounts of the husband and the wife while all new titles issued shall be in the joint names of the husband and the wife. All payments shall be made in public to ensure transparency. Disposal of acquired properties shall be carried out as follows:

- ❖ The acquired land and properties shall vest in the Government Department(s) paying compensation for such land and properties.
- ❖ Project Displaced Persons shall be allowed to collect the materials salvaged from their houses and shops etc. acquired by the project even after payment of compensation. The Government would levy no charges upon them for the same. A notice to that effect would be issued to take away the materials so salvaged within 48 hours of demolition of structures. If not collected then the Project Authority without giving any further notice shall dispose the same.
- ❖ The Project Displaced Persons receiving compensation for trees shall be allowed to take away timber from their trees (acquired by the project) for domestic use. Trees standing on Government Land shall be sold by public auction to be organized by the concerned Government Department(s).

The Project Authority can take appropriate action to demolish structures within the project's Corridor of Impact after the expiry of the notified deadline. The Project Authority can also dismantle structures and evict individuals within the Corridor of Impact of the project if it is established that such structures and individuals occupied the public Right of Way after the duly notified Cut-Off Date. Any grievances and objections in this connection would be referred to the Grievance Redress Committee.

Information Dissemination Campaign

Information dissemination exercises for Project Affected Persons may be carried out prior to implementation of the Resettlement Action Plan. This campaign may be facilitated by the Project Authority and executed by the Partner Non-Government Organization(s) that would be appointed to implement the Resettlement Action Plan.

Impact Categories

Project-induced displacement may lead to loss of income or reduced income for Project Affected Persons. The main categories of impact expected as a result of the project include the following types of loss:

1. Loss of commercial establishments,
2. Loss of commercial space,
3. Loss of residential (dwelling) units,
4. Loss of livelihood, and
5. Loss of common property resources.[14]

Loss of temporary commercial structures is a complex problem since the issue of retaining the present customer base must be considered in this regard. Another problem pertains to the tenants and owners. Mitigation measures delivered under this Resettlement Action Plan may include reconstructing demolished commercial structures in an adjacent area so that the present customer base is retained. The Project Authority should duly consider the means of accomplishing this and addressing ownership of the new structures. The Project Authority would make final decision with regard to all aspects of this matter. There is also the need to respond to more generalized impacts of disturbance in the lives and livelihood of Project Affected Persons. Such adverse impacts may be mitigated by payment of Maintenance Allowance. A Rehabilitation Grant (for vulnerable groups) may be considered in the event income restoration cannot be entirely achieved by utilizing the compensation provided. Project Affected Persons may be assisted by the Project Authority to improve or regain their former status of living at no cost to themselves.

Institutional Arrangements

Implementation of this Resettlement Action Plan requires staff, resources and close coordination with different agencies and organizations working in the project area. This Resettlement Action Plan seeks to provide a strategy for developing the required implementation capacity on the part of the Project Authority.

Capacity building and training may be coordinated with the project implementation schedule in order to ensure that skilled staff members are available to implement this Resettlement Action Plan without any delay in civil works.

Orientation workshops may be organised by the Project Authority (Project Implementation Unit) and Partner Non-Government Organisations. An R&R Cell may be established within the Project Implementation Unit. Partner NGOs would be engaged to support the Project Authority and counterparted with PIU personnel to foster transfer of social development expertise. An independent external agency may provide professional services for monitoring and evaluating the R&R process.

The Project Authority may initiate high priority actions to establish institutional linkages necessary for time-bound delivery of the Project Affected Persons' entitlements and assure coordination across agencies as well as between the various social and economic mitigation measures outlined in this Resettlement Action Plan.

Institutional Context

Effective implementation of this Resettlement Action Plan would require institutional relationships and responsibilities, rapid organizational development and collaborative efforts on the part of the Project Authority, State Government, Partner NGO(s) and Project Affected Persons.

R&R Coordination

The Project Implementation Unit would be responsible for coordinating with different Government Agencies. The R&R Cell would establish operational links to facilitate the critical process of project-induced resettlement. It may establish an effective process of dialogue between the Project Authority and the Project Affected Persons/Communities.

The R&R Cell would have to provide the means and mechanisms for coordinating the efficacious delivery of compensation and assistance entitlements to those adversely affected due to implementation of the project.

The R&R Cell would have to contribute social development perspectives and field-level inputs to ongoing project design and implementation by working closely with project planners, contractors and construction supervision consultants.

It would link the project with the concerned Government Agencies, provide liaison with Affected Communities, establish decentralized (grassroots) committees to coordinate social development and resettlement operations in the field, mobilize Partner NGO(s) and motivate local-level Community-Based Organizations to represent and safeguard the interests of Project Affected Persons.

It would also engage training services, oversee a grievance redress process, actively monitor Resettlement Action Plan implementation and cooperate with project evaluation exercises. The R&R Cell would be responsible for disseminating project-related information to the public and providing additional opportunities for civil societal feedback.

Inter-Departmental Coordination

Resettlement Action Plan entitlements for Income Restoration Programmes and Project Affected Groups are exclusively the responsibility of the Project Authority (apart from the land acquisition and compensation components in which the Revenue Department and the Project Authority would jointly provide entitlements). Several entitlements comprise services and benefits ordinarily provided by other government-sponsored social development programmes such as the vulnerable groups' housing schemes.

The R&R Cell may establish liaison with these ongoing programmes to facilitate access of the Project Affected Persons and take advantage of services and programmes already in place. It may negotiate cost-sharing arrangements wherever feasible. Restoration of community assets would require coordination with the Public Health Engineering Department.

The R&R Cell's coordination with the Education Department

would be required in the event schools are adversely impacted. A variety of State and Central Government programmes addressing women's needs may be associated with other group entitlements, including those responding to potential transmission of sexually transmitted diseases as well as reproductive and child health.

Grievance Redress Mechanism

The Resettlement Action Plan's participatory processes as well as its compensation and support mechanisms are expected to enhance acceptance of the resettlement programme and reduce complaints. There may nevertheless be individuals or groups who perceive that they have not received adequate support or that their needs have not been properly addressed.

The Project Authority would, therefore, establish a Grievance Redress Committee. This Committee would have representation from Project Affected Persons, NGO(s)/CBO(s) involved in the Resettlement Action Plan implementation, local-level Government officials and the Project Authority.

This Committee would hear complaints and facilitate solutions. This process is expected to promote settlement of disputes through mediation in order to reduce the volume of time-consuming litigation. The Project Authority would take final decision on different aspects related to grievance redress of Project Affected Persons.

Monitoring and Evaluation

Monitoring and Evaluation are critical activities in the process of involuntary resettlement. Monitoring involves periodic checking to ascertain whether R&R activities are going according to the Resettlement Action Plan. It provides required feedback to the Project Authority to ensure that the Resettlement Action Plan implementation programme runs on schedule. Evaluation is basically the post-project assessment of whether the implementation programme was finally able to achieve its stated objectives. An independent external agency may be engaged by the Project Authority to carry out the (impact) Monitoring and Evaluation of the project with regard to implementation of the Resettlement Action Plan. M&E would measure project performance against project objectives.

Long term impact indicators may be examined during the project evaluation stage. The Project Authority may contract an external agency (such as an academic institution) that would undertake independent evaluation studies at least twice during the lifetime of the project. These evaluations would provide inputs to the mid-term review and the post-project report. Independent evaluation exercises may focus on assessing whether the overall objectives of the project are being met and would utilize the impact indicators as a basis for evaluation. The Project Authority would take final decisions on all M&E (and related) aspects of the project.

Monitoring of involuntary resettlement operations require an application of general project monitoring procedures to the processes occurring in resettlement with particular attention to the specific high risks intrinsic in such operations. This means that monitoring of R&R requires certain specialized skills. To meet this requirement a sub-unit within the R&R Cell may be established.

An external agency may be appointed to monitor and evaluate the R&R programme on a periodic basis. This additional perspective in Resettlement Action Plan implementation is critical because conventional M&E exercises carried out by Government Agencies may not adequately focus on certain aspects of importance to the implementing agencies. This external agency would be required to streamline the R&R process. External M&E studies may synchronize with the implementation of the Resettlement Action Plan. The external agency may submit periodic reports on the progress of Resettlement Action Plan implementation to the Project Authority. It may also identify the issues and concerns that require attention and subsequent action on the part of the Project Authority.

Conclusions

- ❖ Implementation of the Resettlement Action Plan on the part of Non-Government Organization(s) appointed by the Project Authority would require sensitive handling of the critical issue of involuntary displacement that is a necessary result of infrastructural development projects involving roads and highways, flyovers and interchanges etc.
- ❖ Legal owners of land and structures would suffer in terms of loss of immovable assets while their tenants would suffer losses either in terms of residence or livelihood or both.

- Resettlement of affected persons and rehabilitation of their lost assets (land and/or structures) and livelihood are critical yet imperative social development exercises of infrastructure development projects that require displacement of individuals and groups.

Recommendations

- The Project Authority may set up a dedicated office in order to provide information with regard to the R&R guidelines and the Resettlement Action Plan.
- Fixation of compensation to the legal owners of affected land and structures should be based on the present market rate.
- The Grievance Redress Committee may expedite the process of redress of grievances. Project Affected Persons may be counselled by Partner Non-Government Organization(s) as and when required.
- Unauthorized encroachers and squatters as such do not have any legal rights to their occupied land and structures but the vulnerable groups among such illegal occupants may be considered by the Project Authority for R&R support/assistance.
- Illegal encroachers and squatters may be allowed to salvage the dismantled materials. The Project Authority may consider appointing such persons (belonging to vulnerable groups) as casual workers during the construction stage of the project in order to provide livelihood at least on a short term basis in order to mitigate the adverse impacts of involuntary displacement.
- Representatives from the local bodies such as municipalities/Panchayats, officials from the local administration and police, local Community-Based Organizations/Non-Government Organizations may be consulted on a periodic basis to ensure efficacious implementation of the Resettlement Action Plan.
- Involuntary resettlement caused by infrastructure development projects should be informed by comprehensive mitigation measures in order to reduce adverse impacts on the existing social fabric of Project Affected Persons.

APPENDIX I

KEY DEFINITIONS

Corridor of Impact

The Corridor of Impact is defined as the construction width or the operational width plus a safety zone on either side of the road. Within the Corridor of Impact there should not be any structure or other hindrances. The Corridor of Impact would vary depending on site requirement.

Compensation and Assistance

Compensation refers to restitution made to legal property owners in possession of title deeds under the Land Acquisition Act. Compensation is payment made by the Government to legal owners when Eminent Domain is exercised to transfer ownership of private property/land to the State. Assistance refers to all other support mechanisms such as grants, assets, services etc. provided to Entitled Persons (or their groups).

Project Affected Persons

Project Affected Persons are individuals who would be adversely impacted by implementation of the civil works of the project. They would lose land/property/livelihood in this process. So a Project Affected Person is an individual who (as a direct consequence of the project) sustains damages:

1. due to severance of his/her land, or
2. due to negative impacts on his/her immovable properties in any manner, or
3. due to adverse effects on his/her livelihood calculated on the basis of an objective assessment.

Project Affected Persons include Project Displaced Persons. These are individuals who are compelled to change their place of residence/work/business due to implementation of the project. Project Affected Persons are categorized as follows:

1. Private Property Owners,
2. Tenants,
3. Sharecroppers,
4. Squatters, and
5. Encroachers.

Depending upon their category, Project Affected Persons would be entitled to either compensation or assistance or both. Each category is described as follows:

Private Property Owners have legal titles to land, structures and/or other assets. They are entitled to compensation under the Land Acquisition Act. They are also entitled to shifting (relocation) assistance. They may also be facilitated for voluntary relocation to alternative site(s) (if any).

Tenants have *bona fide* tenancy agreements with private property owners to occupy a structure or land for residence, business or cultivation purposes. They are eligible for certain compensation/ assistance as per existing norms.

Sharecroppers are those individuals who have formally or informally entered into an agreement with private property owners to cultivate their lands.

Squatters have illegally occupied Government Land for residential, commercial and/or other purposes. They are not eligible for compensation but would qualify for certain assistance and targeted support if they belong to vulnerable groups (defined subsequently). They would be entitled to shifting assistance. They would also be assisted for voluntary relocation to alternative sites.

Encroachers have extended their buildings, land-holdings, business premises or work places illegally into Government Land. They are not eligible for either compensation or assistance. Vulnerable groups would be entitled for project support.

Persons Losing their Livelihood

Persons losing their livelihood are Project Affected Persons who are at least 18 years of age at the time of displacement and who stand to lose their primary occupation or primary source of income as a result of project interventions. Such persons are eligible for support extended by the Project Authority on the basis of their contributions to household income.

Vulnerable Groups

Vulnerable groups may receive special targeted support and assistance under the project because they would be unevenly impacted by developmental interventions. It is desirable that such groups receive special support from the project in order to ensure social safeguards. The human face of the project would be duly maintained if adequate attention is paid to these vulnerable groups. The following categories may be considered vulnerable:

- ❖ Women Headed Households,
- ❖ Landless Agricultural Workers,
- ❖ Scheduled Castes,
- ❖ Scheduled Tribes,
- ❖ Persons from households with income less than 20 per cent above the Poverty Line,
- ❖ Elderly Persons (above 65 years of age) who are the single earning members of their respective households,
- ❖ Persons with Disability, and
- ❖ Orphan Children.

Project Affected Households

Project Affected Households are those that would be adversely affected by implementation of the civil works. Project Affected Households are entitled to certain benefits as a household unit.

Project Affected Groups

Project Affected Groups are communities (with a focus on the more vulnerable and weaker sections) that may be adversely/ disproportionately affected by the project.

Entitled Persons

Entitled Persons are Project Affected Persons who qualify for (or are entitled to) assistance/compensation since they would be resettled or otherwise be negatively impacted by the project. Entitled Persons include Project Affected Households and Project Affected Groups.

Cut-Off Date

The Cut-Off Date would be announced in consultation with the concerned District Magistrates in order to ensure that squatter settlements do not proliferate in the affected area due to lack of proper information. A Project Affected Person not identified at the Cut-Off Date may be considered for support if he/she can produce the necessary documentary evidence of his/her residential proof (of not less than three years) before declaration of the Cut-Off Date. The Cut-Off Date identifies Project Affected Persons (within the existing/proposed Right of Way) who are entitled to compensation and/or assistance. Persons occupying the Right of Way after the Cut-Off Date would not be considered as Project Affected Persons under this project. Such persons would not be entitled to any assistance. The list of Project Affected Persons may be made public to ensure that Entitled Persons are duly covered under the project. Project Affected Persons may be allowed to lodge complaints (if any). Appropriate measures may be taken by the Project Authority to avoid any further encroachment(s) or squatter settlement(s) in the project area after announcement of the Cut-Off Date. Information dissemination exercises are critical to make the Cut-Off Date credible *vis-à-vis* the general public. The Project Authority may ensure that the Cut-Off Date is suitably publicized in the project area. Public Notifications in this regard should be prominently displayed in Government offices, post offices, market places, telephone booths, shop windows, public notice boards in the local language. Word of mouth may also be spread by deploying public address systems.

Household Unit

The Household Unit is defined as all persons living and eating together as a single unit. The household as a collective entity shall be entitled to compensation and assistance in certain cases.

Family

A family shall mean the husband, wife and their minor children. Every son or unmarried daughter who has attained 18 years of age on or before the Cut-Off Date would be treated as a separate family. Every divorced or widowed daughter living separately or with the family on or prior to the Cut-Off Date would be treated as a separate family. Orphans in one single household would be clubbed together as one single family. Mentally handicapped persons irrespective of age and sex would be treated as one single family.

Landless Agricultural Worker

A landless agricultural worker is a person who does not hold any agricultural land and who has been deriving his/her principal income by working on the lands of others as a sub-tenant or as an agricultural labourer prior to the Cut-Off Date.

Small Farmer

A farmer holding 2 hectares of non-irrigated or 1 hectare of irrigated land shall be treated as a small farmer.

Marginal Farmer

A farmer holding 1 hectare of non-irrigated or ½ hectare of irrigated land shall be treated as a marginal farmer.

Minimum Economic Holding

The Minimum Economic Holding is equivalent to 2 hectares of non-irrigated or 1 hectare of irrigated land.

Income

The Income of a Project Affected Person shall mean the amount of income as shown in his/her Income Tax Return prior to the Cut-Off Date. His/her income shall be calculated (in the absence of any Income Tax Return) by an objective assessment applying the same method as adopted by the Government Agencies to identify Below Poverty Line families.

REFERENCES

1. *Source*: National Policy on Resettlement and Rehabilitation for Project Affected Families 2003 (published in *The Gazette of India Extraordinary Part I, Section 1, No. 46, Dated 17th February 2004*), Chapter VI (R&R Benefits for Project Affected Families).
2. *Ibid.* Chapter I (Policy: Preamble).
3. *Ibid.* Chapter III (Definitions).
4. *Ibid.*
5. http://www.ciel.org/Ifi/wbinvolresettle.html
6. http://wbln0018.worldbank.org/Institutional/Manuals/OpManual.nsf/toc2/CA2D01A4D1BDF58085256B19008197F6?OpenDocument#foot
7. http://www.indiahousing.com/general/acquisition.asp
8. Public sector organizations have in certain cases directly purchased land/property through negotiations due to project exigencies.
9. Identification of encroachers and squatters may be sought from the voters' lists or from any other legal documents or information from the community (in the absence of ration cards/photo identity cards).
10. Replacement cost shall be equivalent to an amount required to acquire substitute land of equal productive value as well as to replace any structures or other assets. The difference is to be paid by the project in the form of assistance in case the replacement cost is more than the compensation at market price as determined by the Project Authority.
11. Vulnerable categories include Women Headed Households, Landless Agricultural Workers, Scheduled Castes, Scheduled Tribes, Persons from households with income less than 20 per cent above the Poverty Line, Elderly Persons (above 65 years of age) who are the single earning members of their respective households, Persons with Disability and Orphan Children.
12. The Minimum Economic Holding is equivalent to 2 hectares of non-irrigated or 1 hectare of irrigated land.
13. This provision would be applicable in those cases where relocation site(s) may be developed for Project Affected Persons/Project Displaced Persons.
14. Common Property Resources may include playgrounds, community meeting platforms, bus bays, public stand posts, hand pumps, wells, vats, cattle grazing areas, solid waste disposal sites, sewerage and drainage systems, water supply and sanitation systems, electrical infrastructure, educational institutions, primary health centres, local markets etc. that are utilized by the affected community members for their everyday civic requirements.

10

An Exploration of the Feminist Critique of Contemporary Medical Practice using Childbirth as a Case Study: A Review of the Literature

LOUISE WARWICK-BOOTH

Introduction

The relatively recent emergence of feminism as a theoretical perspective within sociology has led to several shifts in focus within the discipline generally. Within sociology feminism has had an impact upon particular subject areas, gaining women a more prominent stance in a number of sociological contexts. Furthermore, feminist ideas have addressed *via* sociology a number of issues including the historical construction of knowledge, the social construction of gender roles, male dominance and sexism. A particular area for feminist concern in relation to female health has been the medicalisation of pregnancy and childbirth (Oakley, 1981; Annandale & Clark, 1996). The emergence of the feminist movement within medical sociology has raised awareness around several issues specifically relating to the medicalisation of childbirth; the social and cultural meanings attached to childbirth, the male take over of the supervision of birth, the extension of medicalisation over female reproduction, general female life and the role of health in social control, problems with scientific knowledge and the use of technology, problems with medical research, the position of the female voice within childbirth, the social construction of gender roles and illness behaviour and the designation of women as particular kinds of patients. Feminists is challenging the medicalisation of childbirth also challenge the medical profession and contemporary medical knowledge at its very core. This article will examine this critique of medicine *via* an analysis of the feminist literature discussing childbirth.

The Social and Historical Context of Childbirth

Common to all feminisms is the argument that women's experiences of health are a social construction (Annandale & Clark, 1996) Childbirth and its management are located within a specific social context because different cultures have invented ways of living and then have defined the meaning of birth, a biological event, based upon this (Oakley, 1979). Thus, although birth is a salient fact of nature, its practices within different societies reflect diversity. Clearly, pregnancy and birth are bodily experiences, which have different negotiated realities within different cultures (Oakley, 1984) reflecting that pregnancy and childbirth practices are socially located. Hence, an examination of childbirth and its associated practices needs to take place within the context of an analysis of wider cultural beliefs, attitudes and societal location. Nevertheless the complexity of the relationship between childbirth and cultural influences must also be recognised. Indeed, there is a danger in discussing childbirth simply as a cultural theme because where women's biological reproduction is linked with the social mothering of children the mystique of childbearing is created as a feminine self-fulfilling occupation (Oakley, 1980).

Historically within western societies childbirth took place within the home where midwives or experienced women were on hand to assist in the process. Until the seventeenth century, birth in most parts of the world was firmly located in the exclusively female domestic arena and hospital birth was uncommon before the twentieth century (Johanson *et al.*, 2002). Feminist theorists point to changes in childbirth practices whereby appropriation of control took place by a male-dominated medical profession (Rich, 1975). Jordanova (1999) also discusses this, arguing that women from all social strata practiced techniques in relation to childbirth but this led to unease about the demarcation between male and female practitioners. This led to midwives being in an uncomfortable position and a professional struggle ensued around who should be in charge of birth. Consequently, a hierarchy was established where women acted under the supervision of men. This male take over of childbirth can also be related to the growth of the medical profession and its associated influence; new forms of analgesia, anesthesia, caesarean section and safe blood transfusion. These changes in the management of childbirth techniques have been criticized by feminists but many argue that such developments have made hospitals safer places in which to give birth.

However, for women who are at a low risk, planned home birth is still as safe as hospital birth (Macfarlane *et al.*, 1999). Moreover, women giving birth at home use less pain relief medication, experience less prolonged labour and less fetal distress (Chamberlain *et al.,* 1997). It is in this context that much literature argues that the experience of women also needs to be considered (Wolf, 2002). Meta analysis demonstrate that women tend to be most satisfied giving birth in a low-tech environment with care by a mid-wife or general practitioner (Villar *et. al.,* 2000). However powerful the influence of the expanding medical profession, the social context of giving birth still remains important; women with generally supportive partners are less likely to receive medical interventions during birth (Fox and Worts, 1999). Here is the central component of much of the feminist critique of biomedical childbirth; its iatrogenic properties (Annandale and Clark, 1996).

Another problem highlighted by contemporary feminists is that women undergo childbirth whilst men supervise. Despite changes in childbirth practices and shifts from the private domain (home) to the public domain (hospital), from female care (experienced woman) to professionals (often male doctors) and from birth as a natural event to a technological and medical event (Oakley, 1984). However, the question of the control structure of female reproduction is more problematic than some feminists have posed. There are anthropological and historical examples to demonstrate that the control structures of reproduction have always been male dominated. Within small-scale societies although women may have responsibility for childbirth, they are still positioned within cultural systems of ideas and practices reflecting dominant power structures, which may be detrimental to them (Calloway, 1993). Furthermore, the literature reflects a dichotomy of experience between modern mid-wife care and obstetrics, with the alternative mid-wife approach perceived as more positive (Annandale and Clark, 1996). This depiction marks potential exploitation in the midwife-client relationship (Hardy, 1993) and obscures the location of contemporary mid-wifery practice, which is firmly situated within biomedicine (Annandale and Clark 1996).

In addition, the historical picture of childbirth can be idealized and can fail to take account of wider cultural systems and ideas. Furthermore, the development of the medical profession and its influence on childbirth can be demonstrated to be positive as maternal mortality in the West fell substantially during the twentieth century. The World Health Organisation has estimated that almost fifteen per cent of women develop complications during childbirth serious enough to require rapid and skilled intervention if they are to survive without lifelong disabilities. Thus, some women need access to medical services during childbirth (Johanson *et al.,* 2002) and technological advancement in such circumstances can arguably be positive. However, some feminists remain certain that the benefit of medical interventions cannot be proved scientifically (Finkelstein, 1990).

Medicalisation

For feminists, science and technology are connected with social change in the western world. Industrialisation led to an increase in the use of science and technology, creating new focuses on health, disease and illness. Consequently, medicine gained an increasing influence in everyday life. Feminist theorists propagate that under certain circumstances virtually any human activity and habit can become medical concerns: specially trained health professionals are deemed to have expert knowledge on how people should live and conduct themselves (Miles, 1991). Furthermore, the increase in technology, drugs, health promotion and health education have led to a general acceptance within western societies that life and quality of life are legitimate concerns of medicine. Medicalisation, it has been argued has affected some groups more than others. Feminists have argued that on women, the impact of the growth of medical influence has been considerable, highlighting the medical focus upon psychiatric problems, the medicalisation of biological processes and the intervention of health practitioners within childcare and the family. It is within this context that the increasing influence of medicine has impacted greatly upon women's lives and most specifically upon their reproductive capabilities (Miles, 1991). Women's embodiment, differentiated from that of men is crucially anchored in reproduction, which links to attempts to control women; the medical profession functions to ensure conformity to social roles and norms (Annandale & Clark, 1996). Consequently, the label 'illness' can be applied to behaviour and then an appropriate treatment can be prescribed, ensuring conformity (Miles, 1991). Thus, feminist theorists argue that the medicalisation of childbirth is part of a wider goal of social control as it has been separated from other social events and reconstituted as a specialist, technical subject under the jurisdiction of an expert authority (Oakley, 1984). Oakley (1984) argues that antenatal care is not about educating women, it is about controlling them; antenatal care is both an exemplar and a facilitator of the wider social control of women. In these circumstances the wombs of women are containers to be captured by the ideologies and practices of specific individuals with specific beliefs and practices. This is clearly demonstrable in contemporary society–legal injunctions can be taken against women who do not readily consent to medical or surgical procedures imposed upon them or who deviate from medical advice (Oakley, 1988). Here feminists are criticising medicine as a form of knowledge, practice and social control.

Feminism and the Deconstruction of Science and Gender Roles

Feminists further critique the medicalisation of childbirth based on scientific knowledge because for feminist theorists there are no such things as medical facts. The progress of science through the centuries has been so spectacular that it carries with it the implied assumption of an ultimate presentation of knowledge that can be free of cultural meanings and the vested interests of the dominant power structures (Calloway, 1993). However, feminist theorists argue that science is tainted with social structure, therefore, it is inherently sexist, racist, classiest and a culturally coercive practice and form of knowledge. Feminists criticise the way in which the construction of scientific and medical knowledge omits both the female perspective and experience (Oakley, 1993). Thus, the nature of scientific and, therefore, medical knowledge is interpreted differently within feminist sociology. The sociology of health and illness have to be understood in relation to the dominant paradigm of western medicine, biomedicine (Nettleton, 1995). The boundaries of biomedicine and the medical profession are viewed as the outcome of socio-political struggles rather than being based upon factual and evidenced scientific knowledge. The professional development of medicine has been closely associated with a patriarchal culture, wherein the sexuality of women has been a crucial issue in the definitions of their medical problems (Turner, 1987). Thus, what counts as legitimate medical knowledge is decided through social processes and socio-political pressures (Nettleton, 1995). Feminists show that science and medical knowledge are clearly contentious and leave the question open as to whether science, medicine and technology are the best resources for dealing with the world. In relation to childbirth and scientific advancements, feminists argue that the history of medical care and the surveillance of women is not one of proven and tested effectiveness (Oakley, 1993).

Furthermore, medical care is problematic for feminists because women's health is conceived of as different to men's; women are treated as exceptional to men because men are taken as the standard reference point (Radley, 1994). The distinction between women as natural and men as cultural appeals to a set of ideas about the biological foundations of womanhood (Jordanova, 1999). Childbirth then, for feminists is a site for the focus and representation of societal rules and practices, which define and reinforce the classification of male and female. Historically, sex roles became constituted in scientific and medical language during industrialisation (Jordanova, 1999). Consequently, to speak of women within medical terms is simply to speak of the body—femininity is located within the body. For some feminists, science has unclothed the female body, to make women easier to understand and this has resulted in women's bodies becoming objects of medical enquiry, brought under the penetrating enquiry of male reason (Jordanova, 1999). Furthermore, a woman's status as a child bearer has been made into a major fact of her life (Rich, 1977).

Consequently, female problems such as pregnancy and childbirth are fields of ambiguity and conflict because the definition of female illness is based on assumptions about the place of men and women within society (Radley, 1994). Here the literature demonstrates the social construction of health and illness to be gendered with sexual stereotypes of women showing them to be both the product and the prisoner of their own reproductive systems, resulting in a particular approach to female illness. Furthermore, findings of medical studies are argued by feminists to be reported in such a way as to create a picture of women that is congruent with such social stereotypes of female weakness and instability (Scrambler, 1997). Feminists discuss childbirth as a contemporary example of this phenomenon but also highlight a lengthy history of female illnesses depicting weakness specifically related to gender (See Scrambler, 1997).

Some feminist theorists argue that biology indirectly influences women's destiny through the way in which it is socially constructed, whilst others argue that biology has a more direct influence upon the destiny of women because of their reproductive capabilities (Sayers, 1982). Whichever viewpoint is accepted, biological differences between the sexes in relation to reproduction do affect the situation of women and men within society. Consequently, pregnancy and childbirth have been pathologised and turned into illnesses that require treatment (Birke, 1980).

Consequently, many different strategies for women attempting to reclaim the female body from the experts, such as obstetricians, who position it as an object, have been proposed (Sayers, 1982). Theorists working within a liberal feminist framework believe that sexual inequality is the result of structural factors within society. Thus, liberal feminists attempt to debunk the official discourse associated with the female body to demonstrate that health is not a straightforward product of biology, but is socially constructed from gender-roles and experiences (Annandale, 1998). One of the problems with this argument according to other feminist perspectives is that liberal feminists are willing to work within the patriarchal system. Radical feminist theorists break completely with this perspective by arguing that patriarchy is the root of women's oppression and by calling for feminised control over reproduction. However, this is again open to criticism, as this perspective has been accused of universalizing the experience of women. These criticisms have led to arguments by some commentators that radical feminism is arguing for fundamental differences between the sexes, actually buys into the male-defined world-view that it is attempting to criticise (Annandale, 1998). Whilst these perspectives cover a wide range of thought, much feminist work has been critiqued for adopting an essentialist position which defines the body based upon gendered difference and as a result adopts some of the problems of natural science (Annandale and Clark, 1996).

Technological Usage

Following on from the deconstruction of science and medicine as medical fact feminists argue that another critical area for concern is the use of technology within childbirth. Doctors and the medical profession portray the scientifically determined benefits of technology for women in childbirth as medical facts, however, they may well be as transient as fashion. Thus, feminists have also critically focused upon the use of technology by doctors as a routine aspect of childbirth arguing that consideration is not given to the effect it has upon the female recipients. Oakley (1979) argues that processes benefiting a few women are applied unthinkingly to the majority who do not require them. The desire to create better, safer facilities has led to women being processed in similar patterns (Birke, 1980). However, public expectations have changed in line with the development of medicalisation and the use of technology. Thus, there is now a 'blame and claim' culture in which people believe that most, if not all deaths in childbirth could be prevented. Consequently, professionals feel disempowered and increasingly use technology as a safeguard in childbirth (Johanson, 2002). Furthermore, feminists have argued that when childbirth was taken into the hospital setting the positive aspects of home care were discarded and that everything is now done for the convenience of the doctors, including the use of technology (Wolf, 2002). Indeed, within contemporary western pregnancies and childbirth, technology is routinely used. Some women find the presence of technology reassuring, however, many find that medical attention is focused not on their own judgments but on messages from machines. Thus, some women are relieved to have their babies 'safely' delivered whilst others often feel uncared for, having received no support or factual information (Kitzinger, 1978). Consequently, feminists argue that medical technologies have led to a significant deterioration in personal care (Doyal, 1995). Feminists have also argued that technology may have more benefits for obstetricians rather than the women experiencing childbirth; new technology has enhanced the profile of the obstetrician in terms of professional status and it has also bolstered the scientific respectability of obstetrics within the wider medical profession. Comparatively, the implications of the use of technology for women and their babies remain debatable as the psychological effects of such use have yet to be researched (Doyal, 1995). The use of technology within childbirth for feminists reflects the colonisation of birth by medicine as one aspect of the wider cultural dependence upon professional health care within contemporary society: doctors are saviours, miracle workers and culture-heroes (Oakley, 1979). The unbridled medical enthusiasm for new techniques is a general feature of modern medicine. Thus, it may not be that obstetrics is a special case but that medical attitudes simply see female reproductive patienthood as a particularly passive and appropriate site for their introduction (Oakley, 1984).

The whole edifice of the routine medical surveillance of pregnant and labouring women using technology rests on an untested assumption that this is the best way to provide mother and infant well-being (Oakley, 1988). The medical profession and the associated technology it has developed has indeed been credited with the decline of infant and maternal mortality in relation to childbirth, however, there has been a failure to account for women eating differently, living more hygienically and having fewer children (Oakley, 1979). Evidence suggesting that poverty, social support, education and employment impact significantly upon pregnancy is also overlooked in most circumstances (Oakley, 1988). Moreover, contemporary measures of mortality such as statistics are open to differing interpretations.

From a feminist perspective, maternity services are not as effective as they might be. Furthermore, the use of technology raises ethical concerns within the feminist critique. At the heart of feminist concerns about obstetric technologies is a fear that the medicalisation of childbirth has all too often been against the interests of mothers (Doyal, 1995). By involving an array of technological equipment in a hospital setting, medicine for feminists makes childbirth into an illness type of experience, with women taking the sick role as patients. Much feminist debate has argued that women dissent from this position and view birth as part of the world of health rather than illness (Graham and Oakley, 1986). Consequently, in recent years feminists have argued that the solution to asserting the right to choose how, where and in what way women give birth is in demanding that women's role as midwives needs to be reinstated so that women again become the prime supervisors over childbirth

(Birke *et al.,* 1980). Furthermore, feminists have also called for demedicalisation through increased home births and alternative pain control (Rajan, 1996). Current UK policy means that by 2009, women will be able to choose between home births, giving birth in a midwifery-led unit, or with midwives and doctors in hospital (McCawley, 2007). However, the reality is much more complex than the theory that given good information, women would make a decision to deliver their babies in a home-like setting. The policy picture is more complex, despite increasing UK birth rates, financial problems are seeing the closure of maternity-led units and there has been a media focus upon the shortage of midwives and the impact this is having upon services for labouring women (McCawley, 2007). Furthermore, given choice, some women may choose to deliver babies by caesarean (Carlisle, 2006).

As Reisman (1983) argues women have not simply been the passive victims of technology as feminists so often illustrate. Rather they collaborate with this process to satisfy their own needs thus, women's relationship to technology is not as simple as it might first appear, as they are not always passive. The medical management of pain and the use of technology within childbirth clearly raise a number of critical issues surrounding the ownership and control of the female body and the extent to which both technology and pain relief constitute a form of oppression or a potential means of liberation (Rajan, 1996). However, this analysis has received criticism. Such analyses are limited in their focus upon medical *versus* natural and consequently overlook practices impacting upon both maternal and infant health, such as elective cesareans. Furthermore, the implication of such practices in relation to the consumption of health care resources also needs consideration (Beckett, 2005).

The Female Voice

Another focus for feminist concern and criticism has been located on the way in which the medical profession excludes the female viewpoint within the birth process. Kitzinger (1992) argues that in any culture those with the power to define the meaning of birth also write the script for how it is to be handled and how different participants should behave. For many feminists in technological cultures, male doctors define birth whilst women experience it. Thus, a central concern located within the feminist critique of the medical practices associated with childbirth is that the female voice and experience of childbirth is lost. Indeed, the National Childbirth Trust argues that women do not so much make informed choices as find themselves constrained by the culture of the unit they attend (Johanson *et al.,* 2002). Savage (2006) argues that childbirth educators may wish to include instruction on negotiating power differences in relationships during birth in order for women to ensure they receive the care they want.

Furthermore, Oakley and Graham (1981) argue that conflict is a fundamental feature of the relationships between the providers and users of maternity services. This is the result of the significant and powerful relationship existing between the expectant mother and her care provider. They argue that doctors and mothers have different ways of looking at the nature, context and management of reproduction. During pregnancy and childbirth, doctors and mothers look at the event using different frames of reference relating to their differing social positions. Most women see pregnancy as a normal healthy process. Comparatively, doctors treat it as if it were potentially an illness (Scrambler, 1997). The woman's relationship with others, her body concept in giving birth and the significance of the birth experience in the context of her whole life are lost (Oakley, 1980). The medical view of childbirth is that of a separate event, whereas women see it within the context of their own biographies (Radley, 1994). Childbirth gains its social meaning through individual female perceptions—it has a lasting meaning for the mother because it is both a turning point and a transition—a baby turns a woman into a mother and mother's lives are incurably affected by this status of motherhood (Oakley, 1979). Thus, for feminists the way childbirth is treated by the medical profession reflects a societal discourse that has shifted its focus from belief, onto the individual and then onto the body as simply a machine (Radley, 1994).

Furthermore, feminist theorists extend this argument to critique research into the female perspective by the medical profession. Thus, it has been argued that such research adopts a patriarchal paradigm and a male-centred worldview (Smith, 1992). Other research into women's attitudes towards birth, discuss women simply as patients whose lives have no context and meaning other than as patients (Kitzinger, 1992). Doctors then, view their female patients in limiting ways. Women complain of unsatisfactory communication throughout their pregnancies resulting from their requests for information being treated as requests for reassurance; doctors simply view women as anxious patients (Scrambler, 1997). Hence, for many women childbirth is a process in which they are disempowered—control of their bodies is removed from them (Kitzinger, 1992). Scrambler (1997) argues that most women see themselves as having expert knowledge about their bodies. Comparatively, doctors believe that the only useful knowledge is medical knowledge. Thus, women having babies are considered not to know what is best for them (Oakley, 1979). Indeed, women are perceived in the same way as children—vulnerable and incapable—throughout their pregnancies and labour (Oakley, 1988). Thus feminists see the male dominated medical profession reduces female feelings, emotions and wider experiences to irrelevant details. In the medical gaze women become passive objects rather than active subjects. Scrambler (1997) argues that women often express a wish to control what happens in childbirth; however, doctors act as if all of the decisions are theirs to make. Hence, some women find themselves stripped and exposed, with their legs splayed and their sexual organs on display. Their bodies become fragmented with all of the attention focused on the space between their legs. Consequently, birth can be likened to rape in a number of ways. (Kitzinger, 1992).

Following on from these criticisms feminists have argued for a refocusing on women's experiences, allowing women to define the meaning of birth, what it is like to be a mother in the context of their own lives and their own values. Research then should not be on women rather it should be for women (Nicolson, 1986). Thus, feminists argue for research that relates to an understanding of women's position as an oppressed social group and which adopts a critical perspective towards approaches to females that render them either invisible or subject to categorisations of any kind (Oakley, 1993). Oakley and Graham's (1981) research suggests that women experiencing childbirth feel that what medical management does above all is to prevent them from taking responsibility for their own behaviour and decisions during childbirth. Thus, feminist research on how women experience maternity services reveals an iceberg of dissatisfaction, lack of information, poor communication, long waiting times and an absence in the continuity of care (Oakley, 1993). In response, some feminists have called for resistance to technological intervention. However, resistance to obstetric intervention is not confined to feminist theory alone, with the development of the natural childbirth movement (Moscucci, 2003).

This approach has to be recognized as an ideology underpinned by the notion that pregnancy is not pathology (Wolf 2002).

Conclusion

The feminist critique of the medicalisation of childbirth shows that any attempt to understand the determination of female fertility must begin with an examination of the complex web that constitutes the social relations of reproduction because social, cultural and economic circumstances clearly shape reproductive experiences (Doyal, 1995). The way in which birth is managed has implications for a society as a whole, for its view of reproduction, for the position of women, for family relationships and for child socialisation (Oakley, 1993). Thus, women as reproducers are socially defined in a specific way within contemporary advanced western industrial society. Evidently, reproduction is one of the structures that contribute to the position of women. As well as production, sexuality and socialisation, reproduction expresses and determines a cultural role and ideology for women (Oakley, 1980), which is arguably problematic for those females experiencing it.

Thus, in answer to the problem of the medicalisation of childbirth, feminist theorists have suggested a number of solutions such as the redomestication of birth, a return to female controlled birth, research for women on childbirth and the provision of therapeutic support for women after childbirth (Oakley, 1980). What is known about women's wishes and fears should also be addressed so that women-centred, clinically effective services can be developed (Johanson *et al.,* 2002). The highest rates of normal birth seem to be associated with successful community focused approaches. Hence, this may be another way forward (Johanson *et al.,* 2002). Furthermore, Johanson *et al.* (2002) have suggested that UK practitioners may need to take heed of other countries, which use a less medicalised approach to childbirth.

Although feminist theorists have made some suggestions to improve the experience of childbirth within contemporary society, the question remains as to whether the 'feminist sisterhood' really has the necessary solutions and answers to this problem (Oakley, 1980) because the wider problem for feminists is patriarchy and this problem is not so simple as to be eradicated.

Clearly, all feminists criticising the medicalisation of childbirth share a common objective of identifying the ways in which patriarchy undermines women's health. However, there are nonetheless significant and highly politicised differences between some of these theorists (Annandale, 1998). Women and related gender issues are everywhere; consequently the subject-matters of feminist theories are not containable within any single disciplinary framework or any set of them (Harding, 1987). Furthermore, particular perspectives shift to accommodate new challenges resulting from social change and indeed competing theoretical frameworks (Annandale, 1998). Thus, an analysis of the literature reveals that the feminist critique of the medicalisation of childbirth is multi-faceted because feminism is a multi-faceted theory with theorists holding differing theoretical positions and different epistemological assumptions.

However, despite the differing feminist approaches, the critique of contemporary childbirth through medicalisation is both comprehensive and relevant to other areas of medical practice, knowledge and treatment within modern biomedicine. The exclusion of women from the process of childbirth and their general treatment at the hands of the medical profession is mirrored in other areas of health care, with other patients (Nettleton, 1995). Thus, the medicalisation of life in relation to social control is an issue for many individuals, not just women experiencing pregnancy and childbirth. Furthermore, the construction of scientific medical knowledge as superior and factual, the depiction of patients as passive who are routinely processed in similar ways, the decline of care due to the increased use of technology, the lack of research on patients needs and the obscurity of the voice of the patient within medical discourse are all relevant criticisms of modern medical practice as a whole, not just the medicalisation of childbirth.

Some feminist theorists have highlighted a degree of initial change within modern medical practice. For example, Nettleton (1995) discusses how professionals are being encouraged to see patients as active participants rather than clinical objects. It is also increasingly common for non-medical males to be present during childbirth and this may have some influence in bringing about change within contemporary practice (Calloway, 1993). As definitions of women and childbirth are inevitably social, their classifications are always being reinterpreted and reconstructed within everyday life. Thus, childbirth practice will not remain static in an ever changing and ever developing world. Indeed, future medical practice and its related developments remain uncertain—there is the possibility that childbirth may be brought back into the arena of social concern and become sensitive to the needs of women, however, there is also a chance that childbirth may become more dehumanised and desocialised (Oakley, 1984). What is required is a context for childbirth that makes it possible for women to feel that they have achieved something of value to themselves in having a child (Oakley, 1980). Thus, the remaining dilemma for medical services at the current time in relation to childbirth is to respect the integrity and autonomy of each woman and baby, in their own unique social context, while at the same time using the most appropriate resources to provide safe, sensitive and effective care (Oakley, 1993).

REFERENCES

Annandale, E. (1998), 'Health, Illness and the Politics of Gender' in Field, D. and Taylor, S. (eds.) *Sociological Perspectives on Health, Illness and Health Care (eds.),* London; Blackwell Science Press.

Annandale, E. (1998), *The Sociology of Health and Medicine: A Critical Introduction*, Cambridge, Polity Press.

Annandale, E. and Clark, J. (1996), 'What is Gender? Feminist Theory and the Sociology of Human Reproduction', *Sociology of Health and Illness,* 18(1) 17-44.

Ardener, S. (1993), *Defining Females: The Nature of Women in Society (eds.),* Leamington Spa, Berg Publishers.

Beckett, K. (2005), 'Choosing Cesarean' *Feminist Theory,* 6 (3): 251-275.

Birke *et al.*, (1980),*Alice Through the Microscope: The Power of Science over Women's Lives (eds.),* London; Virago Press.

Carlisle, D. (2006), 'Safe in Their Hands?' *Health Services Journal,* 30th November 2006.

Chamberlain, G.; Wraight, A.; Crowley, P. (1997), *Home Births: The Report of the 1994 Confidential Enquiry by the National Birthday Trust Fund,* Carnforth; Parthenon.

Chesler, C. (1988), *Sacred Bond: Motherhood under Siege,* London; Virago Press.

Calloway, H. (1993), 'The Most Essentially Female Function of All: Giving Birth' in Ardener, S. (eds.) *Defining Females. The Nature of Women in Society* Leamington Spa; Berg Publishers.

Doyal, L. (1995), *What makes Women Sick: Gender and the Political Economy of Health,* London; Macmillan Press Ltd.

Ehrenreich, E. and English, D. (1979), *For Her Own Good: 150 Years of the Experts, Advice to Women,* New York; Pluto Press.

Finklestein, J. (1990) 'Women, Pregnancy and Childbirth' in Schutt, J.A. (eds.), *The Baby Machine. Reproductive Technology and the Commercialisation of Motherhood,* London; Green Print.

Fox, B. and Worts, D. (1999), 'Revisiting the Critique of Medicalised Childbirth', *Gender and Society,* 13 (3) 326-346.

Graham, H. (2000), *Understanding Health Inequalities,* Buckingham; Open University Press.

Graham, H. and Oakley, A. (1986) 'Competing Ideologies of Reproduction: Medical and Maternal Perspectives on Pregnancy' in Currer, C. and Stacey, M. (eds.), *Concepts of Health and Disease,* Leamington Spa; Berg Publishers.

Harding, S. (1987), 'Is there a Feminist Method' in Harding, S. (eds.), *Feminism and Methodology,* Buckingham; Open University Press.

Hardy, J. (1993) *Challenging Childbirth. How should Midwives Respond?* Unpublished MA Thesis, Warwick University.

Johanson, *et al.*, (2002), 'Has the medicalisation of childbirth gone too far?', *British Medical Journal,* 324: 892-895.

Jordanova, L.J. (1999), 'Natural Facts; A Historical Perspective on Science and Sexuality' in Samson, C. (eds.), *Health Studies: A Critical and Cross-Cultural Reader,* London; Blackwell Publishers.

Kitzinger, S. (1978) *Women as Mothers,* London, Fontana.

Kitzinger, S. (1992), 'Birth and Violence against Women: Generating Hypothesis from Women's Accounts of Unhappiness after Childbirth' in Roberts, H. (eds.), *Women's Health Matters* London; Routledge.

Macfarlane, A.; Cambell, R.; McCandlish, R. (1999), 'Data on Babies Home Births are being Ignored, *'British Medical Journal'*319: 1008.

McCawley, M. (2007) 'Labour's Vision for Maternity', *Health Director* 5 (2), London; A GovNet Communication.

Miles, A. (1991), *Women, Health and Medicine,* Buckingham; Open University Press.

Moscucci, O. (2003), 'Holistic Obstetrics: The Origins of the Natural Childbirth Movement', *Post-graduate Medical Journal* 79, 168-173.

Nettleton, S. (1995), *The Sociology of Health and Illness Cambridge*; Polity Press.

Nicolson, L. (1986), *Gender and History,* New York; Columbia University Press.

Oakley, A. (1979), *Becoming a Mother,* Oxford; Martin Robertson & Co. Ltd.

Oakley, A. (1980), *Women Confined: Towards a Sociology of Childbirth,* Oxford; Martin Robertson & Co. Ltd.

Oakley, A. (1984), 'Doctor knows Best' in Black, N. *et al.,* (1984), *Health and Disease: A Reader (eds.),* Buckingham, Open University Press.

Oakley, A. (1984), *The Captured Womb: A History of the Medical Care of Pregnant Women,* Oxford; Basil Blackwell Ltd.

Oakley, A. (1993), *Women, Health and Medicine,* Edinburgh; Edinburgh University Press.

Oakley, A. and Graham, H. (1981), 'Competing Ideologies of Reproduction: Medical and Maternal Perspectives on Pregnancy' in Roberts, H. (eds.) *Women, Health and Reproduction,* London; Routledge & Kegan Paul.

Orr, J. (1987), *Women's Health in the Community (eds.),* Chichester; John Wiley & Sons Ltd.

Radley, A. (1994), Making Sense of Illness*: The Social Psychology of Health and Disease,* London and New York; Sage Publications.

Rajan, L. (1996), 'Pain and Pain Relief in Labour: Issues of Control' on Williams S. and Calnan, N. (eds.), *Modern Medicine; Lay Perspectives and Experiences*, London; UCL Press.

Rich, A. (1977), *Of Woman Born: Motherhood as Experience and Institution,* London; Virago.

Savage, J.S. (2006), 'The Lived Experience of Knowing in Childbirth', *The Journal of Perinatal Education,* 15 (3) 10-24.

Sayars, J. (1982), *Biological Politics: Feminist and Anti-Feminist Perspectives,* London and New York; Tavistock Publications.

Scrambler, G. (1997), 'Women as Patients and Providers' in Scrambler, G. (eds.) *Sociology as Applied to Medicine,* London; WB Saunders Company Ltd.

Smith, J. (1992), 'Pregnancy and the Transition to Motherhood', Nicholson P. and Ussher, J. (eds.), *The Psychology of Women's Health and Health Care,* London; Macmillan Press.

Turner, B. (1987), *Medical Power and Social Knowledge* London and New York; Sage Publications.

Villar, J.; Carroli, G.; Khan-Neelofur, D. *et al.,* (2000), 'Patterns of Routine Antenatal Care for Low-Risk Pregnancy', Cochrane *Database Systematic Review* see www.cochrane.org/reviews/en/ab000934.html

Wolf, N. (2002), *Misconceptions: Truth, Lies and the Unexpected on the Journey to Motherhood* London; Vintage.

Yearly, S. (1998) *Science, Technology and Social Change,* London; Unwin Hyman Ltd.

11

Community Currency : An Alternative Microfinance in Social Capital-Building and Poverty Alleviation

SAM WONG

Introduction

Community currency, as an alternative form of money, facilitates the exchange of goods and services among the cash-poor population (Aldridge *et al.*, 2001). Akin to other microfinance interventions, community currency programmes aim to combat financial exclusion in access to credit, achieve poverty reduction and generate income by creating employment opportunity. This approach, however, has received scant attention in mainstream literature on microfinance.

The possible reasons for this are that community currency is not regarded as 'credit', and that it has largely been applied in the developed world, such as the United States, the United Kingdom and Australia. It is not certain whether it is applicable in the less developed countries. The community currency approach is also accused of being a 'plaything for the affluent middle class' (Williams, 1996). It is unclear whether it can bring any benefits to the poor, working class. Drawing upon an intensive case study of a community currency project in Hong Kong, this chapter is intended to illustrate how community currency can be 'alternative money' for the cash-poor population. It also examines closely the impact and potential of the approach in the Asian context.

Recognising the multiple objectives of the approach, this chapter will only focus on social capital-building and its effects on poverty alleviation. Social capital is defined as resources generated from social relations (Woolcock, 2001). It is measured by two indicators: social networks and level of trust (Putnam, 2000). By improving the survey design and triangulating qualitative methods, the objective of this chapter is to examine whether, and how, the community currency intervention is effective in re-embedding local social relations, building inclusive community and improving the livelihoods of the poor.

This chapter starts by reviewing the origins, features and objectives of the community currency projects. It then highlights the similarities and differences between the mainstream micro-finance interventions and the community currency approach. After introducing the background of the case study in Hong Kong, it examines the motivation of participation and the impact on social network and trust. The final section will discuss policy implications.

Contrasting Mainstream Microfinance and Community Currency

Community currency approach is defined as 'local system[s] of production, multilateral exchange, and consumption, articulated through a local currency, a single-purpose money—independent of, but often related to, the prevailing national currency' (Lee, 1996, 1377-8). It is also known as 'green money' in Australia and 'local exchange and trading system' (LETS) in the United Kingdom.

The first LETS was established in 1983 in Canada. It was a response to the cause of poverty: the poor lacked cash to engage in productive activities and social lives. It encouraged a different form of trading and financial system. This new medium of exchange, Thorne (1996) explains, 'is a local money valued according to the principle of abundance which breaks with the scarcity discourse of neo-classical economics made hegemonic through global money' (p. 1374). In other words, this approach poses a challenge to the existing economic system that money, as a scarce commodity, restricts exchange, and thus has a negative impact on low-income communities.

The community currency schemes help the poor to form networks to trade goods and services that they need. The 'price' is reached through mutual agreement between buyers and sellers. The transacted currency is purely notional since it cannot be used outside the scheme. Pacione (1997) views this approach as a grassroots-level initiative to confront the globalisation of capitalism and the associated consequence of credit exclusion. It urges us to re-think existing credit relationships and the asymmetrical power dynamics in exchange. Claims have been made that this approach offers a new source of work and credit for the poor (Williams, 1996). Trust is re-built by increasing face-to-face interactions. The disadvantaged are empowered by gaining a sense of control and self-worth as they feel that they make contributions to the local economy (Aldridge *et al.*, 2001).

Similar to other micro-finance interventions, such as credit associations, rotating saving schemes and village banks, the community currency projects form groups and rely on membership to develop networks. However, they have many differences. The community currency scheme is more critical of the existing economic system. It adopts a different type of currency, rather than the prevailing national currency. It is more common in the developed world and shows more concern with environmental protection. While the World Bank and the IMF are the key players in the micro-credit programmes, NGOs, such as the Oxfam, are more willing to experiment with community currency (Table 11.1).

Microfinance and Social Capital

Research on exploring the relationships between microfinance, community currency and social capital have been mushrooming since the mid-1990s. The debate on the effectiveness of micro-credit programmes in building social trust, enlarging social networks and improving the livelihoods of the poor, however, remains contentious. While some studies show the positive results (*e.g.* Karlan, 2001; Seibel, 2000), others suggest the opposite (*e.g.* Dowla, 2005). The disagreement often lies in the definition of social capital and the methodology to measure it (Fine, 2001). In this chapter, I adopt Putnam's definition of social capital as 'features of social organisations, such as trust, norms and networks that can improve the efficiency of society by facilitating coordinated actions' (1993,167).

Table 11.1: Comparing and Contrasting Mainstream Microfinance Interventions and Community Currency

	Mainstream Microfinance Approaches	*Community Currency Approaches*
Similarities	• delivered by teams or groups • claim to be a new source of credit for the poors • usually community-oriented • aim to combat financial and social exclusion, create employment opportunities and generate incomes, alleviate poverty, build social capital and achieve empowerment	
Differences	• use prevailing national currency • aim to address market failure in the micro-credit practice, but work along-with the present economic systems • more focused on livelihoods of the poor • more common in the developing countries • key players include the World Bank and IMF	• adopt an alternative currency, independent to national currency • question the conventional concept of 'credit' and 'money', highlight the exploitative nature of the capitalist system, and urge the re-valuation of conventionally low-paid skills and work • more focused on 'green' ideas • more common in the developed countries • key players include international charities, such as Oxfam

Source: Ideas adapted from Simanowitz, 2003; Dowla, 2005; Seyfang, 2004.

The Trilogy of Social Capital: Bonding, bridging and linking, is useful in examining the inclusiveness of the community currency programmes. Bonding social capital refers to linking to people 'like us', such as our own family, kin and friends of similar class backgrounds. Bridging social capital, in contrast, is connections with people 'unlike us'. Bonding social capital, as Woolcock (2001) asserts, is less desirable since strong ties are characterised as exclusive, inward looking and private-regarding, while bridging social capital is a weak tie which is more inclusive, outward looking and public-regarding. Linking social capital is to forge alliance with people or organisations in power.

Regarding the methodological issues, questions as to how trust and norms of reciprocity are best measured by surveys are often raised. Data generated from qualitative studies are also often challenged by their representation and generalisability. The crux of the problem, I argue, lies in the mistaken dualism of quantitative and qualitative research methods. The research design in this chapter (which will be discussed in the subsequent sections) is intended to address these issues.

Case Study: Community-Oriented Mutual Economy Project in Wan Chai

Background

The economic downturn in the early 2000s, along with the economic restructuring, the Financial Crisis in 1998, the IT bubble burst in 2000 and the SARS epidemic virus in 2003, has worsened poverty in Hong Kong. The income inequalities were worsened as the Gini Coefficient was upto 0.43 in 2003—higher than in many developing countries. Unemployment hit an unprecedented level of 8 per cent in 2003. Wong and Lee (2001) estimate that 800,000 households experienced a 10 per cent to 30 per cent reduction in average incomes. Hong Kong Oxfam (2001) suggests that 600,000 employed workers are in a situation of a high incidence of unstable contract work, high working hours, low salaries and minimal benefits. The informal social networks which formerly provide the poor with financial assistance are severely weakened by the economic hardship. For example, nearly 24 per cent of the Mainland Chinese migrants reported that they borrowed money from their relatives when facing financial difficulties. A year later, it dropped to nearly 13 per cent (HKSAR, 2002).

Hong Kong society also fits into the 'social capital lost' story which shows a picture of collapse of trust and reciprocity. Ng and Hills (2000, 24) use the term 'dwindling social capital' to describe the situation:

> *'Hong Kong is a city of workers, more than a city for citizens. People's security seems to be built on monetary wealth rather than social relationships. Rapid economic take-off in the last two decades has seen the rapid erosion of social networks built in the post-WWII years. Old residential buildings have been bull-dozed for new commercial blocks. Residents have been redistributed to different places' (p. 25).*

The study on social capital by the Hong Kong Federation of Youth Groups (2002) also illustrates a grim picture: nearly 80 per cent of respondents have not involved themselves in community-related activities and 64 per cent suggest that not even one neighbour can be trusted.

In the light of this, with the sponsorship of Hong Kong Oxfam, the St. James Community Centre in Wan Chai experimented with the first community currency project in Hong Kong in 2001 which is called 'Community-Oriented Mutual Economy' (COME). Wan Chai was chosen since it is an old urban centre and has undergone community regeneration since the 1990s. While 45 per cent of households earn more than HK $30,000 monthly, 18 per cent live below the unofficial poverty line which is set at the half of the median income. New arrivals and single elderly are the poors who are geographically excluded (Smith, 2003). The massive scale of regeneration programmes also triggers rapid internal migration which undermines the sense of neighbourhood and community. Facing keen competition, some local retailing businesses are forced to close down.

Organisational Governance and Activities

This project is social capital explicit in objective. It aims to build networks for diverse disadvantaged groups, such as migrants, social benefit recipients, single parents, the unemployed and the elderly, and encourage them to trade. It states clearly in the funding proposal to 'instill new cultural values [to members] which foster reciprocity, mutual respect and community building' (The Proposal, 2000, 10). Exchange is through a currency called 'hour-credit'. Everyone receives 60 free 'hour-credit' when they register as new members.

This project is run by one manager and three social workers. About 500 members were recruited within a year. The bottom-up approach is adopted, and the Central Committee, as the decision-making body, is composed of different disadvantaged group representatives, with the support of academics, accountants and lawyers.

Sunday bazaars are organised once a month to facilitate face-to-face interactions between members. Second-hand goods are traded, and services, such as haircutting and food stalls, are provided. The Monthly *Community Hour-Credit Newsletters* (Figure 11.1) list the offers of, and requests for, goods and services. The price is reached through mutual agreement between buyers and sellers. Social workers put a lot of effort into helping the poor to earn 'hour credits', for example, they recruit migrants and the elderly to run food stalls and to sell second-hand toys. English and computer classes are also organised to enhance members' human capital to seek formal employment.

Figure 11.1: *Community Hour-Credit Newsletter* (Issue of April, 2002)

Four Features

Drawing on overseas experiences and failure, the COME has made many alterations in design and operation which differentiates itself from other community currency projects. First of all, it promotes a 'time-based', rather than a 'money-based', accounting system. It imposes a uniform rate for work of all kinds. Everybody's work receives one time unit for each hour worked. This means that 'it values time spent on work equally an hour is an hour', regardless of the work involved (Lee, 1996, 1383). As Williams (1996) argue, this approach intends to create greater equity in exchange relations and to re-value different skills.

Secondly, widely known as 'green money', community currency projects are often accused of being 'environment-oriented' and neglect the livelihoods of the poors. The COME plays down the messages on environment protection and emphasises issues relevant to the poors, such as job creation and fair trade. Thirdly, many projects design and name their currencies in locally significant ways, such as

Bobbin in Manchester, UK[1]. However, this promotes regionalism and risks creating geographical exclusion. The Wan Chai project makes the design very simple to reach a wider audience (Refer to Figure 11.2). Sketches on the currency, such as pawn and shoe-repairing shops and local snacks, are old features in Hong Kong. They intend to create a sense of nostalgia.

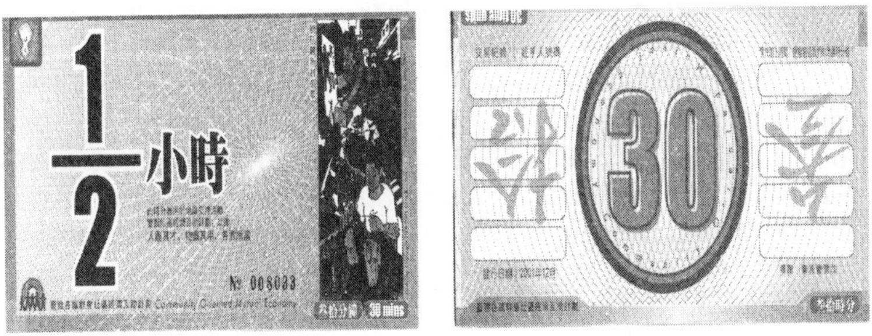

(Front) (Back)

Figure 11.2: ½ Hour-Credit Currency Samples

Fourthly, social workers are enthusiastic in creating bridging and linking social capital. In order to build connections 'unlike us', they draw the middle class and non-Wan Chai residents to the scheme. Not only does it widen the scope of services, such as medical, financial and legal supports, it also facilitates inter-class understanding and cross-region interactions. As Seyfang (2004) argues, the involvement of the middle class is not a one-way donation, but fosters long-term reciprocal social relations. Using the slogan 'We are one Family' also brings members of different gender, age and other social backgrounds together.

Making connections with local retail business diversifies the range of products and services being provided and re-vitalises the local economy. A cafe shop, for example, donates 60 packs of sandwiches daily to the community centre in return of free advertising in the newsletters. The very poor members are recruited to collect and sell the sandwiches to earn 'credit-hours'. The project attracts the attention of local politicians, the government and the media. The project organisers were invited to share their experience in the Legislative Council in 2001. The frequent visits of politicians increase the exposure of the programme. While building linking social capital, however, social workers are aware of the power dynamics since they do not want to be used as the government's propaganda to reduce its investment in local communities.

Evaluation

In the following, I draw on the findings of a survey I conducted in 2001 which was designed to examine the social impact of the COME project. About ten ordinary members were recruited to carry out the questionnaires on the phone. This was intended to offer them an opportunity to earn 'hour-credits', as well as to get involved with the research.

Questions in the survey were set to explore the exchange patterns, motivations and barriers of participation. 5 out of 16 questions were social capital-specific, and two aspects: social network and trust are closely examined. In most social capital surveys, respondents are asked how many friends they meet generally in the group (Roberts and Roche, 2001). This easily causes confusion whether the friends they meet are 'new' or from their established networks. To address this problem, I break the question down into three: total friends in the project, the number of 'new' friends met after joining the project, and the contact with these new friends. I also measure the level of trust from two dimensions: within the group and beyond the group. The latter is also known as 'generalised trust'. Dividing trust into two levels is intended to examine whether internal solidarity is so strong that it creates exclusion.

Along with the survey, ethnographic research was undertaken for eight months. Participant observations were supplemented by semi-structured interviews, focus group discussion and documents, such as the funding proposals, newsletters and minutes. The advantages of triangulating quantitative and qualitative research methods are to offer an aggregate view of social capital building without disregarding the contextual understanding. During my fieldwork, I got assistance from project organisers, and they highlighted my role as a student volunteer who needed to do some 'homework' for the project, rather than a professional researcher, which made me less threatening to ordinary members.

Diverse Motivations

By random sampling, 86 respondents completed the questionnaires.

65 per cent of the respondents were existing members of the St. James Community Centre. 39 per cent learnt about this project from the Centre's social workers. The majority of the respondents were female (74%). Only 40 per cent lived in Wan Chai where the project was based. Regarding the education level, 40 per cent had received primary education or below, while nearly 16 per cent had received tertiary education. Most of the respondents were students and house-wives, 30 per cent and 24 per cent respectively. 18 per cent had a full-time job, 7 per cent was part-time, 5 per cent unemployed and 1.2 per cent under-employed.

The reasons for their participation were mixed. 11.8 per cent of respondents were economically-motivated, and they hope the project could improve their livelihoods. 38.2 per cent were ideologically-motivated who wanted to help the poor and build a more cohesive community. Only 8.8 per cent mentioned widening their social networks by meeting more friends. The rest is the majority (about 40%) who had no particular reason. Some joined it merely out of curiosity, and most of them were invited by their family members and friends. Statistically, the low-income, social benefit recipients and people living within Wan Chai were more economically-motivated. Those who had full time employment and lived outside Wan Chai had a stronger ideological rationality. Gender also played a role in shaping motivation. While economic motivations are more commonly cited amongst women, men were more passive in their involvement, and most of them did not know what they could get from the project.

The items most commonly offered and purchased in Sunday bazaars were food and toys. Asking for domestic services, such as cleaning, was popular outside the bazaars. These three items shared more than half of the total exchange. Only one-third of respondents had made transactions in their everyday lives. Nearly one in four explained that they were too busy to exchange, and 10 per cent said that they did not need any goods and services listed in the newsletters.

More New Friends, but Low Contact

The survey shows that the project helps to enlarge social networks of the poors. Members on average have nine friends in the project, and meet 2.6 'new' friends after joining the project. Housewives, migrants, low-educated members find it easier to make new friendship.

The survey, however, also demonstrates a less rosy picture: firstly, nearly 40 per cent of respondents did not make any 'new' friends at all, and most of them were middle-aged men. They felt marginalised owing to the skewed membership. Only 26 per cent were men and most of them were students. In interviews, they suggested that the Sunday bazaars were tailor made for women where they could share their family life and exchange food and second-hand things. They did not see the 'hour-credits' as 'real' currency which helped them out of poverty. My analysis suggests that the strong gender stereotypes hinder men's participation in the COME project. How to make the project more 'men-friendly' without intimating women needs to be addressed by the project organisers.

Secondly, amongst the members who succeed in making new friendship, 63 per cent of them did not make contacts at all in their everyday life (Figure 11.3).

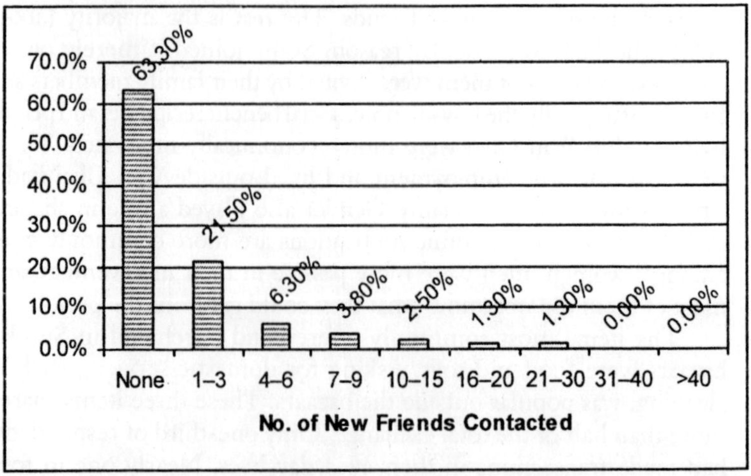

Figure 11.3: Total Number of Friends Contacted over the Past 3 Months

This finding is not quite what social capital theory predicts. Underpinned by the rational choice model, the theory assumes that once individuals build social networks, the contact becomes their assets, and they will consciously and strategically draw upon the social relations to improve their own well-being. Ostrom and Ahn, for example, claims that social capital can be appropriately modelled as 'a self-conscious investment process'. She explains that: 'there is really little question about the conscious choice made when one joins associations, forgoes an immediate payoff in order to follow a norm of reciprocity' (2003, xxxi). This individualised and optimistic agency and instrumental view of social capital, however, are inadequate in understanding a more complex social context (Wong, 2005).

Individuals do not automatically become active and participatory agents, and their involvement in the exchange of goods and services is influenced by their psychology and subjectivity. Williams (1996) argues that members require some degree of self-confidence and self-worth to make the community currency projects work. Having been struggling in the hierarchy of dependence, as Cleaver (2004) suggests, the poor do not suddenly feel liberated from independence. Agents' subjectivity also affects their daily interactions. By exploring agents' subjectivity, it shows that ordinary members perceived that making further contacts with new friends required extra time, energy and resources. They feared that they were not able to reciprocate in the long run.

Institutions, rules and norms also shape interactions between members. Mainland Chinese migrants, for example, were constrained by 'right' norms of articulation and ideas of conflict avoidance. Their accents prevented them from striking bargains with the locals in public since they did not want to sound foolish in front of the locals. They perceived open negotiation about price as threatening and rude, and thus was highly undesirable. They wanted to be accepted and seen as friendly, rather than as trouble makers. Encouraging members to earn 'hour-credits' by all means has a backlash. Some members expressed a strong belief that helping each other should be altruistic. In their own words, it was the right way of doing things in the community. Seeking rewards by purposeful interactions, from their perspective, was too 'money-minded', and this undermined, rather than built, everyday coordination.

High Trust, But Trust What?

The survey asked respondents how much they trust their group and non-group members by rating (5 as most trustworthy and 1 as least trustworthy). While the mean score for the within-group trust was 3.7, it was 3.1 for the generalised trust. Groups, such as the female, the low education and non-Wan Chai residents, tended to show a higher level of trust in both of these levels. The only difference was that housewives and the existing members of the St. James Community Centre had a higher level of generalised trust. These findings appear to suggest that the community currency programmes need a good trustworthy base with strong internal solidarity, but this does not necessarily cause exclusion. The success lies in how messages on inclusive community are delivered and how easy the 'outsiders', such as people of different class and gender backgrounds and residents living outside the areas, gain access to the projects.

The complexity of the meaning of trust is further explored by focus group discussion. To unpack the high level of within-group trust, participants were asked what, and who, they actually trust. The participants expressed their high level of trust in the social workers and the St. James Community Centre as an entity since 'they have done so much good things for us'. This high level of trust in the 'authority', however, does not automatically lead to the same level of trust in their fellow members. They showed caution in their everyday interactions since, in their own words, 'you never know what they (other members) are thinking'.

Mistrust was manifest between class. The lower class members cast their doubt on the motivation of the participation of their middle class counterparts. Rumours were that the rich members sold things that they did not want. The inter-class hostility can be explained by the differential earning capacity since the middle class, having a higher level of human capital, know better how to earn 'hour-credits'. This finding resonates with Williams's study in Manchester where the lower class feels the project is for people other than themselves (1996). This indicates that, despite good intentions in building bridging social capital, we need to put a lot of effort into reconciling the intrinsic differences and interests.

The dilemmas between trust and privacy and between trust and size are worthy of close examination. The project organisers, like many social capitalists, hold a strong assumption that, by increasing information flows between members and by enhancing organisational transparency, they reduce transaction costs of exchange which help to build trust. In doing so, they encourage participants to put advertisements in the newsletters to request for, and to offer, goods and services. Unlike other community currency projects, the central committee is far more decentralised since they normally do not do the matching for the members. In theory, the project is bounded and exclusive to members. In reality, however, it is open to everyone since non-members can read the newsletters and learn the names and contact details of the advertisers. This openness has scared the group members off because they do not feel comfortable about being contacted by strangers. Furthermore, trade relies on reputation and words-of-mouth. Social workers expect that housewives with children are set free to join the labour market since childcare services are provided by other members. Nevertheless, this is not the case because most mothers are unable to make judgement and recruitment merely based on the advertisements.

It also shows a trade-off between the size of the group and the level of trust. To increase the diversity and the scope of goods and services, it is necessary for the COME project to expand its size by reaching a wider audience. However, with the fixed budget and limited numbers of volunteers, this inevitably increases the workloads of the social workers. Worse still, this diverts their attention to meet the ever-increasing demand of work, rather than to resolve the more urgent and complex issues, such as inter-class mixing. The expansion of the group size also undermines the intimacy and understanding between members, and eventually erodes mutual trust.

Conclusions

Community currency programmes have long been ignored by mainstream micro-finance practices. This is largely because community currency is not regarded as the conventional form of 'credit'. It is beyond doubt that community currency is not 'credit', but it is 'alternative money' which plays a critical role in offering additional 'cash' to the poor. The community currency approach shares similar objectives of other microfinance to improve the livelihoods of the poor by intervening in the demand and supply of 'money' through a small-scale monetary system and by addressing the limitations and inequalities of the credit and labour markets. In the light of this, community currency should be treated with equal importance as other microfinance schemes.

My research has shown mixed results about the impact of the community currency project on social capital-building and poverty alleviation. While social networks are built through the project, there are signs that the poor are reluctant to 'use' them. The high levels of within-group and without-group trust are achieved in statistics, but the inter-class mistrust is concealed.

Despite all these, it is a mistake to completely deny the potential of the community currency programmes. The project in Hong Kong has demonstrated some success in creating social capital by enlarging the members' social networks and generalised trust. It has also re-embedded interpersonal relations in the community (Pacione, 1997). The success lies in the effort in reaching the poor and simultaneously not excluding the middle class. The design of community currency also plays down the negative impact of regionalism. This experience is highly relevant to the developing world in that the community currency, as Seyfang (2001) suggests, is a grassroots-level response to global changes.

What we have learnt from the case study is that we should not merely aim to build ***more*** social networks for the poor, but look into whether they are willing to use the new networks, and how they can use them more effectively. The interplay between individual subjectivity and institutional norms is useful in illuminating what social and cultural factors enable and constrain interactions in their everyday lives. Neither should we simply aim at high scores of trust. We need to explore further the complex meaning of trust and uncover the elements of mistrust.

Policy Implications

Literature on community participation tends to assume that the creation of democratic and participatory space facilitates collective action and then fosters trust. The over-emphasis on negotiation and free agency, however, risks idealising the process of bargaining and concealing the unequal power relationship. Aldridge *et al*., (2001) warn that: '...... the way power interweaves during these negotiations is multiple and dynamic' (p. 565). The differential capacities of individuals affect how they negotiate the value of their services and work. As discussed before, the trade patterns in the community currency projects are shaped both by members' own sense of worth and confidence and also by social norms about what behaviour is acceptable and how participants should be behaved. Some individuals face more constraints in making social connections, for example, the elderly are restricted by mobility from attending the Sunday bazaars. How we promote fair participation without disregarding different life circumstances of individuals poses a great challenge to the design of inclusive participatory programmes.

Highlighting the role of sanction in constituting institutional governance in collective action literature assumes that setting up clear enforcement mechanisms facilitate the generation of trust by penalising free-riding behaviour (Ostrom and Ahn, 2003). Alkire and Deneulin (2002), however, are highly critical of the hypothesis that individuals are law-abiding simply from a fear of sanction. They are aware of the inadequate understanding of mixed and complex motivations of human beings. My observations in the case study support this critique. As discussed before, the trust of members is more based on their trust in the social workers rather than in their group members. This, however, does not mean that they have a strong desire to punish their free-riding members. The idea of sanctions, from their point of view, causes anxiety within the group. Penalty undermines, rather than builds, trust and cooperation, and thus is undesirable.

The link between social capital-building and poverty reduction alleviation also needs critical scrutiny. It is generally claimed that the norms of reciprocity alleviate poverty and improve livelihoods (*e.g.* Woolcock, 2001, World Bank, 2000). My case study, however, has shown that the limited range of goods and services offered in the project are inadequate even in meeting the basic needs of the poor. In addition, group participation is not cost-free. It requires the poor to devote considerable time, energy, and most importantly, money to build and maintain social contacts. Therefore, Cleaver (2004) argues that we should first meet the materialistic needs of the poors as a primary condition of participation, and not the other way round.

To conclude, development workers need to be critical about the assumptions and the process of the community currency, so as to avoid creating exclusion. Donors of the community currency programmes should also note that the project approach hinders, rather than facilitates, the building of the long-term trust. The tight time-frame and short-term funding are not sufficient to meet the multiple objectives of the community currency approach. It is also important to highlight that combining community currency with other micro-finance interventions may generate a more positive impact on the poors.

NOTE

1. 'Bobbin' links back to Manchester's historical position as the former centre of the UK cotton-spinning industry when the cotton was wound on bobbins.

REFERENCES

Aldridge, T.; Tooke, J.; Lee, R.; Leyshon, A.; Thrift, N. and Williams, C. (2001), 'Recasting Work: the example of local exchange trading schemes', *Work, Employment and Society*, Vol. 15, No. 3, pp. 565-579.

Alkire, S. and Deneulne, S. (2002), 'Individual motivation, its nature, determinants, and consequences for within-group behaviour' in Heyer, Judith, Stewart, Frances and Thorp, Rosemary (eds.), *Group Behaviour and Development: Is the Market Destroying Cooperation*? Oxford: Oxford University Press.

Cleaver, F. (2004), The social embeddedness of agency and decision-making, in Samuel Hickey and Giles Mohan (eds.) *Participation: from Tyranny to Transformation? Exploring new approaches to participation in development.* London: Zed.

COME (2002), *Minute of the Central Committee, Community-Oriented Mutual Economy Project*, 7th February.

COME (2002), *Newsletter of the Community-Oriented Mutual Economy Project*, January.

COME (2001), *Funding Proposal, Community-Oriented Mutual Economy Project*, 7th October

Dowla, A. (2005), 'In credit we trust: building social capital by Grameen Bank in Bangladesh', *Journal of Socio-Economics*, forthcoming.

Fine, B. (2001), Social Capital *versus Social Theory: Political Economy and Social Science at the turn of the Millennium*. London: Routledge.

Hong Kong Oxfam (2001), Recent Development of Marginal Workers in Hong Kong (in Chinese).

HKSAR (Hong Kong SAR Government) (2002), Surveys on New Arrivals from the Mainland (First quarter of 2002). Hong Kong: Home Affairs D

'Assessing the 'wider' social impacts of microfinance services: hods and findings', *Institute of Development Studies Bulletin*, pp. 106-114.

ocial Capital and Group Banking. Processed, Department MIT.

ral Money? LETS and the social construction of local phies in Southeast England', *Environment and Planning*, -1394.

Ng, M.K. and Hils, P. (eds.) (2000), *Hong Kong: World City or Great City of the World*? Centre for *Urban Planning and Environment Management*, University of Hong Kong.

Ostrom, E. and Ahn, T.K. (eds.) (2003), *Foundations of Social Capital*. Cheltenham: An Elgar Reference Collection.

Pacione, M. (1997), 'Local exchange trading systems as a response to the globalisation of capitalism', *Urban Studies*, Vol. 34, No. 8, pp. 1179-1199.

Putnam, R. (2000), *Bowling Alone: The Collapse and Revival of American Community*. London: Simon and Schuster.

Putnam, R.; Leonardi, R. and Nanetti, R. (1993), *Making Democracy Work: Civil Traditions in Modern Italy*. Princeton: Princeton University Press.

Roberts, M. and Roche, M. (2001) 'Quantifying Social Capital: measuring the intangible in the local policy context', *Radical Statistics*, Vol. 76, Winter, pp. 15-28.

Seibel, H. (2000), How Values Create Value: social capital in microfinance—the case of Philippines. *Rural Finance Working Paper*, No. B8, International Fund for Agricultural Development.

Seyfang, G. (2004), 'Working Outside the Box: Community currencies, time banks and social inclusion', *Journal of Social Policy*, Vol. 33, pp. 49-71.

Seyfang, G. (2001), 'Working for the Finland Dollar: An Evaluation of Local Exchange Trading Schemes as an Informal Employment Strategy to Tackle Social Exclusion', *Work Employment Society*, Vol. 15, September, pp. 581-593.

Simanowitz, A. (2003), 'Micro-finance, poverty and social performance: Overview', *Institute of Development Studies Bulletin*, Vol. 34, No. 4, pp. 1-9.

Smith, C. (2003), 'Wanchai: In search of an identity', in David Faure (ed.), *Hong Kong: A Reader* in Social History. Hong Kong: Oxford University Press.

Thorne, L. (1996), 'Local exchange trading systems in the United Kingdom: A case of re-embedding?', *Environment and Planning*, Vol. 28, pp. 1361-1376.

Williams, C. (1996), 'Local exchange and trading systems: A new source of work and credit for the poor and unemployed?', *Environment and Planning*, Vol. 28, pp. 1395-1415.

Wong, H. and Lee, K.M. (2001), Deadlock, exclusion and future: Qualitative research on Hong Kong *Marginal Labour*. Hong Kong: Oxfam (in Chinese).

Wong, K.F. (2005), 'Inclusion by institutional designs? Rethinking agency, livelihoods and institutions in urban community participation', in K.R. Gupta (ed.) *Urban Development Debates in the New Millennium: Studies in Revisited Theories and Redefined Praxes*. New Delhi: Atlantic Publishers, Vol. 2, Ch. 7, pp. 112-135.

Woolcock, M. (2001), 'The place of social capital in understanding social and economic outcomes', *ISUMA: Canadian Journal of Policy Research*, Vol. 2, No. 1, Spring, pp. 11-17.

World Bank (2000), *World Development Report 2000/2001: Attacking Poverty*. World Bank: Washington D.C.

Index